Greenland

Greenland
Basin

3884

Bjørnøya Barent

357

Jan Mayen

810

405

Voring
Plateau

Icelandic
Plateau

Denmark Strait

G

Irminger Basin 2830

Iceland

Reykjanes Ridge

H

550

Faro
Island

Iceland Basin

Baltic Sea

K

L

ap Isua

3208

Rockall
Bank

North
Sea

238

British
Isles

31

Celtic Shelf

London

EUROPE

Rhine

678

Porcupine Abyssal Plain

38

English Channel

Biscay Abyssal
Plain

4938

Danube

Adriatic Sea

Corse

E A N

Azores-Biscay Rise

5943

Lisboa

Islas Baleares

Sardegna

2875

MEDITERRANE

Arquipélago
dos Açores

Horseshoe Seamounts

56
Ampere
Seamount

Strait of Gibraltar

Alger

265

Arquipélago
da Madeira

Monaco
Basin

238 Great Meteor
Tablemount

Islas Canarias

5491

Tropic of Cancer

AFRICA

Krylov
Seamount

1273

Cape Verde
Plateau

Ilhas do
Cabo Verde

Dakar

Niger

Cape Verde

Basin

Lagos

Sierra
Leone
Rise

5036

Sierra Leone
Basin

1627

Gulf of Guinea

Niger Cone

Bioco

A Pearl in
the Storm

A PEARL IN THE STORM

HOW I FOUND MY HEART
IN THE MIDDLE OF THE OCEAN

TORI MURDEN MCCLURE

COLLINS
An Imprint of HarperCollinsPublishers

HarperCollins books may be purchased for educational, business, or sales promotional use. For information please write: Special Markets Department, HarperCollins Publishers, 10 East 53rd Street, New York, NY 10022.

FIRST EDITION

Designed by Emily Cavett Taff

Library of Congress Cataloging-in-Publication Data has been applied for.

ISBN 978-0-06-171886-1

09 10 11 12 13   OV/RRD   10 9 8 7 6 5 4 3 2 1

Hilaire Belloc wrote, "There is nothing worth the wear of winning, but laughter and the love of friends." Without laughter and the love of friends, none of the journeys contained within this book would have been possible. After spending a summer in Kenya, I asked a Masai friend why he wore so many beads. He replied, "Each bead represents a friend." It was not long after this that I adopted the habit of wearing pearls. Not only do they represent friends, but they also represent the dreams that are shared by friends. Dreams are like the grains of sand that work their way into oysters. At first they irritate. Then they aggravate. If one takes up the challenge of the dream, if one works at it and works at it, the grains of sand may be transformed into pearls. The boat that carried me across the Atlantic is named the American Pearl. I dedicate this book to all the friends, all the pearls, who helped me to transform possibility into fact.

Contents

PART II
The Journey Home

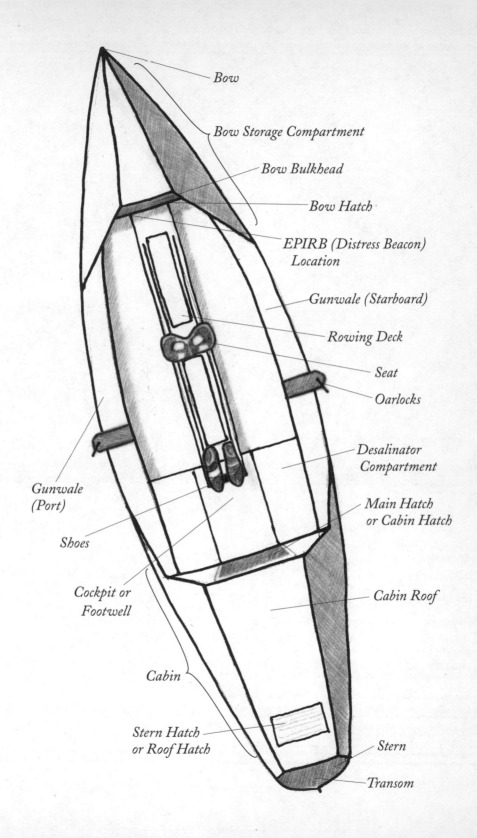

Bow

Bow Storage Compartment

Bow Bulkhead

Bow Hatch

EPIRB (Distress Beacon)
Location

Gunwale (Starboard)

Rowing Deck

Seat

Oarlocks

Desalinator
Compartment

Main Hatch
or Cabin Hatch

Gunwale
(Port)

Shoes

Cockpit or
Footwell

Cabin Roof

Cabin

Stern Hatch
or Roof Hatch

Stern

Transom

PART I

THE JOURNEY OUT

Let Us Have Faith

Security is mostly a superstition.
It does not exist in nature,
nor do the children of men as a whole experience it.
Avoiding danger is no safer in the long run than out-
right exposure.
Life is either a daring adventure, or nothing.
To keep our faces toward change and
behave like free spirits
in the presence of fate is strength undefeatable.

—Helen Keller

CHAPTER 1

The Quest Begins

June 14, 1998
latitude north 35:52, longitude west 75:34
the Outer Banks of North Carolina

IN THE END, I KNOW I ROWED ACROSS THE ATLANTIC to find my heart, but in the beginning, I wasn't aware that it was missing. In January 1998, I asked my uncle, "If I write a book about my explorations, should I write it as a comedy, a history, a tragedy, or a romance?" With a twinkle in his eye, he said, "A romance—it must be a romance." He explained that I was too young to write my life as a history: "Who wants to read the history of half a life?" Tragedy, he explained, was "boring." Anyone over the age of thirty can write his or her life as a tear-soaked muddle. "There is no challenge in that," my uncle counseled. "Comedies are fine, but the greatest stories in life are about romance."

I didn't doubt that my uncle spoke the truth, but there was a problem. I had no experience with romance. None. I was thirty-five. Tragedy, I could write. Comedy, I could write. Even history, I could write. Romance was out of my depth. If I had charted a map of my life, I would have placed romance on the far side of an unexplored ocean, where ships would drop off the edge of the world and the legend at that edge of the map would read, "Here there be sea monsters."

I considered myself a thoroughly modern woman. As a graduate of Smith College, I embraced the notion that our culture had evolved to the point where a woman might openly take on the role of an Odysseus. Like the epic hero in Homer's *Odyssey*, women could be clever. We could set out on epic quests of our own choosing. Like men, we could be independent and internally motivated. Women could be tested and not found wanting in trials of courage, resourcefulness, endurance, strength, and even solitude. What I did not know was that exploring these vaguely masculine qualities would not be enough for me. I am, after all, a woman. It was not until my boat dropped off the edge of the world, into the realm of sea monsters, that I began to understand some of what I had been missing.

LET'S FACE IT: NORMAL, well-adjusted women don't row alone across oceans. According to the records of the Ocean Rowing Society, in London, England, no woman had ever rowed solo across an ocean, but I didn't let this worry me. About midday on Sunday, June 14, 1998, I drove my old gray pickup truck towing a rowboat to the Oregon Inlet Fishing Center, a few miles south of the sleepy beach town of Nags Head, North Carolina.

I'd already made the obligatory stop at the Coast Guard station. The officer in charge had done his best to talk me out of making the trip. More men had walked on the moon than had successfully rowed alone across the North Atlantic. Nonetheless, I stood squarely behind a very simple legal precedent: men had been allowed to leave the coast of the United States in rowboats bound for Europe. They couldn't very well stop me just because I was a woman. Once my boat passed the Coast Guard inspection, I was free to go.

I backed my twenty-three-foot rowboat down a ramp and launched the *American Pearl*. The boat was six feet wide at its widest point. The tallest part of the rear cabin sat four feet above the waterline. In the center of the vessel was a rowing deck about the size of the cargo bed in my Ford F-150. The rowing deck was open to the sky, but there was a watertight cabin at the back of the boat. I would enter the cabin through a waterproof Plexiglas hatchway that was nineteen inches square. This window-sized door between the cabin and the rowing deck was the main hatch.

To call the stern compartment a "cabin" exaggerates the space. The watertight sleeping area was slightly larger than a double-wide coffin. I couldn't sit erect without hitting my head on the ceiling, but I could lie down with a few inches to spare. In the floor that served as my bed there were eight small hatches. These opened into little storage compartments that contained my electrical equipment, tools, clothing, and other gear. Between the cabin and the rowing deck was a cockpit that was two feet wide and sixteen inches deep. This little footwell would serve as a kitchen, bathroom, navigational center, and weather station. There were two small benches on either side of the cockpit. One bench housed the desalination system that would turn salt water into drinking water. In the other, I stored my stove and cooking gear when they were not in use. Like my rowing station, the cockpit was uncovered and open to the weather.

I knew every inch of the boat, which I'd built with the help of friends in the bay of an old warehouse in Louisville, Kentucky. We'd conjured the vessel out of twenty-three sheets of marine plywood following a British design by Philip Morrison. The rowing deck was twelve inches above the surface of the water, and the tops of the gunwales, or sides of the boat, were two and a half feet above the waterline. If the boat hadn't been small enough to ride up and down on ocean swells like a cork, any wave bigger than two and a half feet would have washed over the sides. Water that washed in over the gunwales ran out through four scuppers, or drain holes, at the level of the rowing deck.

The boat was designed like an old egg crate. Nine mahogany ribs ran from side to side. Eight of the ribs were divided by bow-to-stern stringers, one on each side of the centerline. These ribs and stringers separated the inner hull into a checkerboard of watertight compartments. We glued the sections with epoxy, reinforced the seams with fiberglass, and filled the voids with urethane foam. On the salary of a city employee, I couldn't afford to build a lighter, sleeker craft out of carbon fiber or Kevlar.

Of the eleven compartments under the rowing deck, seven stored food, two housed my sea anchors, and two larger compartments in the center of the boat next to the keel held my ballast tanks. For ballast, I would use seawater. Each of the two ballast tanks held just over twenty-five gallons. In rough weather, I would fill the tanks, placing four hundred pounds of water weight next to the keel at the bottom of the boat. This weight would lower the vertical center of gravity, making it more difficult for the boat to flip upside down. If the boat did flip, this ballast would help it to self-right. No one had ever rowed across the North Atlantic without capsizing.

The *American Pearl* was laden with gear and food for a hundred days. My sponsor, Sector Sport Watches, had chartered the motor launch *Sinbad* for members of the press, and they had hired a fishing vessel named *Handful* to tow the *American Pearl* to the center span under the Bonner Bridge, which connects Hatteras Island with the mainland. About a dozen friends had traveled from my hometown of Louisville, Kentucky—home of all great ocean rowers—to see me off. A few of them were with me aboard the *Handful*, but most were relegated to watching from the press boat.

I wished that Gérard could have been there. Gérard d'Aboville was the only person in my circle of friends who could truly appreciate the labyrinth I was about to enter. This world-renowned Frenchman had not only rowed solo across the North Atlantic but also rowed alone west to east across the Pacific. Gérard had traveled to North Carolina to assist me with final preparations.

Standing next to my six-foot frame, Gérard had seemed almost diminutive. He was no burly Hercules, but rather a small man with refined features. His manner was easy and unassuming, but at the same time entirely elegant. To apply a phrase I learned at Smith College, I lusted after his mind. Gérard had definite opinions about the technical elements of my journey. When he saw the *American Pearl* for the first time, Gérard had exclaimed, "It is a barge!"

As Gérard and I discussed knots, hardware, the rudder, and cables, he made suggestions to improve the margins of my safety. He was very concerned about the strength of my parachute-shaped sea anchors, and he spent the better part of two days making improvements to them. When the wind was against me, I would deploy the sea anchors at the back of the boat, and like the parachutes that slow race cars or the space shuttle, the sea anchors would slow the drift of the *American Pearl*.

The anchors would help to keep the boat perpendicular to the oncoming waves, making the boat less likely to capsize. I had three different sizes to use in varying conditions. In adverse winds, but relatively calm seas, I would deploy my biggest sea anchor. This anchor would firmly hold the boat. In rough water, the boat must be able to move with the waves or the sea anchor will either tear apart or break the fitting to which it is attached. So, my storm anchor was my smallest of the three. When conditions made it difficult to decide between the largest parachute or the smallest, I went with the one that was medium size. After all his work, Gérard wasn't satisfied. Doubt tinged his voice when he told me, "I hope they will do the job."

We discussed the dangers of capsizing. Gérard explained, "You think you will become used to it, but you never do. When the boat is upside down, every time is as frightening as the first time." He told me that he'd been on deck during one of his capsizes on the Pacific. He'd lost his temper and gone outside during a storm. With classic understatement he said, "This is not good," but the pain of the memory was written on his face. I waited, hoping that Gérard would tell me more, but he stopped himself. It was as if he didn't want to encumber my experience with too much foreshadowing. I told myself, *I'll not be going on deck during any storms,* but when Gérard suggested I lengthen my safety tether so I could get out from under the boat in a capsize, I doubled its length.

Gérard was a member of the European Parliament, and duty called him home just before my departure. Saying goodbye had been difficult. We didn't exchange many words, but Gérard's eyes were eloquent. I imagined he envied me a little, but there was something else, a sense of sorrow. The lessons of the ocean can be difficult. I think Gérard understood that I was the kind of person who is inclined to go the hard way, and I think he recognized just how much it was going to hurt. As an athlete, I understood physical pain. Rowing twelve hours a day, day after day, for months would not be easy. What Gérard could not tell me was that crossing an ocean of solitude would tax more then muscle and joint.

Standing on the deck of the *Handful* and looking down on the *American Pearl,* I was proud of my little red, white, and blue rowboat. The *American Pearl* might have been a homemade barge, but she was my homemade barge. The tide chart indicated that the high tide would crest at 1:00 P.M. After we reached the bridge, the captain of the *Handful* explained that the tide at the bridge wouldn't turn for another hour. Not wishing to row a 2,800-pound boat against an incoming tide, I turned to my friend Molly Bingham and asked her to wake me up after the tide shifted. Then I stretched out on the deck of the *Handful* and took a nap. A little after 2:00 P.M., Molly woke me.

I rose and began the task of hugging friends goodbye. Noreen Powers and Scott Shoup had been invaluable captains in the team of people who helped me to build the *American Pearl.* Bob Hurley, the other chief builder, hadn't been able to make the trip from Kentucky to the coast. I asked Noreen and Scott to tell Bob goodbye for me. Noreen and another friend, Louise Graff, wished me well. Scott pulled the *American Pearl* alongside and held her steady. Then I climbed over the rail of the *Handful* and took my place aboard my little "barge." Scott tossed me the bowline and gave the *American Pearl* a gentle pat on her nose.

At precisely 2:18 P.M., I dropped my oar blades into the salt water and pulled three colossal strokes. The boat didn't move. I wondered if some joker had anchored the *American Pearl* to the bridge while I'd been napping. The boat with the photographers snapping pictures and shooting video hovered less than twenty yards away. *This is not good.* I was already self-conscious. My sponsor had uniformed me in a blue polo shirt and lime green shorts. The ill-fitting shorts accentuated the extra fifteen pounds I'd deliberately packed on before the trip. I felt ungainly.

I'd better get this barge moving. The sliding seat allowed me to use my legs. These weren't dainty limbs. I'd been training for this trip for almost three years, logging endless hours rowing my single scull up and down the Ohio River. I could pull twice my body weight on the seated row. I did sit-ups holding a 45-pound plate, and I could leg-press more than 650 pounds. Even the football players in the weight room had stopped trying to hassle me. I slid my seat as far forward as possible, placed my oars in the water, and shoved with all the force my legs could muster. The boat began to inch toward France. After a few more strokes, the boat picked up speed, but I wasn't exactly flying. At four-and-a-half miles per hour, I would cross the 3,600 miles of the Atlantic Ocean at a walking pace.

It took me a full twenty minutes to row the first mile to the sea buoy that marked the separation between Oregon Inlet and the Atlantic Ocean. Boats in the flotilla that accompanied me began to turn around long before I reached open ocean. As I was about to pass the sea buoy, the last two vessels navigated around me in slow circles. The friends aboard the press boat said their goodbyes, and they headed back toward the bridge.

The *Handful* was the last vessel to leave. The crew aboard the *Handful* had supervised my sea trials, and they were reluctant to bid me farewell. Finally, even the *Handful* showed me her stern. Because rowers row facing the direction of where they have been, rather than the direction they are going, I could watch *Handful* getting smaller and smaller as it motored toward safe harbor. I rowed for another half an hour before I stopped to change out of the blue polo shirt covered with Sector Sport Watches logos and into a white shirt that would reflect the heat of the June sun.

When I returned to rowing, I noticed a sport fishing boat alter course and head out toward me. A few minutes later, the boat came alongside. Two middle-aged men sat with beers in hand; one asked, "Are you the woman who's trying to row across the Atlantic?"

"Yes," I answered, pulling hard, trying to place some distance between our vessels.

"We just came over to tell you that you're completely nuts."

As they zoomed off, leaving me in a cloud of engine exhaust, I considered the merits of their claim. That morning, a radio interviewer had thrust a microphone into my face and peppered me with one obnoxious question after another. He opened with "Why?"

This is one of my least favorite questions. If someone approves of what you do, he will not ask you why you do it; no one says, "Doctor, why do you want to cure cancer?" With the question "why" comes a subtle accusation that one is doing something wrong. "Why" is not a simple question, and I couldn't produce a simple answer, only simple evasions. The best evasion ever uttered came from George Leigh Mallory when he was asked, "Why do you want to climb Everest?" He answered, "Because it's there."

Beginning my evasions, I responded to the interviewer with questions of my own: "Why does an acorn strive to become an oak?" "Why does a caterpillar lock itself into a cocoon before it becomes a butterfly?"

Either missing the point or choosing to ignore it, my inquisitor followed with a different question: "Why *row* a boat across the Atlantic when you can sail?"

"Why sail when you can fly?" was my return.

My inquisitor talked about the deprivation and the pain that I was letting myself in for. "Why *do* it?"

It was easy to see that this man prided himself on his intelligence. Sharing this fault, I looked him in the eye and answered, "The pathway to enlightenment is through the room with a thousand demons." A look of surprise skidded across the interviewer's face. His eyes widened, and for an instant he seemed to understand that my journey was not about rowing a boat from point A to point B. My goals were as intellectual as they were physical, and for one precious moment that interviewer seemed to understand.

Through solitude and exposure to uncertainty, I believed I would confront my demons. Beyond this confrontation, I expected to find a doorway to some higher intellectual awareness. Had I known the true nature of the demons I would duel, I never would have had the audacity to go looking for them. It was my first day; I was still blissful in my ignorance.

As the sun began to set, I watched seagulls and terns head back toward shore. A band of red splashed up from the western horizon, and streaks of orange, yellow, and purple striped the sky above. As the sunset faded, the light from the 156-foot tower of the Bodie Island Lighthouse served as the last reminder of civilization. I wanted to row until the curve of the ocean rose to extinguish this light, but I lost my duel with the lighthouse for the unglamorous reason that I was hungry.

Cheese enchilada ranchero was the first freeze-dried dinner in the stack of meals under the rowing deck. Ocean rowers, like high-altitude mountaineers, need to consume between 4,000 and 5,000 calories a day to avoid losing muscle mass. Typically, this is about two pounds of food per day, but because I packed freeze-dried dinners, I was able to reduce the weight to about 150 pounds of food for the one hundred days.

Not only does freeze-dried food provide high caloric value at a minimum weight, but the packaging also "swims" well. No one had ever rowed across the North Atlantic without capsizing. My deck hatches were weathertight, but experience taught me that this did not mean waterproof. If the boat flipped upside down, water would get into my food compartments. Before the trip, I tested various food packages by running them through my washing machine. As I've said, freeze-dried food swims well; Hershey's chocolate does not.

Luckett Davidson had helped me with my nutritional plan. She was worried that, as a vegetarian, I'd have trouble getting enough protein. She added protein supplements to the vitamins she packed for each day. We consulted experts in sports nutrition, but the most helpful expertise came from Gérard d'Aboville. He told Luckett, "Just fill the boat with things she likes to eat. The trip will be three months. She can eat like a teenager, it will do no harm." With this, I took out the food list, crossed off the oatmeal PowerBars, and wrote in chocolate PowerBars.

For breakfast each day, I would eat some variety of granola. I didn't plan to stop for lunch. Instead, I would graze on a variety of food bars throughout the day. In the middle of the afternoon, I would have some special snack. Crackers, nuts, candy—these snacks were not so much about nutrition as they were about breaking up the monotony of food bars. For liquid calories we packed powdered Gatorade, hot chocolate, and a variety of dried soups.

After dinner, I lashed down my oars and secured everything on deck. The wind blew from shore at about eighteen miles per hour, and the night sky looked as dark as a cavern. Soon a noisy thunderstorm overtook me. Rain beat down, and lightning darted from cloud to ocean. I climbed into my cabin, stretched out on the mat, and turned off the flashlight. As I lifted a knee it bumped against the ceiling, and a drop of cold water fell into my eye.

I lunged for the light. We'd constructed the roof from a 3/8-inch-thick sheet of mahogany plywood, reinforced with a layer of six-ounce fiberglass. Twelve brass bolts secured two solar panels to the roof. Rainwater dripped in through one of the bolt holes. *That's just great. My first day at sea and I have a leak already.* Gérard had warned me about such things. "At sea in a boat, there is always something that needs repair. If you stop rowing every time you hear a squeak or some imperfection draws your attention, you will never reach France." Gérard had recommended I set aside Sunday mornings for such tasks. *I'll plug the leaky bolt on Sunday.* With this issue settled in my mind, I rolled away from the annoying drip.

I was twenty miles from shore. Once I entered the Gulf Stream, the current would be so powerful that it would be easier to row to France than it would be to row back to North Carolina. When Gérard rowed from the United States to France, he left from Cape Cod, Massachusetts, which is nine hundred miles closer to France. I picked North Carolina because it is closer to the Gulf Stream.

In the 1760s, while he was the postmaster general of North America, Benjamin Franklin noticed that American ships could make the journey from the colonies to England in an average of four weeks. The average for English ships was six weeks. When Franklin investigated, he learned that Nantucket whaling captains had mapped a current of warm water that traveled north from Florida and the Carolinas before it turned northeast toward Europe. American sea captains knew enough to take advantage of this warm-water current going toward Europe and avoid it as they came home.

I was counting on the Gulf Stream to push me two-thirds of the way across the Atlantic. Two British rowers, David Johnstone and John Hoare, had tried a similar route in 1966. Their boat reached Europe; the men did not. I had studied their scientific reasoning, and I believed it to be sound. *Just because Johnstone and Hoare died doesn't mean they were wrong. Right?* To refine my research on the matter, I had taken a seminar on the Gulf Stream from Jenifer Clark, a distinguished scholar who maps ocean currents. Jenifer had convinced me that the benefits of rowing with the Gulf Stream would more than make up for the added distance. Gérard seemed less certain, but he didn't debate the issue.

In my barge, I would need all the natural assistance I could get. I closed my eyes and listened to the echoes of thunder. *In 49 B.C.E., as Julius Caesar crossed the Rubicon River with his army on the way to conquer Rome, he said, "Jacta alea est" (the die is cast). By tomorrow evening, I will have crossed my Rubicon and there will be no going back.*

Each time the thunder and lightning shattered my sleep, I pulled out the flashlight and checked the compass. It read 45 degrees; the thunderstorm was blowing the *American Pearl* toward the northeast. At its closest point, the Gulf Stream was southeast, but France was northeast. *If every squall blows me toward France, I'll be praying for rain.* I set the alarm for 5:30 A.M. and went back to sleep.

The next thing I heard was the beep of the alarm. Time to row! For well over a decade, I'd rolled out of bed before dawn to go rowing, but this was different. I pulled on my life vest and poked my head out the main hatch. The smell of salt air filled my nostrils. I clipped my safety tether into the steel cable that ran the length of the rowing deck. Then I stood to scan the horizon. The wind tousled my hair. The sky to the east was just beginning to shift from black to gray. I searched the southwest horizon, trying to find the light from Bodie Island. There were no landmarks. There was no land. *I'm committed now; no diving overboard, no swimming back to shore.*

I stared into the black water. No rope on board could reach the bottom. I placed my oars in their oarlocks and screwed the gates closed. Then I sat down on the rowing seat and slipped my feet into the shoes that were bolted onto a footplate. Rowers call this plate a foot-stretcher, but no six-foot-tall woman who wears size-twelve shoes wants to think about having her feet stretched.

By this time, the eastern sky glistened pink, and I was ready for my first full day at the oars. Like most rowers, I started at the finish. That is, I began by sitting in the finish position: legs straight, shoulders and head high, arms bent, with the oars drawn into my ribs. The first motion was to send the hands away from the body and out over the knees. Next, I pivoted from the hips to swing my torso forward.

Once my shoulders were as far forward as I could comfortably reach, I let my knees bend.

Approaching the catch is like doing a deep knee bend in a seated position. The sliding seat rolled forward until my torso touched my knees. At that point I lifted my hands and allowed the oars to drop and catch the water. Then the process reversed itself. I pushed off the foot-stretcher, driving my legs down until they were nearly straight. Then I swung my body open until my shoulders passed over my hips, and I leaned back until my stomach muscles tightened. Just before the end of the body swing, I pulled the oars toward my ribs using my arms. Before the oar handles actually hit my ribs, I pushed my hands down. This action triggered a seesaw motion of the oars against the fulcrums of the oarlocks. As the handles went down, the oar blades went up, rising out of the water. *That was one stroke—only one million and a couple of hundred thousand more to go.*

I rowed until 7:00 A.M., then stopped for breakfast. I mixed a cup of powdered milk and dumped a sandwich bag full of granola into it. I munched through breakfast in less than seven minutes and returned to the oars. There were calluses on my hands and on my backside from years of rowing in flat-water racing boats. I rowed until noon. By that time, my heels were beginning to blister.

Blisters grow. Blisters break. Broken blisters can become infected. Infections at sea are bad. Ergo, blisters are bad. I folded myself through the main hatch. In the cabin, I retrieved the first-aid kit and covered my heels with a layer of moleskin to reduce the friction and avoid full-blown blisters. For lunch, I mixed up some powdered Gatorade and grabbed two food bars.

The palatability of food bars is inversely related to their nutritional value. I had bars from Mountain Lift, PowerBar, Clif Bar, Tiger's Milk, and a half dozen other companies. My favorite energy gel was GU. Some bars and gels tasted good and some did not. Some were good for me and some were not.

By 12:15 P.M., I was rowing again. If I planned to cross the ocean in less than three months, I couldn't afford to be leisurely about the rowing schedule. For each hour at the oars, I allowed myself a five-minute break. If a bathroom break ran longer than five minutes, I would subtract time from the next break. At first this seemed a little hard-nosed, but five minutes every hour translated into an hour of daylight lost in a twelve-hour day.

When one is rowing a barge across an ocean, every ounce counts. Not counting my sponsor's polo shirt and shorts, which I packed away for my arrival in France, I had three shirts and three pairs of shorts on board. I had a Gore-Tex jacket and trousers for foul weather. For cold, I packed two fleece jackets and a warm cap. For the heat, I had a white sunsuit and a baseball cap with flaps to protect my neck and ears. I had a thin fleece sleeping bag and a heavier Polarguard sleeping bag. Packing an extra jacket or an additional sleeping bag was out of the question. When the Coast Guard had inspected the *American Pearl*, I'd had a life raft aboard. After the inspection was complete, Gérard questioned whether I actually planned to take the forty-pound raft.

Technically speaking, the Coast Guard specifications for a twenty-three-foot vessel didn't require a life raft. Admittedly, the Coast Guard didn't have rules for transocean rowing boats. According to their records, no American, male or female, had ever rowed solo across an ocean.

Gérard argued that, unlike my food stores, the forty-pound raft wouldn't get any lighter. The extra weight would slow me down. Even if it added only a week to my trip, that might mean the difference between success and failure. Gérard was clear: "A heavy boat is a slow boat." With the storms certain to arrive in the fall, he told me, "a slow boat is more dangerous than a fast boat."

The *American Pearl* was, Gérard argued, "an extremely well-equipped lifeboat." Constructed from wood and foam, the boat might break up, but it wouldn't sink. Sailors have an adage: "The only reason to use a life raft is if you have to climb up into it." In the end, I elected to leave the life raft behind. This allowed me to justify a simple trade: the forty-pound raft went out, and a ten-pound library came in. I knew I could spend a quarter of a year without people, but going a quarter of a year without books was unimaginable.

In a compartment under my sleeping pad, in dry bags of black vinyl, I stowed away books by Plato, Shakespeare, Milton, Melville, Emerson, Viktor Frankl, Martin Buber, Dante, Anne Morrow Lindbergh, and many others. I packed books about Alexander the Great and Winston Churchill. I even took along my grandfather's Bible. Books were such an indulgence that I kept the extent of the library a guarded secret. I certainly didn't tell Gérard about the books. I was less secretive about the small library of books on tape and educational lectures. These were relatively light, and because I could listen to them as I rowed, no one questioned whether they would merit their weight.

THAT EVENING, I REACHED into the compartment under my mat and pulled out John Ciardi's translation of Dante's *Inferno*. I reread the opening line. "Midway in our life's journey, I went astray from the straight road, and woke to find myself alone in a dark wood." *I am thirty-five: midway in life's journey. Have I gone astray from the straight road? I am alone on a dark ocean.*

At the entrance to the Inferno, Dante's guide, the poet Virgil, tells him, "Here must you put by all division of spirit and gather your soul against all cowardice." I believed I was fully prepared for my ocean journey. The first circle of Dante's hell was reserved for the "virtuous unbaptized." The ocean had not yet baptized me; I still thought of myself as virtuous. I hadn't any concept of how deep into the inferno the ocean would take me. Rowing into hell was not my intention. I wish I could say that the devil made me do it, but I took up the quest all by myself.

IT SEEMS AS IF I have always found curiosity to be more compelling than fear. My mother insists that my explorations started as soon as I could walk. I was born in Florida. My father was the superintendent of schools. Mother did her best to raise three children. Mother insists that she took me out of the crib and put me into a bed because I had developed the habit of climbing the sides of the crib and sleeping on the railing.

I don't remember crib climbing. The earliest climb I recall was my first ascent of the pedestal. There was a stone pedestal in the front hall of our Florida home. It was perhaps four feet high and had a platform at its top about fifteen inches square. When my brothers or I wandered into trouble, Mother punished us by making us sit on top of the pedestal. As soon as Mother walked away, the troublemaker was trapped. I hated being stuck in one place. The worst part of sitting on the pedestal was that sooner or later my father would walk through the front door. If he found me on the pedestal, it would announce that I was in trouble.

It became a mission in my two-year-old brain to learn how to climb down off this stone pinnacle. One day while my mother was busy with my brothers, I decided to explore the ominous pillar. The pedestal stood at one end of a long planter. Using a box as a step, I climbed into the planter. Then I teetered along the edge using Mother's plants as handholds. Soon the top of the pedestal came into view at eyeball height. Now it was merely a matter of wiggling up the same way I wriggled into my father's lap when I wanted him to read to me. Before I knew it, I'd inched my way to the top of the pedestal.

Once on the summit, I learned a lesson known to cats and climbers: climbing up is easier than climbing down. I was trapped, just as I would have been had my mother put me there. Calling for help was out of the question. I'd gotten myself onto the pedestal; I must get myself off. I sat in silence searching for a way down, but escape eluded me.

Time slowed to a crawl. I felt lonely, and the stone made my bottom cold, but I dared not cry out. Then my worst nightmare came to pass. Father came through the front door. Not having sufficient vocabulary to explain either my achievement or my predicament, I burst into tears. Father put down his briefcase, took me in his arms, and went to find my mother. Mother looked at the two of us as if we'd lost our minds: "She's not in trouble." But, Father told her, he found me on the pedestal. They summoned my older brother Duke, who was eight years old. Duke claimed that he'd had nothing to do with my being on the pedestal.

My brother Lamar came in; he was six. He tried to tell my parents that I'd climbed up on the pedestal all by myself. As usual, Lamar saw everything, but Lamar had a speech impediment. I could understand him, but for some reason no one else could. By this time, I was content to enjoy the confusion. I even added to it by babbling all the words I knew: "Daddy, peanut, swim, swim, swim, Daddy, peanut, swim, swim, swim." This was the way of the world. My parents thought they knew all, but they didn't. Lamar spoke the truth, but no one understood him. Duke was blamed for something he didn't do, and I learned that life on a pedestal is cold, hard, unforgiving, and best avoided.

CHAPTER 2

Women and Stomachs First

June 16, 1998
latitude north 36:15, longitude west 74:36
full days at sea: 2
progress: 60 miles

AT 2:45 A.M., I WENT ON DECK TO CHECK THE CONDITIONS. One set of waves ran from the southwest toward the northeast, while another set charged out of the north barreling south. The collision of opposing forces tossed the *American Pearl* like a salad. Watching the intersecting waves, I imagined that the dark ocean looked the same to me as it did to Leif Eriksson, Christopher Columbus, and James Cook. Indeed, this view of things predates the existence of man. The ocean might not have looked any different to *Homo habilis*, *Homo erectus*, or Cro-Magnon man. I wondered if they had turned their heads as I did, to let the wind brush the hair out of their faces.

The evening was warm. I stretched out in the narrow space between the port gunwale and the rowing station and gazed up at the stars. I imagined I could feel the rotation of the earth and sense the isolation of our planet floating in the void of space. *What did the ocean teach the many pilgrims who passed this way before me? Are there new worlds yet to be explored or better worlds yet to be discovered?* As I was busy pondering the measure of human progress, the clash of two opposing waves sent a cap of white spray over the gunwale. Suddenly feeling small, wet, and irrelevant, I abandoned my supervision of the earth's rotation and went back to bed.

The morning of June 16 snuck up on me. I didn't make it to the oars before sunup. The wind was strong, and the swells were eight to ten feet. It took several hours for me to find a rowing rhythm that would allow the *American Pearl* to surf the crests of the waves without dropping its nose into the troughs.

A few minutes before noon, I paused to log my location. I pulled out a small brass sextant and a global positioning system unit. I'd had poor experiences with early GPS units. In 1989, I skied 750 miles across Antarctica to the South Pole. The expedition team carried a satellite navigator. This precursor to the GPS was a "brick," my term for anything you lug on a journey that doesn't merit its weight. One evening, a hundred miles from the South Pole, the satnav told us we were in Nairobi. The thing was the size of a four-slice toaster, and it was a brick. The GPS was much smaller than the satnav, but I wasn't willing to trust my life to anything that depended on batteries.

With the sextant, I measured the angle between the sun and the horizon in a boat that was bucking up and down and rocking side to side. Then I did my best to record the precise time, but this was always a bit of a guess. After I had those figures, I spent several minutes doing calculations, with which I plotted my position within a radius of roughly fifty miles. After finishing this lengthy exercise, I picked up the GPS, held it out toward the sky, pushed a button, and waited thirty seconds, and it delivered my latitude and longitude within fifteen feet. *The satellite navigator may have been a brick, but, despite its dependence on batteries, this GPS is worth its weight in . . . chocolate.* (Gold has no value to a woman alone in a rowboat on the ocean.)

The deck was unbearably hot. To get out of the sun, I ate lunch in the cabin. My rowing life would have been more comfortable if the deck had been equipped with a canopy, but my sponsor insisted that I not have anything aboard that might be turned into a sail.

No kite, no wind generator, no tarps, not even a space blanket with grommets at the corners. I had bolted the solar panels flat against the hull instead of mounting them on pivots, where I might have turned them to catch the sun. Pivoting solar panels might also be turned to catch the wind.

The power generated by the solar panels ran my water maker— a desalination unit that turned salt water into fresh water. The panels powered my satellite telephone, running lights, radar target enhancer, and laptop computer. They would power the video camera that Sector had supplied and insisted that I bring along. The Frenchman who taught me to operate the camera said, "You must treat it as you would your best friend." I had thought, *Can I leave my best friend in a waterproof box for three months?* The water maker was not working, and I feared that it would turn into an expensive twenty-five-pound brick.

The system worked by pumping seawater at high pressure through a fine ceramic filter that removed salt and other impurities. A backwash through the pump purged salt and other elements out of the filter. Salt water entered the system through a fitting in the bottom of the hull. The desalinator had worked well when we tested it in the harbor, but now air was entering and breaking the suction. In the harbor, the boat had always been in contact with the water, but in ten-foot swells the hull bounced like a child on a trampoline. Sometimes the intake was in contact with the ocean, while at other times it was bounding in the air.

Fixing this problem couldn't wait until Sunday; I needed water. I knelt in the cockpit, dropped my head into the compartment that held the water maker, and disassembled the intake valve. With my head upside down, the heat, and the rolling motions of the boat, I began to feel seasick. *This isn't the time.* Fighting nausea, I took a section of spare hose and spliced it to the prefilter. Then I weighted the end of the hose by duct-taping a wrench to it, and dropped the hose over the side. I purged the air out of the system and turned the desalinator on. Knowing it would take several minutes for it to pressurize, I went back to rowing, which settled my stomach. Minutes later, the prefilter was full of air. *This will never do!* I shut off the water maker and pledged to work on it on Sunday.

Fortunately, I had a manual hand-pump water maker in reserve, no batteries needed. Two days before I was to leave, we'd realized that my manual desalinator wasn't working. Gérard d'Aboville and another friend, Kathy Steward, flew to Virginia to get another one. Kathy was the only member of the team we trusted with this mission. This fiery redhead was both resourceful and persistent. If Kathy couldn't find a hand-pump desalinator to purchase, she'd track down somebody to build one. Not only did Kathy and Gérard return with a new hand-pump desalinator, Kathy also found a spare waterproof VHF radio. An accident during the week of sea trials had drenched one of my two VHFs, and I hadn't been able to repair it.

Once the sun went down, I used the hand pump to make water for dinner. It took a full half hour of pumping to purify the few liters I needed for the evening. I had an eighteen-liter tank of fresh water, but I held that in reserve for foul weather or emergency use.

The morning of June 17, I was up well before dawn. My hands were stiff as I took up the oars, but the only serious protests came from my backside and my heels. Blisters on my hands and feet were not a concern; I would be able to keep an eye on these areas. Blisters on my backside were more troubling. Until I developed a good set of calluses all around, I would need to be vigilant about keeping my butt as dry as possible. Warm, moist environments breed infection. My seat felt like a bed of nails and my shoes like the mouth of an alligator, but once I got the boat moving, the pain diminished to a dull ache.

The restroom aboard the *American Pearl* was "bucket and chuck it." I had two two-gallon buckets. The blue bucket was for washing and bath water. The red bucket was for other business. It was a low-tech but efficient system.

The highest-tech system aboard was the satellite telephone. As a rule, I cannot abide telephones. My father had inherited nerve deafness from his mother, and my brother Lamar had inherited it from Father. My father has never claimed to read lips, but he hears better through his glasses than through his hearing aids. Like our father, Lamar hears with his eyes. As a consequence, if I can't see a person, I do not believe we are actually communicating.

Aboard the *American Pearl*, I had to force myself to use the satellite phone. I might be perfectly content with silence, but I didn't want to worry my friends. After lunch, I telephoned Gérard in France. Then I talked to Diane Stege, the central contact person for my support team in Kentucky. Diane would pass the word among my friends that all was well. These two short conversations used 20 percent of my battery power, but the solar panels would recharge the batteries by evening.

Over the course of the day, I wore a heart rate monitor to track my exertion. Rowing at a steady pace, my heart rate ranged between 120 and 130 beats per minute, but as I made dinner, my heart rate exceeded 160 beats per minute. I'd never thought of cooking as aerobic exercise, but standing in the cockpit was like tap-dancing on a teeterboard. When I spilled hot soup into my sock and hopped around the deck, my heart rate reached 180. *I've always known it, and now I have proof: cooking is dangerous.*

To make up for the hour that I spent hand-pumping water, I rowed for an hour after sunset. The sky was cloudy, obscuring any light from the moon or stars. Every few minutes, the boat would surf down the face of the wave and plow into a trough. When the nose of the boat submerged, it spun the boat sideways. Sitting on a rowing deck two feet above the water looking sideways into ten-foot swells is not my idea of a good time. After finishing my obligatory hour, I lashed down the oars and went to bed. Lying in the cabin, I thought of home. *I wonder how Lamar is doing.*

IN ADDITION TO BEING hearing-impaired, Lamar is developmentally disabled. I was Lamar's self-appointed guardian long before a court of law appointed me to be his legal guardian. When I was four, our family left behind the sandy soil of Florida and moved to the grassy hills of Connecticut. Lamar and I were delighted to discover that the boy next door had a sandbox. We were busy playing in the sand with the neighbor boy when I heard my brother's new name for the first time. The boy's mother stood behind the screen door shrieking, "He's a retard, he'll dirty everything—get him out of there!" The boy pushed my brother and told him that he had to leave. Lamar left, and I went with him. I didn't know what my brother's new name meant, but I didn't like it.

Minutes later, I was climbing a weeping willow a little farther down the street. Lamar didn't climb trees, but he watched me scramble up the branches. Soon a gang of boys gathered around my brother. I heard Lamar say, "Stop hurting tree." The next thing I knew, seven or eight boys were switching Lamar with branches they'd pulled from the willow. Like the woman behind the screen door, they called him "retard." I shouted down, "His name is Lamar!"

One of the boys whipped my brother across the face with a willow switch, and Lamar started to cry. I jumped out of the tree and knocked the boy to the ground. Another boy pushed me down. As soon as I hit the dirt, I grabbed a pair of feet and pulled them out from under their owner. In an instant, I was engulfed in an array of fists and feet. At the center of the fray, I punched and kicked with all my might. After a few minutes, the pile lifted. Several older boys pulled us apart. As they began to lecture the younger boys about it not being proper to "fight a girl," Lamar and I ran home.

Because Lamar is four years older, I grew up with his special language along with the language of my parents. Because I had no trouble understanding Lamar, I often served as his interpreter. Seeing Lamar with a welt on his face, Mother asked, "What happened?"

My brother told her that some boys hit him with a tree branch, and that I beat the boys up. Mother didn't look to me for a translation. Instead, she spanked me with a belt for several minutes and threw me out into the fenced dog yard so I could "learn some manners." I couldn't decide whether Mother thought I'd hit Lamar with the willow switch or I was being punished for fighting with the boys who had.

I remember the feeling that descended on me as I stood in that dog yard: I felt helpless. This feeling would haunt me and would grow into a nemesis. As clear as any enemy, helplessness would lie in wait for me down every dark alley. Learning to joust with helplessness became a passion.

BEFORE DAWN ON JUNE 18, I checked my position and noted it in my deck log. The winds had driven me well offshore, but I was north of the Gulf Stream. I took up the oars and rowed east at four knots per hour. After an hour and a half, I stopped for breakfast and checked my position. I expected to have covered six miles toward the east. Instead, the GPS told me that I had traveled less than three miles east-southeast. I turned the GPS off, waited a few seconds, then turned it on and tried again. The result was the same. I wanted to throw the GPS into the ocean. *I am in an adverse current that is pushing me southwest at 2.3 miles per hour.* I adjusted my course, but I knew I was rowing up the down escalator.

By late afternoon, I'd rowed my hands bloody trying to beat the countercurrent. The Gulf Stream was forty-six nautical miles to the east. Each hour, I rowed the equivalent of four-and-a-half nautical miles forward while the current pushed me two-and-a-quarter miles back. It would take twenty hours of nonstop rowing to reach the Gulf Stream. If I stopped rowing, the adverse current would carry me in the wrong direction. For the first time in the trip, I wondered, *What am I doing here?*

ANY PERSON WHO LEAVES the comfort of civilization is des-
tined to ask this question from time to time. Still, asking it so early
in the trip struck me as a lapse in mental fortitude. *Don't let the "have
you ever . . ." people win.* The "have you ever . . ." people are the mall
muffins of a spectator society.

"Have you ever been alone, on the ocean?" they ask.

"No."

"Have you ever been alone, on the ocean, at night?"

"No."

"Have you ever been alone, on the ocean, at night, in the dark?"

The penchant for redundancy among the "have you ever . . ."
people is enormously irritating. *How are we human beings to progress
without testing our limits or going beyond what is known? I must prefer
risk over stalemate. Why am I supposed to be afraid of the dark? People die
from hunger, from cold, from injury and illness, but what peril is there in
the sun going down? It is an interior darkness, the darkness of mind, that
is deadly, not the dark of night.*

Reporter: "So, are you crazy?"

Tori: "Probably. Aren't we all?"

Reporter: "Was there some trauma in your childhood that
makes you want to do this?"

Tori: "As a girl, I wasn't allowed to play baseball. I never
got over it."

Reporter: "Are you an adrenaline junkie?"

Tori: "You try rowing twelve hours a day, every day, for
three months and see how much adrenaline you get
out of it."

Reporter: "If you aren't going to get any money out of this, are
you after fame?"

Tori: "Can you name the first woman to climb Mount
Everest?"

Reporter: [Silence]

Tori: "Her name was Junko Tabei. Can you name the first woman to ski to the North Pole?"

Reporter: [Silence]

Tori: "Her name was Ann Bancroft. Can you name the first woman to ski to the South Pole?"

Reporter: [Silence]

Tori: "A woman named Shirley Metz and I were the first women to ski to the geographical South Pole. We touched the pole at the same time so we could each claim to have been the first. Had you ever heard of either of us?"

Reporter: [A silent shrug]

Tori: "Men occasionally garner fame out of expeditions. Women do not. Men are sometimes rewarded for their rugged individualism. Women are not. When a woman is too robust or too independent, she gets asked what her boyfriend thinks about it. No one genuinely cares what the boyfriend thinks; they just want to know whether or not she has a boyfriend."

Reporter: "Well, okay then."

Tori: "Okay then."

Exhausted from battling the current and in need of better things to occupy my mind, I decided I would give myself thirty minutes to work on repairing the desalinator. Hand-pumping a useful quantity of water would take at least thirty minutes, so it seemed like a wise investment of time. To fortify myself for the undertaking, I opened a bag of peanut M&M's. Munching M&M's as I went, I pulled out my roll of tools. To make room for the tools on the floor of the cockpit, I laid the bag of M&M's on the starboard gunwale. Once I unrolled the bag on the floor, an empty pocket reminded me that one of my adjustable wrenches was still taped to the intake hose as a weight. I detached the intake hose and laid it on the gunwale beside the M&M's.

This finished, I began disassembling the prefilter system on the water maker. Soon I needed the wrench that was taped to the intake hose. As I reached for the hose on the gunwale to retrieve the wrench, the boat lurched toward the starboard side. I had my fingers around the hose when the M&M's started to slide. Without thinking, I let go of the hose and grabbed the bag of M&M's. Then I watched as gravity carried the hose over the side and down into the water. I leaned out over the gunwale in time to see the wrench, the hose, an O-ring, and the fitting that attached the hose to the prefilter system sink into the water. For a spilt second I considered diving after it, but stopped myself. *The water is several hundred feet deep. How long can I hold my breath? Not long enough.*

I sat down on the gunwale and glared at the bag of M&M's as if my situation were their fault. *All hands on deck: women and stomachs first.* There were other bags of M&M's aboard, but four critical pieces of equipment were spiraling to the bottom of the ocean. *Brilliant.* If I couldn't fabricate a new O-ring, scavenge another section of hose, concoct a fitting to connect the scavenged hose to the desalinator, and find a weight to sink the hose into the water without using my last wrench, I would be hand-pumping my fresh water all the way to France.

IF LAMAR COULD HAVE seen me, he would have shrugged, raised an eyebrow, laughed, and flipped his hands palms toward the ceiling. When I was young, the hearing aids that my father and brother used were not technologically sophisticated. Conversations were kept short and to the point. Extraneous noise made even the simplest exchanges impossible. Because of this, Lamar and I shared a nonverbal vocabulary. A shrug, raised eyebrow, and silent laugh meant, "Oops, it's broken." *Lamar was good at breaking things.* His palms-up hand gesture would ask, "How you gonna fix it?" *I was good at fixing things.*

DARN THE M&M'S, I need water. I pulled the rubber bladder out of my spare bilge pump and carved out a rough O-ring with my Swiss Army knife. Next, I scavenged a length of hose from the saltwater ballast tanks under the rowing deck. To connect the hose to the desalinator, I cut a section from an irrigation syringe that was in my first-aid kit. Finally, I weighted the hose with a fishing weight from my survival bag.

Using these conjured parts, I reassembled the water maker, purged the air out of the system, and flipped the power switch. The pump sputtered to life, and, after the unit pressurized, it produced the first solar-powered water of the voyage. I leaned against the bulkhead and smiled as I imagined Lamar nodding his approval. Instead of the thirty minutes I'd allotted, I'd spent a full hour and a half on the task.

To make up for lost time and to fight the adverse current, I pulled hard on the oars with hardly a break until after 11:00 P.M. After cooking dinner and preparing the boat for the night, I collapsed onto my mat in a foul mood. *How could I have allowed the boat to run with the wind that first night? I should have thrown out the parachute of my sea anchor to slow the boat down. My ego got in the way. I wanted to impress the "have you ever . . ." people with miles. Now I am 120 nautical miles from the start. If I'd caught the Gulf Stream on the second day, as I had planned, I might be 250 or 300 miles from the start. I am an idiot. How could I have saved the M&M's and let the desalinator parts go overboard?*

Just as my psyche was sinking low enough to visit the hose on the bottom of the ocean, the sound of clicks and whistles disrupted my thoughts. *Not only did you let your pride navigate this boat, you've left the VHF radio on.* I rolled over and opened the hatch to the electronics compartment, which was under my shoulder. The radio was off, but the clicks and whistles grew louder. I put my hand on the wall and felt it vibrate with pops and whoops. *Dolphins!*

I leapt up, bumping my head on the ceiling. Then I raced through the main hatch and stepped onto the deck. A sliver of moon found a hole in the clouds. Its diffuse light made the water shimmer with silvery blue, and I found myself standing in the middle of a pod of spotted dolphins. Their backs were a purplish gray and their white bellies sported distinctive dots. Twelve or more dolphins circled the boat. One leapt into the air, followed by another, then another. They twisted and spun.

The dolphins gurgled. They whistled. They clicked. One turned on its side and slapped its pectoral fin on the surface of the water. All of a sudden I felt dizzy. My head began to swim, and I realized that I'd been holding my breath. With a sudden intake of air, I started to laugh. My giggles startled one of the larger dolphins. It jerked back as if to swim away, and then it seemed to cock its smooth head to listen. "Hello," I said. I sank to my knees with the dolphin only a few feet away. It lingered with its beak out of the water, the spots on its chin clearly visible.

Then a loud whistle rose from behind me. In a flash of fins, the dolphins were gone. I stood on deck, bathed in moonlight, allowing the boat to sway beneath my feet. After several minutes, I spread my hands and lifted them high above my head, embracing a massive blue cloud in the arc of my arms. My breathing fell into synchrony with the rhythm of the waves. The air smelled clean, with a vague sweetness. In the distance, the splash of dolphins drew me back into myself. I turned to face the sound and cocked my head, impersonating the big dolphin. "Thanks."

Within a minute or two, dark clouds drew a curtain across the slender moon, and the clouds faded from light blue to the color of lead. *Storm brewing.* I checked the lashings on my oars, topped off the ballast tanks, and verified that all the hatches were securely battened down. Then I crawled back into the cabin and listened to the rising wind. Before long it was howling out of the west. Rain pummeled the *Pearl*. I rocked and rolled around my little cabin. Every time I checked the compass it read 90 degrees: my course was due east. The wind was pushing me toward the Gulf Stream. *Go, baby, go!*

At dawn on June 19, a stiff breeze still blew toward the east. When I checked my position, I found myself fifteen miles closer to the Gulf Stream and knocking on the elevator door. The storm had left me a cockpit full of semifresh water. Before taking up my oars, I took a bath and washed my clothes. I'd heard stories about people rowing naked. This was not for me. *The legend that Eleanor of Aquitaine rode bare-breasted toward Damascus during the Second Crusade is just a myth; the windburn could have killed her.*

Wearing wet but clean clothes, I settled in to work at the oars about 6:15 A.M. I enjoyed the sensation of the cool morning breeze chilling my shoulders under the damp shirt. There were three- and four-foot swells. As had become my custom, I rowed the first hour and a half without a break. With the wind behind me, I was skimming across the swells at almost seven miles per hour.

After a quick breakfast, I settled in to my second session at the oars. Before long, the winds died down to nothing and the day became a repeat of the day before, hazy, hot, humid, and flat. By lunchtime, however, I'd covered twenty-five miles. I pulled in the oars and checked my position. The GPS reported that even with the oars out of the water I was moving northeast at better than two miles per hour. I dropped a thermometer into the water. The water temperature was 78°F: five degrees warmer than it had been the day before. *The Gulf Stream: I am in the elevator.*

The water was moving my way. Easy swells lolled the boat as gently as a swinging hammock, and I wished myself to be in no other place on earth. *If there is any truer statement of happiness, I cannot bring it to mind.* I fired up the satellite telephone and sent an e-mail to my support team. Then I rowed until dinner. As I was eating my freeze-dried pasta primavera, dolphins arrived to entertain me. The rainbow of a sunset painted the sky with color that reflected pink and turquoise off the water. These dolphins didn't have spots. In fact, I could see nothing to distinguish them from common dolphins, but when you are alone on a calm ocean at sunset there is nothing common about dolphins of any kind.

I pulled out the video camera and attempted to capture the scene on film. I narrated, "People sit at home in their living rooms and ask me why I do this. Hmm." I hoped that the picture alone would provide an acceptable answer. I felt proud not to be searching for life in the absent corners of weekends. My mind bragged to itself about holding the vitality of existence in my fingertips. Intoxicated by this chest pounding, I felt as if I could ride the crest of a tidal wave while drinking tea. It was early in the trip, the boat was still full of food, and I was still full of myself.

CHAPTER 3

A Shark and an Explosion

June 20, 1998
latitude north 36:46, longitude west 70:48
full days at sea: 6
progress: 282 miles

AT DAWN, THE WATER TEMPERATURE WAS 82°F, WHICH confirmed my placement in the Gulf Stream. Schools of small fish gathered under the boat. I imagined that sea worms, barnacles, and other small creatures had begun to attach themselves to my slow-moving hull. Over the course of several months, this accumulation of growth would increase the drag on the hull and slow me down.

After breakfast, a thought swam languidly through my brain; *I should get in the water and scrub the boat.* Just then my eye caught a shadow moving through the water. The ghostly form rose. Its head and tail swung from side to side like a snake. When the figure passed within a few feet, it took the distinctive shape of a hammerhead shark.

My ears thudded with the sound of my heartbeat. I pulled out my copy of *National Audubon Society Field Guide to North American Fishes, Whales and Dolphins.* After reading about hammerheads, I eased quietly into my rowing seat and slid my oars into the water. I rowed gently, as if I might somehow sneak away from the shark. For the next several hours, the shark carved slow circles around the boat.

I compared the behavior of the shark to that of the dolphins, and I came to understand why humans tend to anthropomorphize dolphins as the "good guys" and sharks as the "bad guys." The dolphins visited; the hammerhead lurked. The dolphins played; the shark stalked. For the dolphins, my boat and I provided novel entertainment; for the shark, my boat was an impediment to the prospect of a juicy meal. By late morning, the hammerhead lost interest and moved off. *I am not getting out of this boat. If I arrive in France with a two-inch-thick shag carpet of marine growth on the bottom of the boat, so be it. Some say hammerheads will attack humans; some say they will not. I'm not willing to experiment.*

After lunch, I heard spouting in the distance. A hundred yards away, a pod of whales lounged on the surface of the ocean. When one blew, I saw two columns of mist. *Baleen whales: two blowholes.* Toothed whales have only one blowhole. I rowed toward the whales, but my seat squeaked so loudly that the whales submerged. The day of my departure, well-wishers had tracked sand onto the deck of the *American Pearl.* Some of the sand worked its way into my seat tracks, which caused my seat to grind and squeak with each stroke. This irritation fell to the Sunday repair list. It was only Saturday. *Sorry, guys. I'll take my seat apart and clean it in the morning.*

As I put a teapot of water on the stove for dinner, more spotted dolphins stopped for a visit. There was a small unspotted baby in the pod. I focused on the baby dolphin with such intensity that its mother whisked it away. I turned my attention back to the stove. The single burner swung from side to side and front to back on two gimbaled pivots. The whole contraption was not much larger than a basketball. My friend Luckett had given me the little kettle to boil the water that I poured into my freeze-dried meals. The fuel was propane. Several advisors had encouraged me to locate the stove inside the cabin, but I'd had a bad experience with carbon monoxide.

WHEN I WAS IN the Antarctic, we cooked all our meals in one central tent, called the transportable utility retractable dome, better known as the TURD. One stormy afternoon, I spent too much time with the stoves in the TURD. My face turned bright red, and before I knew what was happening I was outside in the snow wolfing up my dinner. It was classic carbon monoxide poisoning. I had a powerful headache that lasted for days. To avoid revisiting that experience aboard the *American Pearl*, I located the stove outside in the cockpit near the main hatch. If the weather became inclement, I could sit in the cabin and reach out into the cockpit to stir a meal or to refill the teapot.

FROM SUNSET TO SUNSET, I progressed more than ninety miles. "I love the Gulf Stream!" I shouted. At midnight, a wind blew in from the northeast. When the wind opposes the current, the Gulf Stream can turn ugly in a hurry. When waves hit from the side, it is relatively easy for a vessel the size of the *American Pearl* to end up bottom up. For safety, I dropped my large sea anchor over the side and watched the parachute of its fabric drift off the stern. The sea anchor would keep the boat perpendicular to the waves, making it more difficult for a wave to capsize the boat.

Sunday, June 21, to honor the Sabbath as a day of rest, I planned to sleep in for an extra hour or two, but I was eager to get to my repair list. I cleaned and oiled each element of my sliding seat until it no longer sounded like a chorus of whining harpies. When the sun was high enough to power the desalinator without drawing down the batteries, I started the water maker and ran the fresh water into my blue laundry bucket. While the bucket was filling with water, I plugged the bolt holes in the cabin roof with epoxy putty.

Next I took a bath. I washed my shirt, then my shorts, and then my body. After these were relatively clean, I dunked my head into the bucket of cold water and lathered my hair with Joy dishwashing detergent. Once clean, I put my wet shirt back on and pulled out a dry pair of shorts. The shirt would dry while I rowed, but I didn't want to risk diaper rash by rowing in wet shorts. I hung the wet shorts on the cabin roof to dry. The cabin roof was only about four feet above the waterline, so I had to keep an eye out for breaking waves.

The last task on my repair list was to find something to block the sun from pouring through the stern hatch and scalding my tender feet. I considered using a few of the foil wrappers from my freeze-dried dinners to cover the inside of the Plexiglas, but then I remembered that I had a small zip-top bag with decorations for a Fourth of July celebration. Because my technical team was French, my major sponsor was Italian, and Kenneth Crutchlow, who would rightly take credit for bringing all of us together, was British, I'd planned to be brazenly American on the Fourth of July. I'd packed a goofy three-cornered hat and miniature copies of the Declaration of Independence, the great seal of the United States, and portraits of U.S. presidents.

I figured I'd rather look up at U.S. presidents than used dinner wrappers, so I duct-taped portraits of George Washington, John F. Kennedy, and Andrew Jackson to the inside of the stern hatch. With those fellows above me, I didn't think it fair to leave all the others locked in a plastic bag. I kept taping presidents to the ceiling until thirteen men stared grimly down. I added the Declaration of Independence and the Great Seal of the United States for balance. Then I decided I should save my duct tape for more important things.

I took up the oars at about 10:00 A.M. and rowed until noon. After a couple of PowerBars and some fruit punch, I decided to send out a few e-mails. One message was for my friends in Kentucky; another was a letter to the Kentucky Bar Association. While preparing for the voyage, I had neglected to get three of the required thirteen and a half hours of continuing legal education classes to keep my license to practice law. I begged the KBA's forgiveness and promised

I would make up the hours as soon as I got off the ocean. I hooked the computer up to the satellite telephone and dialed the number to connect to the computer in Kentucky. Just as the letters were beginning to transfer, a stream of sparks flew up from the bottom of the electrical box and the telephone went dead.

I shut off the power and waited for the smoke to clear. A wire from the back of the telephone's transceiver was lying in the bottom of the electrical box. I reattached the wire and confidently turned everything back on. Nothing happened. I tried other combinations, and soon I was able to restore power to the telephone, but it still didn't work. I ran through all the troubleshooting suggestions in the instruction manual. When I reached the end of the suggestions, the manual instructed me to call a toll-free number to speak with a service representative. *Darn, where's that pay phone when you need it?* With the noonday sun, the temperature inside the cabin rose to 115°F. My temper was rising too. *I hate phones, and they hate me. I'll fix it later.*

I went back to rowing. The wind was against me. It was not strong, only five or ten miles an hour out of the northeast. Still, it was enough to impede my progress. Needing a distraction, I decided it was time to delve into my audio library. I opened the small Rubbermaid container and picked a tape at random. It was a lecture about Isaac Newton.

I've always had a soft spot for dear old Isaac. He invented differential calculus, formulated the theory of gravity (with or without the help of an apple falling from a tree and knocking him on the head), defined terrestrial mechanics, and explained the science of color. The poet William Wordsworth wrote of Newton:

> *Where the statue stood*
> *Of Newton, with his prism and silent face,*
> *The marble index of a mind for ever*
> *Voyaging through strange seas of Thought, alone.*

I admired Newton for the rationality of his scientific mind. Despite the chaos of his personal life, Newton brought the world the light of knowledge. Pride was not among his flaws. Newton thought himself to be like a child playing with seashells, "whilst the great ocean of truth lay all undiscovered before me."

As I continued to row, I gazed out to sea. A flock of dark shearwaters flew over, and one paused to hover just above my head. It was about the size of a crow, and its color was sooty brown with a lighter belly. Still thinking about Newton, I wondered whether a bird would give up the ability to fly for the ability to read and write. *I would not give up my books even to fly free as a bird. The written word is the connective tissue of human experience. Without knowledge, freedom suffocates.*

WHEN I WAS FIVE, we moved to a suburb of Philadelphia. My parents didn't understand Lamar any better, but there was a new rule in our house: if Lamar got into trouble, all three children received a spanking. Whenever Lamar was in trouble, I was usually involved. So it made sense that I would be spanked along with him, but Duke never did anything wrong. He was two years older than Lamar and six years older than I. Lamar and I didn't hang around with Duke; we worshipped him from afar. After school, while Duke did his homework, Lamar and I explored the woods near our home. We knew every rock and tree in those woods.

When I was in the third grade we moved to Uniontown, Pennsylvania. Lamar and I went to Craig Elementary School, and Duke went to the junior high. As Lamar and I walked to school, a couple of kids lobbed rocks in our direction. By that time, I had gained plenty of experience in returning rocks to their rightful owners, and I usually hit what I aimed at.

Before the teachers even learned my name, they sent me to the principal's office. The principal frowned. "You must not throw rocks."

"The kids were throwing rocks at my brother. I was just returning them," I explained.

The principal said it was his job to defend my brother.

Incredulous, I stared up at the man. "Well, you've been doing a piss-poor job of it!"

The principal was too shocked to speak, so I continued. "Where were you last year, and the year before that? Where were you this morning? Where will you be this afternoon when we walk home?"

I was too young to comprehend the hazards of speaking truth to power, but the principal looked strangely sympathetic. He was smiling when he told me that "young ladies should not use the phrase 'piss-poor.'" He explained that he would protect Lamar while we were in school and that my parents would watch out for him at other times. He seemed like a nice man. I didn't doubt his sincerity, but he was wrong on both counts. Adults always thought they were in control, but they were often wrong.

STARTING ON JUNE 22, after that first week at sea, my days started to run together. I'd roll out of the cabin before the sun came up, row all day, and after dark find myself in a place that looked just like the place I'd started in before dawn that morning. I'd crawl onto my thin mat, and the next day I'd climb out to do it all over again.

My ninth day at sea, I went backward. The headwinds were so strong that I spent much of the morning with the boat on its sea anchor. The wind was opposed to the current, and the waves grew steep and threatened to roll the boat. As I lay in the cabin, the force of the waves slammed me into the wall, and a few rollers caused me to have close encounters with the ceiling. By early afternoon, I grew tired of being tossed about.

I went on deck, pulled in the sea anchor, put out my oars, and rowed. It was an exercise in futility. I didn't need Newton or a GPS to tell me the boat was going backward. When rowers take a stroke, the motion of the oars through the water leaves swirls that rowers call "puddles." Normally a rower receives the satisfaction of seeing her puddles fade behind the stern of the boat. When a rower takes a stroke and the puddle does not move, the boat is not moving. When a rower takes a stroke and the puddle moves toward the front of the boat, the boat is moving backward. The boat was going backward.

A white-tailed tropicbird hovered just a few feet above the deck. It was a little smaller than a pigeon, all white except for the dark tips of its wings and a black mask across its eyes. It had two white tail feathers that were almost as long as its body. I imagined it to be an oceanic Lone Ranger. *I wonder, is it lonely? Nonsense—it's just a bird. Just because the phone is broken, that doesn't mean that the bird overhead is lonely. Fix the satphone on Sunday, and the birds will seem perfectly jolly.*

After I cooked dinner, it was time to change the propane canister on the stove. Standing in the cockpit, I couldn't gain enough leverage to unscrew the tank from the stove fitting. To avoid falling overboard, I took the stove into the cabin, where I could lie down to wrestle with it. After several minutes, I managed to twist off the old canister and install a new one. I placed the depleted canister between my feet, reached outside, and hung the stove on its mounting plate in the cockpit. *Time for a nice cup of cocoa.*

I pulled out my lighter, leaned out of the main hatch, and thumbed the sparking wheel of the lighter over the burner of the stove several times. The lighter didn't spark. *I'll be halfway across the Atlantic before I master the child-safety switch on this lighter.* I pulled my hand inside, pushed the safety switch to the side, and fired the lighter. The instant it fired, a whoosh of flame rose up from my feet. *Propane gas is heavier than air.* The old canister may not have had enough gas to cook a meal, but it wasn't entirely empty. As I reached down to grab the flaming canister, I singed my eyebrow with the lighter.

Tossing the lighter into the cockpit, I took hold of the propane canister and threw it out the hatch. There it bounced off the gunwale into the ocean. *Darn it! Now I've got to go and get the thing.* I'd promised a group of schoolchildren that I wouldn't jettison any trash. *Promises, promises.* I scrambled out. The canister was floating on the port side just out of reach. I put my starboard oar in the oarlock and took a few strokes. This moved the boat between the canister and the wind. Once the canister was in the lee of the boat, I let the wind push the *American Pearl* to the little fuel tank. I reached over the side and picked it up. When I had it in hand, I sat down on the gunwale and stared at the canister just as I had stared at the errant bag of M&M's. *A hammerhead shark and a singed eyebrow . . . we are not in Kentucky anymore.*

CHAPTER 4

Baptism by Storm

June 25, 1998
latitude north 37:43, longitude west 69:28
days at sea: 11
progress: 382 miles

THE FIRST FEW STROKES OF THE DAY WERE THE HARD-est. My fingers were raw. My knees creaked. My shoulders were stiff. I didn't need eyes to sense daybreak. I could feel the dawn. As the first rays of the sunrise warmed my back, this early warmth was welcome, but as the sun climbed the vertebrae of my spine, its rays transformed into whips of flame that lashed my back. When the sun reached its apex at midday, radiant energy poured down on my head and my clothes dripped with perspiration. The black straps of my life vest soaked up the heat until I thought the skin beneath my shirt would boil.

Take off the life vest. I can't take it off. The sea is calm, what's the harm? Good weather breeds bad habits. It's too hot for ceremony. Taking off the life vest is a mistake. Who is looking? Who will ever know? I took off my vest with the tether attached and rowed unencumbered.

More than half a dozen men had died trying to row across the North Atlantic. All of their boats survived. If I were to become separated from the boat, a life vest would keep me alive for a few days at most. The life vest was not nearly as important as the safety tether that was attached to the life vest. The tether was fastened to a steel cable that ran the length of the deck. If stormy weather washed me off the deck, or if I tripped and fell overboard, the tether would keep me with the boat. *If I become separated from the boat, which will happen first, drowning or getting eaten? Just today . . . I'll only do it today.*

As the sun sank in the western sky, I pulled my baseball cap low to shade my eyes. By late afternoon my shirt had stiffened with dried perspiration. I fired up the water maker, filled the blue bucket, and took a bath. I was sitting on deck, with clean hair and a wet shirt, enjoying my dinner, when I heard the sound of engines. I looked up expecting to see a plane at twenty thousand feet. The azure dome of the sky was empty. I looked out to sea but didn't see anything. The sound grew louder, and I turned around. A vessel the length of a basketball court was headed my way.

In a flash, the standards of civilized behavior washed across my solitude. *Company! I should make some tea. The deck is a mess, I must tidy up. Wait, my shirt's wet, and I'm not wearing a bra.* I swung my life vest over my shoulders and buckled it in front of me. There was no time to straighten up the deck. The boat was fifty feet away.

A deep, manly voice called down from the deck above me. "Do you need any help?"

Combing fingers through my wet hair, I said, "No, I am doing just fine."

"What kind of boat is that?"

"It's a rowboat. I'm rowing to France." I tried to sound confident.

There was a long pause and a hushed discussion on the deck above me. "How long have you been out?"

"Eleven days," I said.

"How long will it take you?"

"About three months."

"We'll reach the Mediterranean in two weeks," said the man from above.

"My satellite telephone isn't working at the moment. Would you mind contacting my friends in Kentucky to let them know that I am doing just fine?" The man wrote down the telephone number and agreed to send a message. After circling the *American Pearl* a few times they departed. On the stern of their vessel, I read the name *Captain Millions*. The faint cloud of diesel exhaust smelled strangely agreeable.

I rowed until 7:00 P.M. After I lashed everything down for the evening, I leaned over the gunwale to take the water temperature. A nurse shark came within a few feet of my hand. It was about three feet long and perfectly harmless. "Hello, and how are you this evening?" I carried on with what I was doing. The water temperature was 81°F and the air temperature was the same. After noting these figures in my log, I climbed into the damp, stuffy cabin.

Taking off my life vest was one thing, but leaving the hatches open in the cabin was out of the question. Rogue waves had capsized more than one ocean rower on an otherwise calm sea. The ability of the *American Pearl* to right itself depended on having an air pocket in the watertight cabin. If the boat capsized with a hatch open, the cabin would fill with water and the boat would not self-right. This was a risk I couldn't afford to take, so I always slept with the hatches closed. The only opening in the cabin was a three-inch air vent in the ceiling. If the boat inverted, I could shut off that vent in a few seconds.

Writers wax eloquent about the silence of the sea, but I never heard it. Lines for my sea anchor hung coiled outside on the cabin bulkhead. As these ropes swung with passing swells, the sound resonated through the plywood like fingernails scratching along a rough tabletop. The rudder cables ran through PVC pipes inside the cabin. Each time the rudder shifted, the pipes squawked like two angry crows. Fish slapped the cabin walls. My water bottle rolled back and forth, back and forth, back and forth. Flocks of birds resting on the surface of the ocean cackled and cawed.

Not all sounds were bothersome. If I placed my ear low against the wall, I could often hear the deep cello reverberations of singing whales. In my dreams, whale songs brought recollections of hushed conversations, and the clucks of birds transmuted into laughter. Often I woke up from a vivid dream thinking there was a boat alongside. Many mornings I raced onto the deck only to find a raft of chatty shearwaters floating nearby. "How's a woman supposed to sleep?" I scolded them.

June 26. The only drawback to rowing in the Gulf Stream was that there were too many fish; I couldn't row without hitting them. Initially, it was amusing. I'd drop the oar into the water and fish would scurry away. I'd take my stroke and lift the oar out, and the fish would return. A second later, the oar would go back in and fish would scurry away. The oar would come out and fish would return.

At midday, a school of yellowfin tuna vied for positions in the shade of my boat; the school was so thick that the fish couldn't move out of the way when I dropped the oar into the water. Stroke after stroke, my oar hit tuna after tuna. It didn't seem to hurt the fish. In fact, I worried that the spikes of their yellow dorsal fins would chip my oars. "Get out of the way. Look, it's a simple thing—the oar goes in, the oar comes out. *Move!*"

To turn my attention away from the inconsiderate fish, I listened to a lecture about Aristotle's *Nicomachean Ethics*. Aristotle was a Renaissance man eighteen hundred years before the Renaissance. He believed that educated people are as much superior to uneducated people as the living are to the dead. As a teacher, he was conversant with anatomy, astronomy, economics, embryology, geography, geology, meteorology, physics, and zoology. He wrote about aesthetics, ethics, government, metaphysics, politics, psychology, rhetoric, and theology. Socrates taught Plato; Plato taught Aristotle; Aristotle taught Alexander the Great. Aristotle wrote that "courage is knowledge." *I'm not sure which comes first: knowledge or courage. Knowledge certainly fosters courage, but without the courage to put knowledge to work, what is the point?* Aristotle believed that humanity is influenced more by fear than it is by faith.

MY FAITH WAS BORN out of fear. When I was in the third grade, a mock fight broke out between the Catholics and the Protestants. A group of children surrounded Lamar and began screaming at him. I clawed my way to the center of the circle. "Is he a Catholic or a Protestant?" they yelled. "We're Presbyterians," I hollered. There was a pause as the Catholic leader conferred with the Protestant leader. They decided we were neutral and could move to the safe zone along the fence. I wasn't sure what being a Presbyterian meant, but I was delighted to be one.

In Uniontown, church provided the only safe zone in our lives. There were rare exceptions, such as the morning the Sunday school teacher looked straight at Lamar and me and said, "Jesus died for your sins." After church, a boy named David told everyone that Lamar and I had killed Jesus. My status as a Jesus-killer was not easy for my nine-year-old brain to grasp. God had let his son die because Lamar and I were going to be bad, even though we wouldn't be born for a couple thousand years.

I figured it was just like the times Mother had spanked all three of us because we'd be going to Grandmother's house soon and we might "get away with something." I didn't understand the universal calculus, but if Jesus had died for my sins thousands of years ago, I guess it made sense I could get punished for something I might do at Grandmother's house next week.

Adults rarely made sense. Each time my parents learned that I had been fighting, I was rewarded with a sound spanking. "Young ladies do not brawl." This was always spoken as if my becoming a lady were more important than protecting my brother. I didn't see how becoming a lady was very appealing. Ladies didn't run. Ladies didn't jump. Ladies didn't climb. Ladies didn't wear trousers in public places. As far as I could tell, ladies were idle spectators. I didn't like the boys who tormented my brother and me, but I utterly despised the girls who watched and did nothing. I could return a rock, a punch, or a kick, but I was helpless in defending against the apathy of onlookers.

As a third grader, I didn't understand that apathy is a symptom of collective helplessness. When we turn away from people in distress, it is not because we are unfeeling. We turn away because we feel inadequate to lend assistance. Incompetence and helplessness travel hand in glove. They are accomplices in tragedy. Courage is knowledge; knowledge is courage.

All afternoon on June 27, the wind backed around the compass: from the west at fifteen miles per hour, from the southwest at twenty, from the south at twenty-five. When the wind shifts counterclockwise on the North Atlantic, bad weather is usually on the way. Black clouds piled up on pewter clouds. By late afternoon, the wind had risen forty miles per hour and waves began to crash over my starboard gunwale.

One white-tipped wave yanked the oar out of my hand, wrenching my shoulder. *That's it! I'm out of here!* I stopped rowing, lashed down the oars, and retreated to the cabin. The next day was Sunday, but it was not a day for rest. The storm gained strength throughout the night. Thunder rumbled and lightning punctuated the darkness. At dawn, the waves were the size of houses. With the boat rolling precariously from side to side, I grumbled at the video camera, "When I decided to row the Gulf Stream, I didn't imagine that it would be like going over Niagara Falls in a barrel."

The swells were not more than twenty feet high, but they were steep, and many rolled into breakers. The solar panels on the roof generated too much interference for the GPS to work inside the cabin. To log my position, I lay on my back and held the GPS as far out the main hatch as I could reach. Several large swells came and went. Then I heard the rumble of an approaching breaker. *Here it comes!* I drew in my hand and slammed the hatch shut.

The wave hit with so much force that it slid me across the lid of my electronics compartment. My hip caught the handle, levering it to the open position. In the next instant, the boat rolled upside down and my forehead slammed into the ceiling. My shoulder, hip, and knees followed in quick succession. *Ouch!* I pushed up off the ceiling to look out the hatch I'd closed only seconds before. I saw fish. The hatch was under water.

Seawater gushed in through the air vent at my knee. In the few seconds it took to screw the vent closed, several gallons of seawater flooded into my little space. I looked up at the bottom of the cabin, and watched the watertight lid of the electronics compartment swing open. The handset from my satellite phone tumbled out and plopped into the seawater, followed by a cascade of other gear.

I had studied every story I could find about knockdowns and capsizes, but nothing had prepared me for the drooling panic of being six hundred miles offshore, alone, crouched on my hands and knees with the boat's ceiling under me. Adrenaline flooded my arteries, and the instinct to open the hatch and swim clear of the boat was overwhelming.

I grabbed the hatch handles and started to open them. *No, bad idea.* I forced myself to recall a kayaking trip that I'd taken down the French Broad, in Tennessee. My kayak had flipped in a treacherous set of rapids. I missed my first attempt at an Eskimo roll. Then I missed the second try, but I managed to suck in a healthy gulp of air. As I tried to roll a third time, a set of rocks on the river bottom gave me what kayakers call a "full dynamic facial." I lost my nerve, shoved out of the kayak, and swam through the next set of rapids with my kayak in one hand and my paddle in the other. *That was stupid, but a wet exit in the middle of the ocean could be fatal. Stay calm. Stay inside.*

Roll, baby, roll . . . roll, baby, roll . . . please roll . . . please, please roll. One minute passed and then another. *I'll suffocate; I've got to get out of here.* I closed my eyes and wrestled back the impulse to open the hatch. *No, there is enough air in here for hours.* Slowly the boat began to recover. It turned on its side, and I rolled down the cabin wall. A portion of the roof lifted out of the water, and I dropped to the floor.

Another large wave hit and the roof slid back into the water. To stave off another roll I climbed up the floor toward the higher wall.

My hands trembled as I clutched the rudder pipe that ran high along the starboard side. The roof eased out of the water. *It rolled. The* Pearl *rolled. I'm okay.* Slowly the port side rose higher, but the waves outside continued to pummel the vessel. I wriggled into the stern and wedged my body into the smallest part of the cabin. *If the boat rolls again, I won't get tossed around.*

Each time the boat fell off a wave, the water in the cabin sloshed in all directions. Much of the water found its way into the electronics compartment, which held my communications equipment. Outside, the wind was forty-five miles per hour, gusting to fifty miles an hour. Air rushing between the roof and the solar panels caused the ceiling to vibrate like a pipe organ. The bolts that held the panels to the roof wobbled each time waves slapped the roof. The epoxy putty around the bolts worked loose, and it wasn't long before water dribbled through the ceiling and rained down on me.

I crawled out of the stern to get the putty out of my repair kit. I was mixing a small ball of epoxy in my hand when the boat went into the air and came down hard on its port side. I fell toward the ceiling and struck my head against the hasp of the porthole. Dropping the putty, I scurried back into my fetal position against the transom. With a flash of lightning I could see that drops of blood followed me across the cabin. *My head is bleeding.*

With the whoosh of an approaching breaker, I gripped the handles of the stern hatch. The boat rolled onto its roof and then shifted back again to the same side. *Does that count as a rollover? No, it wasn't a three-sixty; it was only a one-eighty. It doesn't count. Breathe, keep breathing. There is just something* wrong *about looking out the stern hatch and seeing fish.* I locked the handles so I wouldn't open the hatch by accident. I yelled at the wind, "Stop. Stop it. Stop it *now!*" Then with a whimper I added, "Please?"

The *American Pearl* rolled onto its side. *Up is good. Down is bad,*

Roll up. Small boats in storms move like bucking bulls, the ends shifting up and down far more than the middle. To use maritime terminology, a boat rolls side to side, pitches end to end, and heaves up and down. If you put your head to one side of the boat, the roll has more heave. If you put your head on one end of the boat or the other, the pitch has more heave. If you don't keep your head toward the middle of the boat, or the middle of the pitch or the roll, one kind of heave may lead to another. I had not felt seasick since the first few days, but a stomach spasm told me that I was about to throw up. I shoved off the transom, rolled onto my knees, and dived toward the main hatch. The instant I opened the hatch I vomited into the outside cockpit.

I closed the hatch, wiped my mouth on my sleeve, and crawled back into my tight spot against the transom. My second trip to the main hatch was not so fortuitous. As I was about to open the hatch, a wave hit. I closed the hatch and puked at the same time. Vomit splashed off the inside of the glass and splattered back into my lap. *Oh, that's just lovely.* Hoping to settle my stomach, I put my feet in the stern and my head closer to the middle of the boat. The boat did another half roll, and I fell onto the ceiling.

There I found myself eye to eye with the portrait of Franklin Delano Roosevelt. In a mildly patrician accent I quoted FDR: "First of all, let me assert my firm belief that the only thing we have to fear is fear itself—nameless, unreasoning, unjustified terror which paralyzes needed efforts to convert retreat into advance." *Forgive me, dear sir, but I am scared. Fear is my life insurance policy, and I am retreating back into the stern, where I will get less battered and where the smell is not so revolting.*

I folded myself back into a tight crouch in the back of the boat. As I clutched the hatch handles, I prayed, begging for my life, pleading for Jesus, Mary, Joseph, the three wise men, and the god Poseidon to save me from the storm.

After I'd been holed up in the cabin for about six hours, nature began to call. With the boat pitching wildly from side to side and waves sweeping across the roof, going on deck to use the bathroom bucket was out of the question.

Fortunately, while climbing in Alaska, I'd developed the skill of being able to use a wide-mouthed water bottle as a pee bottle so I would not need to leave the tent at night. I'd stashed a spare water bottle with my first-aid kit for just this contingency. My friends had sent along enough vitamins to keep an elephant healthy, and I'd taken to stuffing the vitamins I couldn't choke down into the extra water bottle. I dumped the extra vitamins onto my mat and employed the water bottle for its intended purpose. As I pulled up my shorts, the boat rolled again. I had not yet closed the water bottle. It spilled. *No one is going to believe this.* Sloshing water dissolved the vitamins, which added an acrid odor to that of the seawater, vomit, and urine. Later, I would record, "The smell was diabolical."

As the sun went down the cabin cooled and I started to shiver. I opened the compartment that held my fleece sleeping bag, and was disappointed to find it sopping. I had no alternative but to curl up inside the dripping fleece. *Gérard d'Aboville would describe this situation as "uncomfortable but not life-threatening."* I had an emergency position-indicating radio beacon, better known as an EPIRB. If the situation had been genuinely life-threatening, I could set off this international distress signal, and someone would come to my assistance.

EPIRBs are not for times you've made a mess of things and you just want to go home. They are for situations when if someone doesn't come to your aid, life or limb will be lost. I couldn't imagine anything more ignominious than being rescued at sea. Nothing would cause a greater offense to my self-reliant pride. I repeated what I knew Gérard would say: "This situation is uncomfortable but not life-threatening."

If I abandoned ship, how would I face Bob Hurley, Noreen Powers, Scott Shoup, or the others who helped build the boat? I can't leave the

Pearl. *I can't give the "have you ever . . ." people the satisfaction of watching me quit. Most important, how could I in good conscience subject another human being to this vile smell?*

Resigned to the discomfort of my situation, I pulled the wet fleece around my shoulders, cradled my head in my arms, and quivered into a restless sleep. Hours later, a boom of thunder jolted me wide-eyed. It was too dark to see, but I sensed the presence of a wise older friend. In my imagination, Luckett Davidson cupped my face in her warm, strong hands. I had seen Luckett hold the face of Gérard d'Aboville in this same comforting manner.

Luckett was part of my support team. She had been responsible for organizing my meals and the rest of my nutritional plan. More than that, she was an archfriend. Luckett had come to North Carolina for my departure. Ever the protector, Luckett was worried, and she turned to Gérard for reassurance. He responded by saying, "Tori will finish in victory." The statement surprised all who heard it, perhaps even Gérard himself. It was clear that he had made no such predictions about other ocean rowers. In thanks, Luckett hugged Gérard's face in her hands.

The memory gave me the sense everything would work out. A sustained burst of lightning lit the cabin for several seconds. There were no archfriends with me. I was alone.

THE SUMMER BEFORE I entered the fifth grade, we moved from one side of Uniontown, Pennsylvania, to the other. For Lamar and me this meant a new school, a new church, and, I figured, a new group of tormentors. Our older brother, Duke, was in high school and getting ready to apply to college. People described Duke as a loner, but as a teenager he'd gone to five different schools in five years. He simply stopped trying to make friends. Duke was very intelligent, and in Uniontown that made him the odd man out.

Unlike Duke, I used my athletic ability to make friends. I was big for my age and could play football with the best of the boys. There were not so many children under twelve in our new neighborhood that we could distinguish between girls and boys when choosing teams. In football and wiffleball (like baseball, only with improvised bats and a plastic ball) I was always the first girl picked. Football was my favorite. I delighted in lifting boys off the ground and dropping them on their heads. The best athlete in our age group was a tall, handsome boy named Eric Fee.

In our new neighborhood, Eric was king. To his credit, Eric was a benevolent ruler. He treated girls with respect. He was gentle toward animals. One afternoon Lamar and I were at the playground. I was practicing basketball, and Lamar was in his usual place at the edge of the playground watching the action. Out of the corner of my eye, I saw a grubby boy pick up a rock and throw it at my brother. The rock missed. Before the boy could pick up a second rock, I tackled him, pinning him to the asphalt. Eric was on the other side of the playground with a boy named Dale Ellis. When they heard a fight was under way, they came running. By the time they arrived, I was straddling the boy on the pavement, my hands gripping his collar. He was kicking; I was yelling.

Eric thought the boy had picked a fight with me. He peppered my prisoner with questions: "Why are you fighting with a girl? Why did you throw the rock? What did her brother do to you?" Eric and Dale pulled me off my prisoner, and they took him aside.

After a few minutes, Eric and Dale dragged the boy over to Lamar and made him apologize. My jaw dropped; no one had ever apologized to my brother before. Then Eric called all the kids on the playground into a huddle. Once everyone was assembled, Eric explained that Lamar could not defend himself, and because of this, no one was to tease or taunt him for any reason. Further, if someone did something to Lamar, Eric would be the one to "tie up the score." Someone asked whether this applied to me. Eric grinned in my direction and said, "I think she can take care of herself."

Eric Fee's simple decree changed our lives. That day on the playground, Eric blessed my life with a lesson in benevolent leadership. For the first time I could remember, Lamar and I were safe in our own neighborhood. One eleven-year-old boy bestowed peace and justice on two hapless misfits. I knew then what I wanted in life: to gain enough respect to do the same for others.

Eric seemed utterly immune to helplessness. He was faster and stronger than anyone else, so he could make the rules. Eric was an athlete. So I would be an athlete. He was a good student, which gave him authority in the classroom. I would top the boys not just in football but also in science and math. I would grow into my name, Victoria Elizabeth. Like the two great British queens, I would learn to rule. At least, that was the plan when I was eleven. The road that put me on a collision course with the Atlantic had a few more curves and bumps in it.

CHAPTER 5

Death on Deck

June 29, 1998
latitude north 38:33, longitude west 63:54
days at sea: 15
progress: 698 miles

FOR MOST OF THE NIGHT I HAD BEGGED FOR DAWN, but when the light came it was unsettling to see the blood-tinged seawater that sloshed around the cabin. The barometer was rising. *Good news.* The sky had cleared, but the wind was blowing at almost thirty miles an hour from the wrong direction. *Bad news.*

Turning my attention to the boat, I inspected the compartments under my sleeping mat. The electrical compartment that held two 12-volt gel cell batteries was dry, but all of the other compartments were wet. I reached into the murky soup sloshing around my electronics bin and pulled out the handset for my satellite telephone. *I don't think the engineers anticipated someone dunking the receiver in salt water, let alone the things this phone's been soaking in all night.*

I fished out a Sony digital camera. I shook the camera and heard water gurgling inside the housing. *Dear Sony: All I did was drop the camera in salt water and let it sit for twelve hours. What do you mean, my extended warranty will not cover it?*

The VHF radio was wet, but it was supposed to be submersible. *It'll be fine,* I thought as I set it aside. My "waterproof" headlamp turned out not to be. The last item I found in the water was the patch cord that connected the computer to the satellite communicator; the contacts were corroded. As I twirled the cord for the satcom in my fingers, a growing recognition of my situation called to mind a passage from the *Rime of the Ancient Mariner*, by Samuel Taylor Coleridge.

> *Down dropped the breeze, the sails dropped down,*
> *'Twas sad as sad could be;*
> *And we did speak only to break*
> *The silence of the sea!*

I had wished for silence, and fate rewarded me with more silence than I'd bargained for. I would learn what it means to be alone, on the ocean, at night, in the dark.

Nothing in my bag of tricks or tools could help me fabricate a new satphone. I couldn't stop at a mall to pick up a new patch cord for the satellite communicator. There would be no comforting words of advice from Gérard. There would be no updates on the vicissitudes of the Gulf Stream from Jenifer Clark. I couldn't send out messages to benefit my sponsor, so I resolved to be more diligent about shooting video for Sector. *Maybe they can use it after the trip.*

Having checked the weather and assessed the condition of the boat, I used the sighting mirror on my mountaineering compass to locate the cut on my head. Dividing the blood-matted hair, I uncovered the split in the skin. It was no more than three-quarters of an inch long. *How could so much blood have come from such a small cut?*

I rolled onto my back to consider the presidential portraits on my ceiling. Thomas Jefferson had blood on his face, which was better than what was all over Theodore Roosevelt. *My apologies, gentlemen; I will do some housekeeping.* Pressing my feet against the ceiling to keep from bouncing around like a basketball, I sponged every surface in the cabin three times with mixtures of fresh water and dishwashing detergent. When I was finished, the cabin smelled like Joy and soggy vitamins. It was not a pleasing smell, but it was a vast improvement.

After I'd finished cleaning up, I went rowing. The headwind had diminished to twenty miles per hour. I turned the boat forty-five degrees to the swells, quartering the waves, so I could manage the seas. My forward progress was miserable, but I took solace in the routine of the oars.

As I cooked dinner that evening, a food wrapper blew out of my hand and flew into the far corner of the bow. I grumbled after it. As I reached out to pick it up, I noticed the wrapper was stuck to something large and moist, and that the something was looking at me. The creature was a foot long, white and slimy, with a purple tinge around its edges: a dead squid. I did what any reasonable woman would do: I ran.

Two running steps carried me from the bow bulkhead to the stern cockpit, where I sat down to compose myself. *That's disgusting. I can handle a dead rabbit, a dead bird, or even a dead horse, but a dead squid . . . yuck. It must have been trapped when the boat capsized. Maybe the boat will capsize again and it will go away. Tori, get a grip. No slippery dead thing is worth another capsize.*

The situation made me think about the mayor of Louisville, Jerry Abramson. The mayor is a fastidious fellow, and during the time I had worked in his office, I made an effort to dress myself appropriately. Finding stylish shoes in a size twelve had always been a problem. One afternoon as I was walking beside the mayor, he looked down at my feet and noted, "Got your lizard-skin shoes on today." My shoes were not lizard-skin—they weren't even leather—but one didn't quibble with the mayor. "Yes, sir, staying on top of things." Then the mayor turned to a nearby police officer and said, "She probably killed the lizards with her bare hands." *Dead squid? I'm not touching that thing.*

That night, as I was sleeping, I imagined that I could hear the squid whimpering from the other end of the boat. About 3:30 A.M. a loud groan woke me, and I realized it was only the squawking of the rudder lines in their pipes. Wide awake, I slipped into my life vest and went on deck to employ the bucket.

When I looked up, Carl Sagan's voice from the television series *Cosmos* echoed in my mind: "billions and billions of stars." Until that moment, I had no earthly concept of what "billions and billions" actually looked like. The moon had retired for the evening, but the Milky Way painted a highway of light across the night. I couldn't find major constellations because there were too many stars. I faced north to look for Polaris, the North Star. Ordinarily the Big Dipper would point the way; I saw billions and billions of stars. Similarly, Draco and Cassiopeia were lost in a sea of sparklers. I turned toward the east and southeast to look for Venus and Jupiter. Instead of these two nearby planets, I saw billions and billions of stars. Ordinarily, I could find Vega in the west, but that night it was as indistinguishable as a single grain of sand on a beach.

I rinsed the bucket overboard, and a cloud of phosphorescent light filled the water beside my boat. I rinsed the bucket again and watched the water sparkle as if it contained a thousand lightning bugs. Three dolphins arrived. As they leapt into the air and splashed back into the water, flames of phosphorescence trailed their powerful flukes. I couldn't see the dolphins under water, but I could track them by the squiggles of light sparking in their underwater wakes. The dolphins circled the boat several times before swimming off toward the south.

In a speech I wrote for the mayor of Louisville I had used the phrase "a rainbow of excellence that lights the cosmic dark." The mayor said the line was too hyperbolic. As I knelt on deck, encircled by the celestial illumination of the stars above and bioluminescent plankton in the sea below, the hyperbole no longer seemed exaggerated. I reached overboard and stirred the ocean with my hand until swirls of light flowed from my fingertips. *So here I am, alone, on the ocean, at night, in the dark. Lucky me. Without darkness, one cannot see the stars.*

The morning of June 30, the seas were disturbed by waves coming from different directions. Fortunately, these were Tinkertoys compared to the freight liners that had capsized the *American Pearl*. I came to call these short, steep swells "yappy-dog waves." It was easier to row through fifteen-foot rollers than two-foot yappy-dog waves.

Unlike a sailboat, which goes up and down with the swells and shifts from side to side when it changes its tack, my boat went up-down-side-to-side, up-down-side-to-side. In yappy-dog waves, the boat could rock back and forth thirty or forty times every minute. Trying to row with these little waves tangling up the oars was a torture fit for the Spanish Inquisition.

WHEN I ENTERED THE seventh grade, the sky fell in on my world. "Give me your lunch money, or I'll kill your brother." Lamar had gone to the special education classes at the junior high school for two years before I got there. There were five sections of seventh graders: the brightest students went into Section 7E, while the slowest kids went in Section 7A. I'd been one of the best students in my sixth-grade class, but because I was Lamar Murden's sister, I was assigned to Section 7A with the "dumb" kids.

Even worse, in junior high school, girls weren't allowed to play football or baseball. This didn't make any sense. Eric Fee, Dale Ellis, and all the boys could play football, but not me. In autumn in western Pennsylvania, if you can't play football, you are nothing. I was a girl. So I was nothing.

The only socially acceptable team sport that girls were allowed to play was basketball. I was okay at basketball, but Leslie Lyons was better. Girls were not permitted to play football or baseball because these sports weren't "ladylike." It was clear to me that the whole "lady" thing was an evil conspiracy designed to keep girls incompetent and helpless.

Dale Ellis tried to explain this new segregation to me as we walked home from school. He said that there were things he could not do because his skin was black. There were things I couldn't do because I was a girl. "Life's not fair," Dale said, kicking at the dust when we reached his driveway. "Life's not fair," I repeated, kicking at the same dust. *Why not?* I wondered. *Who makes the rules?*

Being thirteen is not easy for anyone, but I was 5'10" in the seventh grade and a full head taller than most of my classmates. My family was not wealthy. What clothes my mother didn't make for me were hand-me-downs from my older brothers. Emulating the example of Eric Fee, I'd succeeded in turning myself into an athlete. I was broad-shouldered and my chest was flat. The same teenagers who called my brother the "retard" ridiculed my androgynous appearance by calling me "it" or "she-it" run together quickly.

Lamar and I could not go through the line in the cafeteria without being harassed. After witnessing an ugly incident, the principal suggested Lamar and I bring bag lunches to school. Students who brought lunch could eat in the auditorium instead of the cafeteria. This was better than running the gauntlet of the cafeteria line, but it didn't stop kids from snatching Lamar's lunch out of his hands.

I contrived a solution for this problem. Lamar and I packed Benedictine sandwiches for lunch. No one in western Pennsylvania had heard of Benedictine (a spread made of cucumbers, onions, and cream cheese, popular in Kentucky). My mother was from Kentucky. Like her mother before her, when she made Benedictine she added green food coloring to the spread.

After a boy stole my brother's sandwich, he asked "Eww, what's the green stuff?"

I announced in a voice loud enough to carry across the auditorium, "It's green because it is made from *boogers!*" No one stole food from Lamar or me again.

Since I couldn't play football, I decided to pick up boys and drop them on their heads on the intellectual playing field. With oversight from my brother Duke, I started building rockets. I entered a small rocket named the "Honest John" in the school's science contest. I painted scenes from colonial history in red, white, and blue on the body of the rocket, and on the nose cone I painted a portrait of John Adams. I won the science contest, but I lost the rocket when it landed on the roof of the local funeral home, never to be seen again.

After a few grading periods, the principal called me into his office and explained that he was going to move me out of Section 7A and into Section 7E. I wanted to ask, "What took you so long?" but I liked this principal and I thought it wise not to annoy him. The best part of my new assignment was that Eric Fee was in 7E.

After school, Eric had to practice for football, basketball, base-ball, or whatever sport was in season. For the hoodlums of the town, my brother and I were always in season. It was in those days that Lamar observed, "Blood is good; you bleed, everybody go home." Lamar was right. When someone drew blood, a fight would end, but because the blood was usually Lamar's or my own this was small consolation.

There weren't rules about kicking a girl when she was down, but blood was a flag of surrender. My greatest asset in those days was the fact that I have an extremely delicate nose. One good punch and my nose would produce a red torrent that would cause even the most obnoxious ruffian to back off. The only worry was that I had to be careful not to get blood on my clothes.

If my mother found blood on my blouse, she would want to know what happened. When my clothes weren't torn, I'd insist that "my nose just started bleeding." If I'd torn a sleeve or lost half my but-tons, I'd pretend I'd been playing some neighborhood game that got out of hand. I had so many bloody noses that Mother took me to the doctor to find out what was wrong. The doctor didn't find anything. I was terrified that the nose drops he prescribed to stop the nosebleeds might actually work. They didn't. *What a lucky nose.*

THE AFTERNOON OF JUNE 30, I heard spouting in the distance. It came from a pod of humpback whales. Their explosive exhalations formed clouds of mist over the water. I stood to watch. The whales lingered. To give myself an excuse for whale watching rather than rowing, I found Scott's thermometer and took the temperature of the water. The thermometer read 70°F. *No, that's wrong.* It felt as if someone had punched me in the stomach. I took the water temperature a second time. It was 70°. *That's too cold. The Gulf Stream should be warmer than that!* The location of the Gulf Stream close to the shore of the United States is relatively predictable, but farther out to sea it shifts north and south like water out of a fire hose. *I've lost the Stream. I need to talk to Jenifer Clark. The Stream, I've lost the Stream.*

Jenifer Clark had provided me with maps accurately identifying the location of the Gulf Stream and outlining its most favorable currents, but she warned that the maps had to be updated every few weeks. No communications meant no updates. When I chose to leave from Cape Hatteras instead of Cape Cod, my calculations suggested that the Gulf Stream route would be faster, possibly weeks faster, than the Cape Cod route despite the added distance. *If I don't get back into the Gulf Stream, all bets are off. Without a favorable current, every adverse wind will push me back toward the United States.*

Spurred on by the cold water, I rowed as if I was racing for my life. I ignored the difficulty of pulling a 2,800-pound boat through yappy-dog waves. I skipped my 3:30 P.M. snack break and didn't stop for dinner. At sunset, my growing hunger turned the sky into a fruit bowl. There were apple and strawberry reds, banana and lemon yellows, oranges and apricots, and even a few kiwis in the western sky. *It is too early to begin thinking about strawberries and bananas; I will not see land or taste fresh fruit for months.* I ignored my hunger and rowed well into the night. Before I went to bed, I took the water temperature: 69°F. The famous line from Joseph Conrad's *Heart of Darkness* came to mind: "The horror, the horror."

On July 1, a menacing counterswell brought with it another gale. It was too dangerous to row. I stayed in the cabin with my feet braced against the wall and wrote long entries in my journal. Thunder, lightning, and rain continued all afternoon. I set the journal aside and started rereading *Moby Dick*, by Herman Melville. When I came to the famous sermon about the biblical story of Jonah and the whale delivered by Father Mapple, I couldn't help thinking that I was in the belly of a whale named *American Pearl*. Melville wrote:

> *The ribs and terrors in the whale,*
> *Arched over me a dismal gloom,*
> *While all God's sun-lit waves rolled by,*
> *And left me deepening down to doom.*
>
> *I saw the open maw of hell,*
> *With endless pains and sorrows there;*
> *Which none but they that feel can tell—*
> *Oh, I was plunging to despair.*

I could not have understood this passage when I read the book as a child, I thought.

At sunset, I went on deck just long enough to refill my water bottle and scrounge a couple of food bars. In the fading light, I noticed that one of my rudder lines was broken. I was about to get out a new length of line when I spotted the faint lights of a ship on the horizon. It looked to be a mile off and moving away. I pulled out my VHF radio and turned it on. Nothing happened. I turned it off and then back on. Still, nothing. *Oh, that's just great.* I climbed into the cabin and disassembled the radio. When I removed the cover, which read "submersible," water dripped out. The electronic components were crusted with salt. I shook the water out of the unit, did my best to remove the salt, used an eraser to clean rust off the contacts, and reassembled the radio. It didn't work.

This meant that the only piece of working communications equipment onboard was the one-watt VHF radio that Kathy Steward had purchased the day before my departure. The radio was in the bow compartment, in a Rubbermaid container, stored inside a dry bag that I considered my "Christmas box." I had not planned to open the bag before I reached the halfway point. The single-watt radio would not transmit more than a mile or two.

Normally, I didn't use my flashlight to read because I didn't have battery power to spare, but that night I plowed my sorrows into the pages of *Moby Dick*. I felt some acquaintance with the miseries of Captain Ahab. "When I think of this life I have led; the desolation of solitude it has been; the masoned, walled-town of a Captain's exclusiveness, which admits but small entrance to any sympathy from the green country without—oh, weariness! heaviness! Guinea-coast slavery of solitary command!" *Captain Ahab at least had a crew for company. Oh, for even the monosyllabic Queequeg to chat with me, a "cannibal" to help this Christian.*

CHAPTER 6

Independence Day

July 2, 1998
latitude north 39:25, longitude west 60:24
days at sea: 18
progress: 899 miles

AROUND 2:00 A.M. ON JULY 2, I FELT THE BOAT RISE ON a heavy swell. The rudder, offset by its broken cable, slipped to one side, and the boat carved a turn like a giant surfboard. *The damage to the rudder—how could I have forgotten?* Realizing that I was broadside to the waves, I reached up and closed the air vent. One wave passed, then another. Just as I started to relax, the *American Pearl* flipped like a pancake. My knee slammed into the ceiling, but by crossing my arms I was able to cushion the blow to my face.

As I was about to launch into a barrage of self-reproach, another wave flicked the boat upright. The motion was so abrupt that I skimmed past the cabin wall and landed with an awkward thud on the floor. I felt the jerk of the sea anchor pulling the stern of the boat around into the next wave.

The storm wasn't particularly fierce, but if I didn't repair the rudder, I'd be doing push-ups off the ceiling all night. I tumbled out into the rain, cut a section of rope from my spare line, and threw it over the roof of the cabin, where it dropped next to the rudder. Then I crawled through the cabin to the stern hatch. My timing had to be perfect. I crouched under the hatch and waited until a wave crashed over the roof. This would give me several seconds before the next wave reached the boat.

I opened the thirteen-by-eighteen-inch hatch and launched myself skyward. My shoulders wedged like a cork in the opening. *Hello? Elementary mathematics: my shoulders are nineteen inches wide, and the hatch is eighteen inches wide. How many times will we repeat this lesson?* Valuable seconds ticked by as I struggled to free myself. Squirming loose, I dropped back into the cabin, then I sent an arm up through the hole. This reduced the breadth of my shoulders enough to clear easily. In a split second, I was up on my knees. In this position, the hatch hit me about waist high. I searched for the line that I'd tossed over the roof, but couldn't locate it.

Then I felt the wind pause. *Uh-oh, too slow.* I looked up into the dark face of the curly-topped wave looming above me. *Bath time!* The wave engulfed the stern of the boat, and water gurgled all the way to my toes. When the stern of the boat emerged from the far side, I shook my hair like a wet dog. The line that I needed emerged from the froth directly in front of me. I grabbed the line, tied a bowline through the starboard eye of the rudder, ducked back through the hatch, and banged it shut. I was pleasantly surprised to find that the slosh in the cabin was not more than a few inches deep. I caught my breath for a brief moment before climbing out on deck to finish tying off the new rudder line.

As I bailed the water out of the cabin and sponged off my sleeping mat, I started to imagine that the line running out to my sea anchor was too long. So every half an hour for the next several hours, I experimented with my sea anchor. When the line was too short, the parachute anchor jerked the boat so violently that it threatened to tear the cleats out of the roof. *Or jar the teeth out of my head.* When the line was too long, slack formed between the boat and the anchor, and the boat didn't stay perpendicular to the waves. In the end, I decided that my original configuration had been about right.

It was almost dawn when I abandoned the experiment to settle back into my cabin for a few hours of sleep. *Ocean rowing is like mountain climbing—you're either working your butt off or you're sitting still waiting for the weather to change. I hope that capsize took the dead squid off the deck. It was beginning to smell.*

After a couple of hours of sleep, I climbed out into a steady rain. The gunwales had scuppers, holes that served as drains to allow water to run off the deck. To keep tools and other items from escaping through these holes, I had covered the scuppers with plastic netting. I was dismayed to find that my dead squid had company: another squid and two large fish stared up at me with dull, lifeless eyes. I could work around one decomposing corpse, but four was too many. I didn't have gloves, so I opened a box of Huggies diaper wipes, which I'd brought along to use as washcloths if I ran short of fresh water.

I groped in the direction of the first fish with the wipe until I felt the carcass. As I lifted it, the fish slid out of my grasp. Using a firmer grip on the second try, I succeeded in tossing the creature overboard. I repeated the process with the second fish and the new squid. When I tried to get hold of the older squid, it stuck to the deck like chewing gum. I had to work my fingers under the carcass and pry it off. Once it was free, I tossed it overboard, but it left behind a gray squid-shaped stain on the white deck.

The rain had slowed to a drizzle. I unlashed the oars and rowed for several hours. At lunchtime, a line of heavy clouds provided me with a chorus of thunder and flashes of lightning. *I don't mind rain, but electrical storms are a different kettle of fish.*

I withdrew to the cabin; a few minutes later the sun came out. I went back to the oars. A half an hour after that, another squall brought more lightning, and this time the lightning was accompanied by the wispy funnels of two waterspouts.

I returned to the cabin. An hour later, I was rowing again. Mountaineers call short breaks in bad weather "sucker holes," and as my climbing friends would tell you, I fall for sucker holes every time.

Despite the weather, the rowing was excellent. The wind had

diminished. The water was rough enough to keep things interesting, but not so rough as to make it dangerous. The large following swells didn't break. Some were twenty feet high, but because their crests didn't roll, they were no bother at all. Surfing the larger swells reminded me of riding towboat wakes on the Ohio River. Occasionally a roller capped off, washed over the cabin, and showered down on me. At those times, I wondered, *What will I lose if the boat capsizes?* When everything was shipshape and I was properly tethered, the answer was nothing.

As I rowed, a storm petrel circled the boat. My visitor was about six inches long with short rounded wings. Its beak and plumage were dark brown, but it had a patch of white on its rump. Petrels live at sea, feeding on small fish, squid, and tiny crustaceans that they scoop from the water as they patter their feet along the surface with their wings outstretched. It was Gérard who told me that petrels are peripatetic: always flying, never resting.

Gérard seemed to know that, despite their diminutive size, I would feel a certain kinship with these birds. They didn't soar easily on the wind like the big shearwaters or gulls. They dodged, darted, and zigzagged almost like bats. They were always on the move. I watched closely to see if I could catch a petrel napping on the surface of the water, but I never did.

On July 3, the water remained cold. My guess was that the Gulf Stream was to the south, but I wasn't willing to alter course on a hunch. *If I row due east toward the southern tip of France, I will meet up with the Gulf Stream sooner or later.* The boat felt sluggish, as if I were rowing uphill. I rowed for an hour and a half, but the boat covered less than half a mile. *I'm in another countercurrent, rowing against the stream.* A wind out of the east-northeast picked up in the afternoon, which made it difficult to hold my course.

To help me row into the wind, I tried to drop the dagger board. A dagger board is much like a center board, but it is removable. If I could get the board down into the water, it would help to keep the boat from being blown sideways, but it wouldn't budge. I sat on it. I pushed. I pulled. I even tried swearing, but nothing shifted it. In exasperation, I reached into the bow compartment and pulled out a Louisville Slugger oar handle. The baseball bat manufacturer had fabricated the handles for my two sets of spare oars. These handles were made of solid white ash and were shaped not too differently from a baseball bat. I took a swing at the dagger board—*bang*. Another swing, a louder bang. Nothing moved.

As my frustration escalated, so did the force of my swings. The improvised bat stung my hands, but I kept on swinging. If I couldn't move the dagger board, I would quell my frustration by breaking something. *Women are perfectly capable of behaving like men when no one's watching.* Fortunately for both the equipment and my feminine dignity, the dagger board moved before I damaged anything.

The next day, I awakened to the sound of rain pounding the roof. I switched on the camera. "Saturday, July fourth, four A.M., dawn's early light. What so proudly we hail is a storm coming from . . . oh . . . you guessed it . . . the northeast." There would be no elaborate Fourth of July celebration. I would not shoot video of me rowing in the goofy three-cornered hat. I wouldn't decorate the rowing deck with the presidents who hadn't made it to the ceiling. I stayed inside. Rowing against the storm would be fruitless. I used the time to plug leaks with epoxy putty. When this task was complete, I pulled out my mountaineering compass to use the mirror.

My face was tanned except for a white strip across my eyes that had been protected by sunglasses. The cut on my head was healing. As my fingers combed through my hair, a long white scar grinned on the left side near my part. In civilization, I took care to brush my hair in a way that hid this scar, but on the ocean, concealing scars was unimportant. The scar was from a broken golf club.

I got the scar when I was about thirteen. A line of boys sitting on a fence, had been taunting Lamar, and, after I could tolerate no more, I decided to make them stop. I grabbed one of the boys from behind, pulled him off the fence, and dropped him into the weeds. Another boy leapt from the fence, knocking me to the ground. The sky spun. Grass flew. I felt the supreme satisfaction of punching and kicking with all my might.

The next thing I knew, I woke up in a puddle of blood. Lamar was standing over me. "Blood is good; Johnny hit you with a golf club; everybody go home." My parents were out, but my brother Duke was "babysitting." Duke used ice to stop the bleeding. After I'd gotten cleaned up, Duke and I had a long talk about whether we needed to say anything to my parents about the injury. We didn't.

Aboard the *American Pearl*, I closed the mirror on my compass and tucked it away. My hands were free of blisters. I'd lost the fat that I had intentionally put on for the journey. There was a large bruise on my right thigh from the July 2 capsize. A sliver of sunlight highlighted a small triangular scar on the side of my thigh. This was the only visible scar that had come from a girl. I don't remember how the fight started, but it ended when Valerie stabbed me in the leg. I told my mother that I'd been bitten by a dog. *It wasn't a lie. Valerie was a mangy, flea-bitten cur. It was certain that she was no lady.* Mother worried that I would get rabies, but I assured her that the dog had been "very healthy."

The boat fell off a wave and slapped down so hard it knocked the wind out of me. It felt as if a gorilla had smacked my back. *I have to get past this adverse current and find the Gulf Stream again. I can't do anything cooped up in this cabin.* A wave . . . a slap. Before long, my mood was as fierce and stormy as the conditions outside. A wave . . . a slap. The wind bellowed. I bellowed back. A wave . . . a slap. *No, now that's enough. I'm going rowing.* I bolted from the cabin. Before I could haul in the sea anchor a wave came over the deck and knocked me down. I kicked at the retreating water.

In a fit of rage, I hauled in the sea anchor, snatched it out of the water, and hurled it onto the deck in a heap. I untied the oars, took my seat, and rowed the boat headlong into the squall. Waves tangled my oar handles and whacked my kneecaps. Ocean spray rained down. As I rowed into the teeth of the storm, my mood grew volcanic. My brain kept dragging me toward the place where memory was all ash and searing ember.

As a dog returns to its vomit, so a fool repeats her folly. Why must I go back to that place? Why must I revisit that original sin?

IT WAS LATE SPRING; I was nearing the end of eighth grade. Lamar and I lingered after school. I practiced basketball so I could watch my favorite teacher get into his car and drive away. He would wave. I would wave. Then Lamar and I would walk home.

It was a stupid teenage crush.

The teacher came. The teacher went.

Danger lurked just around the corner. In my folly, I was blind and giddy with girlish thoughts of love. How could I have been so selfish, so stupid?

Five older boys, each with a length of bailing twine, came around from the side of the school building.

I didn't know them, but they seemed to know Lamar.

The boy in the red T-shirt looked ashamed. His face warned me of danger; his eyes begged me to run.

Lamar couldn't run very fast.

I looked to the teachers' parking lot; the last car was gone. I turned to the playing fields, the teams were away.

"Run, Lamar, run!"

We ran, but the boys caught Lamar and pushed him into the shallow alcove by the back door to the cafeteria. I stood at a distance until I saw them pull Lamar's pants down. I charged back toward my brother.

I wasn't big enough, or strong enough, or fast enough.

The boys dragged me away biting and kicking. Between the pavement and the playing fields stood a tall row of pine trees. The boys tied my struggling arms behind me around a tree. The bailing twine cut into my wrists and elbows. The tree didn't have low branches to provide cover. The boys left me and went back to my brother.

I screamed and I screamed. I pulled and jerked against the twine.

There were houses on either side of the school. Surely someone could hear me. No one came. No one heard my screams. No one heard the grunts and moans that came from the alcove. One boy wouldn't "do it." I could hear the other boys taunting him. I couldn't see.

Maybe it was the boy in the red T-shirt who wouldn't "do it."

When they were finished, they left. I stopped struggling. Twisting around to look for Lamar, I saw that my hands had been tied with a bow. It took such little effort to untie myself that I was paralyzed with shame. I didn't get up. I didn't go to my brother. I wallowed on the ground, burying my face in the dirt.

I had failed him. I failed my brother.

It wasn't long before Lamar came to me. He looked me over and smiled. "No blood," he said. His undemanding expression told me that this had not been the first time.

The bathhouse at the pool . . . Lamar had stopped swimming. Lamar loved to swim.

We walked home in slow silence. There was nothing to say. In my rock-strewn silence, I vowed never again to fall in love. I would stand apart, solitary, independent, singular. Love was too dangerous, too selfish, too irrational . . . too ladylike. Love was blind, and I needed eyes that were cold and clear. To shield my brother from harm, I needed to stay sharp. Sharp as the knife I wished I'd had that day.

Sharp as the knives I've carried ever since.

From that day forward, every fight, every insult, every injury, added fuel to the rage I could not navigate. Every person in need became my brother. Each time I failed to make a difference, it rubbed salt into the unutterable wound of this primary failure.

No longer would I be content to merely joust with helplessness; I would hunt it down and kill it. I vowed to weed incompetence out of every corner of my life. I would become large enough, strong enough, and clever enough to protect the people who needed my protection. I would make a difference. I would be of service. I would not fail, not like that, not again, not ever.

IN MY HOURS OF darkness, mad, raving Ahab had nothing on me. His whale was Moby Dick. My whale had a different name: helplessness. Herman Melville wrote, "With the mad secret of his unabated rage bolted up and keyed in him, Ahab had purposely sailed upon the present voyage with the one and only all-engrossing object of hunting the White Whale."

Moby Dick tore away Ahab's leg. Helplessness tore away my inno-cence.

"Ahab had cherished a wild vindictiveness against the whale, all the more fell for that in his frantic morbidness he at last came to identify with him, not only all his bodily woes, but all his intellectual and spiritual exasperations. The white whale swam before him as the monomaniac incarnation of all those malicious agencies which some deep men feel eating in them, till they are left living on with half a heart and half a lung."

Helplessness took my heart. If I can row alone across the Atlantic, I might succeed in hunting down helplessness and killing it.

I rowed, frothing with fury, through heavy swells until exhaustion allowed me to rein in the wild mustangs of thought. With conscious force, I dragged my mind away from gnawing memory and pushed it toward the light.

IT'S THE FOURTH OF *July: the high holiday of the Enlightenment.* As John Adams once said, "It is a great day; it is a good day." I crawled into the cabin and stared up at one of the documents duct-taped to the ceiling. "In CONGRESS, July 4, 1776. The unanimous Declaration of the thirteen united States of America." Two hundred and twenty-two years ago, thirty British battleships and a few hundred supply ships sat at anchor in New York Harbor. Aboard were 1,200 cannon, 30,000 soldiers, 10,000 sailors, and orders from King George III to bring the colonies back into line with British rule. A hundred miles away, fifty-five men declared the independence of "thirteen united States of America." *And people call* me *crazy?*

I climbed back out on deck, took up my oars, and rowed all afternoon. An hour before sunset, three whales joined me. For about twenty minutes, I thought they were humpbacks. They were black and forty or fifty feet long. In the confused seas it took me a long while to notice that these whales didn't have dorsal fins. This distinguished them as northern right whales.

My mind wandered: *right whales, right hand, right angle, right thinking, right stuff, right brain, civil rights, Bill of Rights, Thomas Jefferson, the Fourth of July.* At Valley Forge with his troops, George Washington watched a performance of Joseph Addison's play *Cato.* Washington had seen the play before. He quoted it in letters. One of his favorite lines was, "'Tis not in mortals to command success, but we'll do more, Sempronius, we'll deserve it."

I reached out to touch the American flag that fluttered on the starboard gunwale. Then I picked up my deck log and wrote in the margin, "Journeys like this are not about what we get out of them, but rather, they are about what we give, and in giving so much to life, we learn the vast expanse of wealth we have at hand."

CHAPTER 7

Sea Lions in the Middle of the North Atlantic

July 5, 1998
latitude north 40:25, longitude west 60:18
days at sea: 21
progress: 1,020 miles

SUNDAY, JULY 5, THE WIND CAME AROUND TO THE SOUTH-
west. The only repair I made was to add padding to the ribs that
supported the cabin roof. Each time the seas became rough the ribs
in the boat rubbed the skin off my ribs. Once I'd padded the wooden
ribs, I opened the storage compartment in the bow and located the
VHF radio that Kathy Steward had purchased. I turned the small
handheld radio over in my hands. *If I break this radio, I'll be reduced to
sending smoke signals to passing ships.*

Once I took up my oars, I rowed for fifteen hours, with nothing more than a five-minute break in any one hour. I didn't stop for
dinner until long after the sun went down. While I was cooking
dinner, fish thrashed near the boat. As I stood to see what was going
on, a large wave from the north intersected with a swell coming from
the west, and together they blanket-tossed me out of the boat. I flew
headfirst over the starboard side.

As I fell, I heard the crunch of my hip smacking the gunwale.
My head went into the water, but before my torso could follow my
harness jerked tight. *Reaching the end of one's tether is a good thing.* I
hooked my legs over the lip of the gunwale, reached up, clasped the

wood rail, and levered myself back into the boat. I shook my gory locks at the next wave. "If I want to wash my hair, thank you, I will use the bucket!"

The next morning my hip was swollen and sported a bruise the size of my open hand, but the wind was with me. I found three flying fish on deck and tossed them overboard. A big dorado gobbled up the smaller fish as soon as they hit the water. By midday the seas were calm, and the *American Pearl* was surrounded by thousands of fish. Besides dorado, there were yellowfin tuna and smaller fish of a dozen species. I fantasized that I'd returned to the Gulf Stream, but neither the water temperature nor the direction of the current supported this fantasy. Finding the Gulf Stream again had become an obsession. I rowed toward stretches of ocean because, like the Gulf Stream, they appeared to be a different color, only to realize that the color variations were caused by clouds.

At 8:30 A.M. on July 7, I saw a ship on my horizon. I leapt to the cabin and grabbed the VHF radio. "This is the rowing vessel *American Pearl, American Pearl*. My long-range communications systems are down, and I'm looking for someone who can relay a message. I see a ship on my horizon; can you hear me? Over." I waited, but there was no answer. "This is the rowing vessel *American Pearl, American Pearl*. My long-range communications systems are down, and I'm looking for someone who can relay a message. Over." I repeated the same message again and again. "They don't listen to VHF radios out here!"

The ship was a quarter mile to my starboard. My heart sank as it passed without a word. "They can't hear me. No one can hear me." I hadn't spoken to another human being in weeks. I pulled out my video camera to record the scene. The ship was a mile off and growing more distant. Before tucking the radio into the cabin, I tried one last time. "This is the rowing vessel *American Pearl, American Pearl*. My long-range communications systems are down, and I'm looking for someone who can relay a message. I see a ship on my horizon; can you hear me? Over." There was a crackle of static, and the radio in my hand began to speak.

"This is the USS *Sea Lion*. What can we do for you?"

In my excitement, I nearly dropped the radio. "Could you make a collect call for me? I have lost long-range communications, and I need to let some folks know I am okay."

The radio went silent for a long moment. The voice became officious. It said, "We don't make collect calls. Are you in any kind of trouble?"

"No, it is just that I am rowing a boat from the United States to France. I haven't been able to tell anybody that I am all right. I just thought it might be nice. Over."

"Did you say . . . *rowing*?"

"Yes, I'm in a rowboat. Over."

A long pause followed. I imagined the discussion that might be taking place on the bridge of the vessel that was now well to my west. The voice on the radio returned, but it was less officious. They agreed to take a message. I asked them to contact Diane Stege in Louisville, Kentucky, to tell her that I was okay. I'd capsized twice, but the boat righted itself, and other than my communications systems not working, all was well.

I pulled out the camera, intending to videotape the ship before it faded from view. As I switched on the camera, a question came to mind. "Do you guys have a weather report? Over."

The third mate said, "Sure do. Hold a minute." The weather report was good. There were no storms or gales. Then the captain came on the radio. His voice sounded friendly. "I just tried calling the number you gave me, and there was an answering machine. I will call a little bit later and try to talk to someone personally. I'll make sure we get hold of them and let them know what your status is. How are you doing, by the way?"

"I am doing ten times better than I was before I saw your ship. Over."

"Roger on that. What size is your boat?"

"My boat is twenty-three feet long and just under six feet wide. Over."

The captain told me his ship was a little bigger than mine, and it covered 465 miles a day. I reported that this was about ten times faster than I was going. Then I asked about the location of the Gulf Stream, explaining, "I aim to stay in the Gulf Stream as much as possible. I lost it a few days ago; I am hoping to pick it up again. Over."

"Roger on that. If you continue in the direction of about eighty degrees, you will pick 'er up. It slowed us down quite a bit. She was moving probably a little over a knot, so that will give you extra miles."

"Yes, that's what I like to hear." The bad news was that it was 180 miles away.

"What kind of radio equipment do you have aboard there?" the captain asked.

"Well, I had a satellite telephone until my first capsize, and I have a satellite communicator, but it is not working either. The serial cable got fouled in some seawater. So I don't have any long-range communications; I am down to just a VHF radio. Over."

"What port of call are you trying to make over in France?"

"Ideally Brest, but I may have to settle for the English Channel."

"Roger on that. As you approach that area, you are going to be running into a lot more ships. Even with these calm seas, we did not pick you up on radar at all."

"Right. I have a high-tech radar target enhancer that obviously isn't working. So I will pull out the low-tech reflective gear and get it up."

"Roger on that. Get it up as high as you can. I wish you the best of luck."

"Thank you—I need all the luck I can get a hold of. Bye."

I had tried to convince myself that losing communications was a good thing because it forced me to live within myself. It is a tenet of monastic traditions that it is only when a life cannot spread out that it is able to rise to greater heights. I valued solitude. Still, the chance to talk to someone was excruciatingly pleasant, even if only for a few precious minutes. *If the ship covers 465 miles per day, they are doing just over nineteen miles an hour. In another three or four minutes they will be out of range; I will be as alone as Adam before the creation of Eve.*

Standing in the cockpit, I caught a glimpse of my reflection in the Plexiglas of the main hatch. I was glad that no one aboard the *Sea Lion* could see me. My hair had taken on a life of its own. I'd all but given up on the unruly mess, dubbing it "the entity." My face and arms were crusted with patches of salt. *I need a bath.* I filled a bucket and washed hair, body, and clothing.

Fifteen minutes later, I was again rowing into the wind, but this time it was with clean hair and a wet shirt. Chatting with the crew of the USS *Sea Lion* had been welcome, but the shallowness of the conversation haunted my thinking. "Tell my friends I'm okay. Are there any storms? Where is the Gulf Stream?" *That was it? No, there was more: I am invisible, imperceptible, undetectable. They couldn't see me.* A half an hour later, my shirt was dry . . . for a moment.

A large tuna slapped its tail against the side of my boat and salt water showered down on me. *Fish spit. The sun is out. In an hour, I will be roasting. I'm hungry.* I reached into the snack compartment under the deck and pulled out a small bag of cashews. Without thinking, I tossed a handful of nuts into my mouth. They had the consistency of mashed potatoes and tasted like vinegar. Inhaling through my nostrils, I gained enough force to spit the nuts out over the gunwale.

"Take that, fish. Human beings can spit too." I snatched up the bag of cashews and found that the nuts had been swimming in seawater. I dumped the cashews over the side and tucked the bag into the garbage compartment. Undeterred, I retrieved another bag. This time I examined the nuts to make sure they were dry before tossing a handful into my mouth.

I laid the cashews on the compass table just above my feet. I took two strokes, dropped my left oar into the water at full reach, then picked up a cashew and ate it in time to catch the oar again before the momentum of the boat brought the oar into my chest. I took a few more strokes, dropped my right oar, snatched up a nut, tossed it into my mouth, and caught the oar again as it came into my side. In this left-right manner I could make a bag of cashews last half an hour without ever stopping the boat.

There was a rush of water beside the boat, and I stiffened to see the top of a wave capped in white foam. *A breaker? No . . . the approaching wave isn't steep enough to break.* I studied the swell, and the mystery revealed itself. Several dolphins were surfing the top of the wave. A second or two before the wave reached my vessel, the line of dolphins charged. In that instant, a cavalcade of fish leapt into the air; some struck the sides of the boat, while others hurdled over my oars. *The dolphins are hunting.* For these adept hunters, catching the fish that were gathered under my boat must have been the equivalent of shooting them in a barrel. I continued to row, and after a few minutes the circus under the boat subsided.

Before long, the white-tipped wave at my stern quarter formed again. Once the dolphins aligned themselves in an orderly rank, they executed another cavalry charge, scattering fish in all directions. One panicked fish leapt into my boat. I picked it up. "Out of the frying pan and into the fire," I mused, and tossed the fish back overboard. The dolphins repeated this cycle every few minutes for well over forty-five minutes.

I approached a raft of birds resting on the surface of the ocean. The dolphins formed up and charged as usual, but one dolphin broke ranks and tore through the flock of shearwaters. Birds and feathers flew in all directions. They squawked. They screeched. They squealed and shrieked. *That dolphin isn't hungry. He's just messing with them.*

As I watched the heckled birds fly off, I noticed a large cargo ship on the horizon. I pulled out my radio and tried to hail the ship. The ship was stacked tall with shipping containers, and it was moving fast. The main part of the hull was painted black, and the bottom paint was red. With every passing minute I could see more detail. I kept trying to hail the ship. "This is the rowing vessel *American Pearl, American Pearl*, do you read, over?" There was no response.

One particular detail began to worry me: I couldn't see the sides of the ship. It was headed straight for me. *If they run me over, will they even feel it?* I dropped the radio on the deck and rushed to my rowing seat. I pulled as hard as I could, rowing a line perpendicular to the path of the ship. Minutes passed, and I still seemed to be looking straight down the barrel. The sport of rowing is renowned for its ability to produce large amounts of lactic acid in every major muscle group—legs, back, arms—and I was feeling the burn. It was with agonizing slowness that I began to see a little more of the ship's starboard side.

When the bow of the ship passed, it was less than eighty yards away. The name painted on the ship in large white letters was *Lykes Challenger*. I caught the bow wave, and by leaning into the front of my boat I managed to surf the wave away from the ship. I gained another eighty yards of distance before the stern wake hit and swamped my deck. If my mother had heard the things I yelled at the back end of that ship, she would have washed my mouth out with soap.

MY POOR MOTHER. The pledge I made to banish love and all trivial emotions from my life fell hardest on my mother. While she and I had never been close, the further I retreated into detached intellectualism, the more distance I placed between my mother and me. Struggling with inner demons, I became indifferent to the influence of the world in general and to my mother in particular. I had never been a talker, but around my mother my silence grew sullen.

In school, my natural shyness and reserve deepened. In the world of my intellect, everything was neatly ordered. I arranged every person, idea, and action in tidy categories of "good" or "evil." I did not allow for messy overlaps of ambiguity. There were no gray areas in the gray matter of my brain. Ideas that did not fit into its well-ordered framework were evicted. People or actions that upset the carefully calculated balance of my mind were banished to the suburbs of thought. As a result, I became absolutely sure about the things I knew. Outwardly, this made me a typical American teenager.

I was about halfway through the ninth grade in Uniontown, Pennsylvania, when my English and algebra teachers suggested that I try to get into something called a private school. My English teacher explained that only smart children went to these schools. The algebra teacher said that I'd scored in the highest rank on a national test. "It might be enough to get you into a private school." I misinterpreted the intent of my teachers. Experience had taught me that smart kids didn't hit as hard as dumb kids. I thought my teachers were trying to help me to win a few fights.

On the advice of those teachers, I timidly asked my parents about going to a private school. Mother said, "If you want to go to a private school, you can move to Louisville, Kentucky, and help to take care of your grandmother." My maternal grandmother had what my parents called "hardening of the arteries." These days, it would be called Alzheimer's disease. When my grandmother wasn't totally confused, she was downright mean.

My father wanted to know who had put the idea of a private school into my head. When I told him, he arranged to have a conference with these teachers. I have no idea what was said, but when my parents returned home from the conference they were upset. Mother took me to my room and closed the door. She sat on the bed and asked me how often I'd been fighting. Over the years, I'd become adept at keeping secrets, but there was no way out of this one. I gazed at the floor. After a tense silence, I admitted that I fought several times a week, "but only to protect Lamar." Mother didn't ask for details, and I didn't volunteer any. She simply left the room and closed the door behind her.

I expected to find myself grounded for life, but instead, my father wrote away for the entrance examinations for the Louisville Collegiate School. The guidance counselor in Uniontown supervised when I took the tests. Each portion of the exam said at the top, "You have one hour to complete this section of the test." The guidance counselor gave me a few extra minutes on each segment, and each time I turned in a portion she said, "Let me look over this and see how you did." While I can't prove it, I believe that the counselor cheated on my behalf. I was accepted by the prestigious school for girls in Kentucky. I was signed up for a blind date with destiny.

CHAPTER 8

Three Strokes Forward,
Two Strokes Back

July 9, 1998
latitude north 40:14, longitude west 57:25
days at sea: 25
progress: 1,184 miles

I OFTEN LOST MILES WHILE I SLEPT, BUT IN JULY THIS would become the rule rather than the exception. On July 9, I lost eight miles. So I rowed forty-six. On July 10, I lost sixteen miles. I'd rerowed the sixteen and added another twenty-eight. The morning of July 11, I'd lost fourteen miles.

The North Atlantic has a reputation for turning the toughest souls into sniveling whiners. I'd studied the logs of the men who rowed across the North Atlantic before me. Each man complained that the winds were against him. Each claimed that the currents were averse, and each rower insisted that his weather was worse than the weather faced by any rower who went before him. I found myself matching their strokes more closely than I wanted to admit.

When I lost communications, I lost the Gulf Stream. When I lost the Gulf Stream, I lost the sense that I was in command of my destiny. The winds and currents became my enemies, and the weather turned perfectly wretched. After weeks without a word from friends, it was easy to imagine that every rower who went before me had had it easy. The evening before I'd left from North Carolina, Barry Bingham Jr. had tried to talk me out of making the trip. Barry was a dear friend. He'd spent most of his life working in journalism. He reported, "Tori, the *New York Times* is predicting that 1998 will be the worst hurricane season on record."

New York Times, *Shmoo York Times—what do they know?* I replied, "Barry, I don't place much stock in long-term weather forecasting."

This statement notwithstanding, I had trusted the pilot charts when they indicated that the prevailing winds for my crossing would be from the southwest toward the northeast. *The pilot charts are turning out to be about as reliable as the* Farmer's Almanac. *The prevailing winds I've encountered are from the northeast.* I rowed into the wind all day, and each night it pushed me back toward the United States. *Do salmon swimming upstream ever get a chance to rest? I think they are called headwinds because of their propensity for messing with one's head.*

I recalled the observations of a sailor: "Once you get onto the open ocean, the swells will all be from the same direction. It is not like in the movies, where the waves come from every direction and crash on you." This was a comforting statement, but it was wrong. Most sweeping statements about the ocean fail to hold water when examined from the modest deck of a rowing boat.

There are storm-generated swells and wind-generated swells. Storm waves are like the ripples that form when a pebble is tossed into a puddle. These swells travel thousands of miles outward from the center of a gale. Sooner or later, storm swells encounter wind swells. Wind-generated swells occur when wind blows across the surface of the ocean for a long period of time. The wind is a shifty thing. It might blow one way for several days, generating waves moving in one direction. Then it changes directions and new waves form, colliding with the older ones.

Perhaps in faster boats, boats with sails, or boats with engines, or boats with sails and engines, fancy the thought, perhaps these boats move so quickly that their occupants can see only one set of swells at a time. I, however, am not dizzied by speed. Most days there was a dominant swell and a chorus of smaller crossing swells: a few Great Danes with lots of little yappy dogs nipping at their heels.

Joining the headwind from the northeast were lightning, thunder, and rain. *Rowing in the rain saves on washing.* The afternoon of July 11, the rain slowed to a drizzle. Pulling out my video camera, I recorded a passage from *Macbeth* as I rowed: "Tomorrow, and tomorrow, and tomorrow, creeps in this petty pace from day to day, to the last syllable of recorded time; and all our yesterdays have lighted fools the way to dusty death. Out, out, brief candle! Life's but a walking shadow, a poor player that struts and frets his hour upon the stage and then is heard no more: it is a tale told by an idiot, full of sound and fury, signifying nothing."

I rowed for thirteen hours and made it thirty-six miles before going to bed. On July 12, the GPS reported I'd lost twenty miles. It was Sunday. I checked all the compartments and pumped water out of several of them. *There was a Frenchman who attempted this journey, and he was rescued because, he claimed, his boat was sinking. Several months later, the boat arrived in France without him. I would not like to be in that position. So I'll keep bailing.* Once the compartments were dry, I took up the oars.

I had not been rowing long when a white-capped wave hurled over the gunwale and slapped me in the shoulder. As I turned to vent my wrath at it, I thought, *Reprimands will not bring the waves into line. Anger will not alter the wind. Sadness will not bring back the Gulf Stream. The greatest freedom allotted to any human being is the freedom to choose one's attitude. Whatever the weather, it is my weather, and I must do my best to enjoy it.*

During dinner, a sea turtle stopped by for a visit. At three or four feet in length, it was the size of a coffee table. Its oval shell was brown and green with yellow striping. When I took up my oars again, the turtle swam alongside for about twenty minutes, its head bobbing just above the surface of the water. Then, with laughing eyes, the turtle passed me. Something about my being left behind by a turtle pricked my competitive nature. I pulled harder, trying to keep up, but I couldn't catch the turtle. Soon I was reduced to laughter. *I'm on the North Atlantic in a rowboat, racing a turtle . . . and losing. Okay, so they can swim thirty miles an hour. Out here, I'm the tortoise and it's the hare.*

In the early evening, a heavy fog rolled in. My Ocean Sentry radar target enhancer was supposed to light me up on any ship's radar, but the captain of the USS *Sea Lion* had told me that it wasn't working. So before I turned in for the night, I assembled a simple aluminum radar reflector, tied it to an oar, and lashed the oar upright against the cabin bulkhead. This was not an ideal arrangement. A wave over the top of the cabin, or a capsize, would either shatter the oar or carry the whole contraption overboard. I logged that I'd rowed thirty-one miles, and went to bed.

By morning the oar with the radar reflector was hanging precariously over the side of the boat. *That didn't work.* I checked my position and noted that I'd lost twelve miles. I was 2,514 miles from France. I decided that I would row at least fourteen miles that day so that I would have only 2,500 miles left. There was a strong headwind. I rowed for fifteen hours, but I was still two miles short of the 2,500-mile mark.

I wanted to tear my pilot charts into little pieces and throw them over the side. I rose out of my seat and attempted to instruct the wind. "You are supposed to blow the other way. The experts told me you would blow *toward* France, not *away* from France." Then I sat down and had a chat with the video camera.

"I will either starve to death or I will get to France. One thing is for sure: a bad attitude isn't going to get me there. So I'll stay diligent about eating, sleeping, and drinking water, putting on my jacket when I'm cold, and taking off my jacket when I'm hot, and I'll get there. I may be a lunatic by the time I get there, but I'll get there."

I brought to mind the teachings of Chuang Tzu. "He who wants to have right without wrong, order without disorder, does not understand the principles of heaven and earth. He does not know how things hang together. Can a man cling only to heaven and know nothing of earth? They are correlative, to know one is to know the other." *I cannot sit on the ocean and expect the wind to blow only from the west. That's not how life works. I must accept the unfavorable winds just as I accept favorable ones.* In ancient China, dragons were considered creatures of great power and positive force. In works of art these dragons were often depicted holding a pearl. The pearl was a symbol of internal change. *I am in the* American Pearl, *on the ocean, surfing the dragon's tail.*

AT THE AGE OF FIFTEEN, I left my parents and my brother Lamar behind and moved in with my grandmother so I could attend the Louisville Collegiate School. Best of all, my brother Duke would be there. He was twenty-one and on his own. Duke hadn't finished college. This disappointed my parents, and returning home was not an option. Duke worked for Radio Shack during the day and built computers in my grandmother's basement half the night. My older brother could make a computer do anything.

My school uniform arrived in the mail. I tried it on; the green plaid kilt was hemmed to hang a few inches below the knee. I arrived for school wearing the kilt, a navy blue sweater, blue knee socks, and white high-top basketball shoes. I'd barely reached the end of the first hallway before I noticed that every girl in the place was staring at me. A lovely blond girl named Gracia Huntington started to giggle the instant I entered her line of sight. "What are you laughing at?" I asked.

"No one wears a kilt that long," she announced with a chuckle. "You clearly don't know how to dress yourself." I looked around. Every other kilt in the building was hemmed well above the knee. Jennifer Broaddus said, "Nice shoes."

I felt like a six-foot-tall billboard whose outfit proclaimed, "This girl does not belong here." Before lunch that first day, I stood in the hallway outside the history classroom trying to roll the waist of my kilt so the hem would look shorter. Noting my dilemma, the history teacher came into the hallway, gave me a knowing smile, and handed me a stapler. I curtsied, took the stapler, and all but ran to the restroom. There I stapled a hem in my kilt until it looked like everyone else's.

Each student was assigned to a lunch table. Ten girls sat at each table with a teacher. I found my table, and when I realized that I would have to sit next to Gracia Huntington, I wanted to melt into the floor. When she saw my kilt, Gracia smiled and called me "resourceful." I didn't know what that word meant, but it didn't sound like an insult.

ON JULY 14, I DID a little jig in the cockpit when the GPS reported that I'd drifted back only two miles during the night. The temperature had dropped. I was nearing the tail of the Grand Banks. I hoped that I might have picked up a section of the cold Labrador Current heading for Europe. I pulled on my heavy jacket and climbed out on deck well before dawn. A chilly wind came out of the north at twenty miles per hour. I rowed for an hour and a half, and the wind swung around to come out of the northeast at thirty-five miles per hour. The barometer was falling, and the wind was rising. Shortly after sunrise, the wind grew too strong to fight. I put out the small storm sea anchor.

To stave off boredom I detached the Ocean Sentry radar target enhancer and took it into the cabin with me. When I removed the first screw from the cover, water poured out of the hole. *That could be the problem.* I drained the housing and disassembled the main components. Then I replaced a series of corroded wires, carefully soldering each connection. When I was finished I reattached the unit to the roof and switched it on. It sprang to life and ran through its testing cycle perfectly.

Now what? I lay in my cabin staring up at the presidents. A ball of black hair was stuck in the duct tape that secured John Quincy Adams to the ceiling. I reached up with the soldering iron and set the hair on fire. Watching the miniature fireworks gave me such satisfaction that I turned to look around my sleeping area. Tiny balls of hair rolled around the cabin like miniature tumbleweeds. One by one, I torched them with the soldering iron.

IT WAS INEVITABLE THAT in my quest to defeat helplessness I would seek out tools to improve my leverage. We are *Homo sapiens*: tool users. My education in all things mechanical came from the Reverend William Leo Deutsch. Bill ran a Presbyterian summer camp just outside of Louisville. When I was about fifteen, I signed on as a camp counselor working with disabled campers, but before long Bill had me soldering wires, fixing roofs, plumbing bathhouses, mixing concrete, mudding drywall, felling trees, and splitting rails. It was Bill who introduced me to power tools. I used a large portion of my first paycheck to purchase a chain saw. "Every woman needs a good chain saw," observed Bill with an approving grin.

I'd never met anyone like Bill Deutsch. He was well educated, read voraciously, and seemed to know a little bit about everything. Despite his soaring intellect, Bill didn't suffer from the shallow sophistication that prides itself on clean hands. Nor did Bill see any reason why a young woman shouldn't learn how to saw, weld, grind, solder, or blow things up. The last was almost always accidental.

Bill would hand me a book about plumbing or mixing concrete, and he'd point me toward a project. One afternoon, he'd asked me to cut the rusty piping out of an old shower house. The rusty pipes were lead and the elbow joints were copper. It seemed to me that the quickest way to remove the plumbing was to cut through all the elbow joints. Hours later, when Bill came to view my progress, his salt-and-pepper beard visibly whitened. In carefully modulated tones Bill explained, "The copper elbow joints were the only valuable parts. We could have reused them." The book he'd loaned me didn't have a chapter on recycling. *Oops.*

I trusted Bill implicitly. When he asked me to climb into a grave-sized trench under the sidewalk beside the swimming pool, to hold the bracing until his cutting torch burned through the metal side of the pool, I didn't think twice about it. When my shoes started to smoke, I asked if it might be a good time for me to exit the hole. Someone up top relayed the question. "Don't bother me while I have a torch in my hand," was the testy reply. Another minute passed, and flames began to shoot through the wall at my feet. Taking this as my cue, I launched myself out of the tunnel. As I turned a water hose on my shoes, Bill said, "I didn't know you were still in there." *Oops.*

Campers came and campers went, but Bill harvested a staff of teenagers who shared one unifying trait: we each walked memory lane with a limp. Bill was the consummate "good shepherd" who created an atmosphere where each of us felt valued and useful. Bill saw the brokenness of Ahab in each of us, but he looked past our short-comings. He made each one of us believe that we were a young King Arthur on the verge of pulling the sword from the stone. He told us that we would achieve great things, and we believed him.

I had a fondness for using levers to move fallen trees, rocks, Volkswagens, and other large objects. More than once Bill called me "Archimedes." Paraphrasing the Greek mathematician and engineer, Bill clapped me on the shoulder and said, "Give you a place to stand and you shall move the world." Not wishing to see me fall, Bill always took care to see that my footing was secure.

I was scheduled to lead a weeklong backpacking trip for a youth group from Elizabethtown, Kentucky. When the group arrived, I was dismayed to realize that they were all male, mostly football players, and that I was younger than many of them. We gathered in the dining hall, where I distributed the food for the trip and supervised the loading of their backpacks. As we were finishing, Bill walked through the hall and asked, "So, Tori, are you going to take these young men for a run around camp in full pack?" I tried to say no, but the gauntlet had been thrown down.

"Yeah, let's go for a run," said one burly fellow.

"Right, yeah, a couple of miles would be great," said another. I could almost hear the "we'll show her" subtext. While my backpack appeared to be full, all it contained was a metal canteen cup, a spoon, and an unfurled sleeping bag. Bill knew I hadn't had time to pack. He gave me a wink as he headed out the back door. I pretended to struggle with my pack as I hefted it to my shoulders. The guys put on their packs, and we jogged out of the hall.

With every step I took, the metal spoon bounced inside the cup. The resulting metallic clang conveyed the erroneous impression that my backpack was filled with engine parts. The gentlemen behind me started to fall out of line before we'd finished the first quarter mile. By the time we reached their cabin, all but a few had slowed to a walk. "You can leave your packs here if you like," I said, fresh as a spring daisy. "Then we can jog back down to the dining hall for dinner." The guys gratefully left their loads and we jogged back to the hall, my "full" pack clanging all the way.

During dinner, I overheard Bill giving advice to the group leader. "Tori isn't much of a talker, so when she speaks, listen. I've never seen her angry, but if she should lose her temper, you better have a shovel ready to bury the bodies."

I spent a week with those guys in Red River Gorge. They didn't give me the least bit of trouble.

CHAPTER 9

Storm Petrels

July 17, 1998
latitude north 41:38, longitude west 54:38
days at sea: 33
progress: 1,379 miles

I TOOK STOCK OF MY SITUATION. I'D BEEN OUT FOR thirty-three days, and I'd covered one-third of the distance to France. I had food for a hundred days. Technically, I was on schedule, but the Gulf Stream and other favorable currents lose velocity as they approach Europe. Unless my luck changed, the second half of the trip would be slower than the first half. The trip could last 120 days.

I had to begin rowing more and eating less. Instead of rowing from dawn to dusk, I would row from 4:00 A.M. to 10:00 P.M. I'd eat one cooked meal a day: dinner. I would save the soup, cocoa, and Gatorade for storm rations. Instead of taking a 3:30 P.M. snack break every day, I would take it every other day. Finally, I would reserve all my peanut butter to use as emergency rations for the end of the trip. That evening I forced myself to eat the three-bean chili that I'd been avoiding out of gastric fear. This concern turned out to have been fully justified. Fortunately, I was alone, on the ocean, at night, in the noisy dark.

On July 18, the alarm sounded at 4:00 A.M., and I climbed out onto a deck that was as dark as a coal mine. Before daylight, I rowed eight miles. The dawn rose, gray and rainy. By lunchtime, I was tired of gray. *I need color.* I thumbed through a series of taped lectures and picked out a cassette about Claude Monet. The lecture recounted a story about Monet traveling to Le Havre to paint the ocean. *I would like to travel to Le Havre to see the ocean.* As I considered that thought, I tripped over the irony of it. I'd been staring at nothing but ocean for over a month. *Well, it would be nice to see the ocean from land.*

At 3:35 P.M., I was eating peanuts when the boat fell out from under me. With peanuts scattering in every direction, I looked up into the face of a towering wave. I grabbed both gunwales and shifted my weight toward the oncoming swell. The *American Pearl* creaked loudly as it scaled the sheer face of the monster. When the boat reached the crest, it did a little spin, teetering precariously on the ridge. I worried that the boat and I would turn a somersault down the far side, but to my relief I felt the rudder bite into the wave and guide us safely down.

I'd never seen a wave like that one. It seemed to rise from nothing, steep-faced and full of foam. There was a moment of raw terror, and then it was gone. I had been diligent about keeping everything tied down, but that freakish wave reminded me that anything could happen. I went back to rowing. By 10:00 P.M., I'd covered fifty-two miles.

On July 19, I rowed thirty-five miles. On July 20, the alarm went off at 4:00 A.M. I threw the clock into the stern of the boat and rolled back to sleep. When I came to my senses at 5:00 A.M., the alarm was still beeping. *No row, no eat.* I forced myself to climb out into a dark and foggy drizzle. With the constant rain, fog, and ocean spray, my rowing shoes were growing tattered. I cut apart the woolen three-cornered hat I'd brought along for the Fourth of July and lined my shoes with the soft felt. The headwind was not particularly strong, but in fifteen hours of rowing I managed to cover only seven miles. *There must be an opposing current.*

At 1:00 A.M. on July 21, I dreamt that there was a mouse in my cabin. Opening my eyes, I realized it wasn't a dream. There was a very definite scratching sound. I switched on the flashlight expecting to find a stow-away rodent, but nothing was there. The scratching continued. I soon realized that the sound was coming from the deck. I shone my flashlight out the main hatch. A small petrel was sitting in the bottom of my cockpit. In the limited space, the bird did not have enough running room to take off. *The poor thing is trapped.*

I pulled on my life vest and went outside. Petrels were accustomed to taking off from water. So, I reasoned, if I filled the cockpit with seawater the bird would rescue itself. After I'd poured several buckets of water into the cockpit, the poor bird was sloshing back and forth, colliding with the walls. *This isn't going to work.* I unlashed an oar and tried to scoop the bird out of the water. After several blundering attempts, the bird stopped moving. *I've killed it.* My heart sank.

Alone, on the ocean, at night, in the dark, I felt abominable. I'd killed another living creature. It is in the nature of our existence that we kill other living things to survive, but as a vegetarian, I didn't usually kill birds. *It was an accident. My intent had been innocent, but the result was murder.*

I looked up. There wasn't a moon, but every star seemed to be watching me; billions of stars staring down in disdain. *I should get the body out of the cockpit while it is dark and I don't really have to see it.* I took my oar, and because I felt no need to be tentative, I scooped up the bird in a single motion. I started to dump it unceremoniously over the side. *No, it deserves better.* In an apologetic prayer, I lifted the oar with the little bird balanced on its blade high over my head. *I am so sorry.* Once the breeze above the cabin hit the bird, it stood up and flew away. "Ahhh," I gasped with surprise and delight at this sudden resurrection. As the bird circled the boat, I smiled up at the stars. They were not full of disdain; they were full of hope.

HOW MANY TIMES HAD *I been that bird?* At the Louisville Collegiate School, Helen Kent Longley was an institution. She made up the entire high school history department. She taught ancient history to the tenth grade, European history to the eleventh grade, and American history to the senior class. History had always been one of my favorite subjects. A few weeks into the semester, when I took my first history test, I thought I'd done quite well, but when the tests came back I'd received a D-minus. Worse, there was a note from Mrs. Longley at the top of the cover sheet. It read, "Please see me." I was devastated. I'd never gotten a D in my life. After class, I bolted from the room. It took me several days to work up the courage to go and see Mrs. Longley.

When I entered her classroom, I was so terrified my teeth chattered. I sat in my usual desk, and Mrs. Longley took a seat in the desk next to mine. She asked, "What happened?"

"I've never taken that kind of test before. At my old school, the tests were always true-false or multiple choice. I thought I did okay."

Mrs. Longley went over the test with me question by question. In the format of a conversation, my answers were flawless. Once she satisfied herself that I knew the material, Mrs. Longley stood up and began to pace the room. Mrs. Longley had been in the Navy in World War II, and her military bearing was impossible to miss. "You've never written answers to a test in essay form?"

Barely raising my voice to a whisper, I answered, "No, ma'am."

She asked, "Have you ever written a term paper?"

My classmates had been discussing term papers since the first day of school. Brimming with frustration, I asked, "What *is* a term paper?"

Before she could stop herself, the words "Oh my" escaped Mrs. Longley's lips. She took several deep breaths. Once she'd steadied her nerves, she sat next to me again and asked about my academic background.

Except for kindergarten and first grade, I had always gone to public schools. "I have never written anything longer than two and a half pages."

"Okay," Mrs. Longley said, raising a hand to indicate that she'd heard enough. Then she sat quietly for a long time.

My secret is out. I don't belong in this school, and Mrs. Longley knows it. They'll send me back to Pennsylvania. Just as I had when my father discovered me on top of the pedestal, I burst into tears. I tried to speak: "I don't . . . I don't . . . I don't belong."

Without looking at me, Mrs. Longley put her hand on my arm as an indication that I should remain silent. Something told me that she was calculating whether I had any scholastic potential. I could almost visualize her turning over my future in her mind. Mrs. Longley was in her sixties. Would I be worth her time? She gazed at the ceiling for a moment, then looked at me. When her decision was made, Mrs. Longley stood with perfect dignity. She walked to her desk, lifted a box of Kleenex, returned, and handed me the box. When I looked up from my desk, Mrs. Longley's steel-blue eyes conveyed assurance. "This is not your fault," she said firmly. "You have intelligence. I believe you are capable of doing this level of work. Your responses this morning prove that you knew the material when you took the test. Your difficulties are mechanical."

I attempted to respond but managed only an unintelligible sob.

"You are behind. Your peers have been writing essays and papers since they were old enough to write."

I sniffled.

"It is understood that Collegiate students will have several hours of homework every evening."

I nodded.

"What might take one of your classmates three hours to accomplish may take you six, but you must do it, and do it all." She stressed that final word.

I sat a little straighter and managed a proper "Yes, ma'am."

"If you study hard and do all of your homework, I will teach you the mechanics of how to take the tests and how to write the papers." Then she paused to be sure she had my full attention. "But I cannot, and will not, do the work for you."

"No, ma'am."

"If there is any assignment you do not understand, you will find me here before or after school."

"Yes, ma'am."

"Now, if you would like to sit for a minute, to pull yourself together, that would be acceptable."

I would have sooner lingered in a burning building. As I gathered my things to leave, Mrs. Longley opened a heavy book on her desk. Without looking up, she said, "For the educated person the world is an open book; to the ignorant, it is an unsolved mystery."

I wiped the last tears away with my sleeve. "Yes, ma'am."

Then Mrs. Longley looked at me over the top of her glasses and said, "You don't like unsolved mysteries, do you?"

"No, ma'am."

ON JULY 22, THE fog was so thick that I could barely make out the bow of my boat. I could hear whales all around me, but I couldn't see them. Around 10:00 A.M., I rowed into a clearing where two humpbacks were lounging on the surface. Until I rowed within twenty yards, they didn't seem to take any notice of me. I paused and shipped my oars. The sound of the oars clunking against the gunwales led one of the whales to slip silently beneath the surface. The second whale lingered for a minute. Then with a gentle twist and an arch of the back the whale started a dive. I thought I'd remembered reading that a whale diving from a dead stop couldn't lift its flukes. So I was more than a little surprised to see the white undersides of a broad tail rise high above my head before the whale slid quietly down. *I guess she didn't read the book.*

I watched the ripples where the whale went down until the fog surrounded me again. I shoved out my oars and returned to rowing. Minutes later, the alarm sounded on my Ocean Sentry. *There's a ship nearby.*

I switched off the alarm and listened. I heard the deep thrum of engines, but I couldn't see anything through the curtain of fog. I pulled out the VHF radio. "This is the rowing vessel *American Pearl, American Pearl.* Does anyone read me?" I gave my latitude and longitude and repeated the question: "Can anyone hear me?" The throb of engines grew louder. *It's getting closer.* I stood on deck turning in circles. The sound echoed off the fog. I couldn't tell what direction the sound was coming from, but it was getting louder.

"This is the rowing vessel *American Pearl, American Pearl.* Does anyone read me?" I pulled the whistle out of my life vest and blew it as hard as I could. The sound bounced off the fog and returned to me sounding weak and feeble. The thump of my heart kept time with the throbbing engines. After several uneasy minutes, the sound of engines grew more distant and faded in the fog.

I rowed for seventeen hours but progressed less than twelve miles toward France. During dinner, I commented on video about the dismal progress. "I don't know what to say, I don't know what to think. I know it's a heavy boat, but for pity's sake . . . if things continue [like this], I'll be here until Christmas."

July 23 brought still more fog. I rowed for a few hours before reaching into my compartment of food bars to get some breakfast. I fished around and pulled up a Clif Bar. It was apple-cherry flavor. *I don't remember requesting apple-cherry.* I dropped the bar back into the bin and dug around for a different Clif Bar. I was hoping for a chocolate chip one or, even better, peanut butter chocolate chip. Instead, I came up with an apricot Clif Bar. *I might have accidentally ordered apple-cherry, but there's no way I ordered any apricot.*

As if the ocean could hear me, I yelled, "I've been had by the nutrition police! Here I am, rowing fourteen to sixteen hours a day, and the staff at Rainbow Blossom, my friendly neighborhood health food store, was worried that I might be eating too much chocolate. So they substituted fruit flavors for chocolate chip flavors. Can't I at least shuffle off this mortal coil eating something other than dried apricots?" *I have nothing against dried fruit, but isn't part of the joy in physical exertion the ability to eat whatever you darn well please?*

As I continued to row, a plastic bag filled with what looked like pink cotton candy inside it floated between the blade of my oar and the boat. *Garbage. I should pick it up.* I reached over the side to grab the bag but noticed something odd. *Tentacles?* I jerked back my hand. This was no plastic bag filled with cotton candy. It was a Portuguese man-of-war with tentacles extending more than twenty feet. This cousin to the jellyfish stings with toxins only slightly less harmful than cobra venom. "Well, I don't think I'll be trying to put you into my garbage bag." I returned to rowing, and before I'd taken thirty strokes the iridescent float of the man-of-war slipped into the fog behind my boat.

Late that evening, I pulled out my journal and wrote, "My life is not lonely so much as unadorned. On the ocean there is no duplicity. I row. I eat. I sleep. I fix things. Insincerity began to fade when my communications system went out. I save my food wrappers but toss all pretense of special virtue overboard."

When I finished these words, I opened the journal to the first page and began to read my entries. "'I, Tori Murden, am rowing under the great dome of the sky' . . . blah, blah, blah." As I turned the pages, I barely recognized the woman who'd left North Carolina bound for France. She believed that arrogance and self-assurance went together, and she would accept both. She confused vulnerability with weakness and would have none of either. She thought that peace was something only lazy people could enjoy. She hid behind impenetrable walls and did not see that they consumed more of life than they preserved.

The all-enveloping fog outside seemed like an apt metaphor for my life up to that point. I had lived behind the walls of a carefully constructed fortress. A few close friends had traversed past the barbed wire and scaled the outer parapets, but only a handful of individuals had gained admittance to the interior. True to my pledge, romance had been barred at the front gate. On the ocean, the barriers of my fortress crumbled from lack of use. For the first time I could remember, my inside self began to match the outside one.

Somewhere in the "silence" of the sea, I learned to listen. I heard whales sing, dolphins chatter, and I listened to the small quiet voices within me. Having practiced listening, I found that I had less to say. As a speck of humanity in nature, I was utterly insignificant. As an individual, I was unique and special. Though I stood by myself, I was never alone.

As I flipped through the pages of my journal, long-suppressed emotions welled up in me and boiled over. I hadn't written anything in my journal that wasn't true. I hadn't written anything that didn't happen. But I couldn't help noticing that every thought was neatly polished for public consumption. My deck log was written on water-resistant Ritchie Wet Notes. In it, I kept a record of the latitude and longitude, wind speed and direction, and temperature. I jotted random thoughts in the margins in no particular order. My leather-bound journal with its cotton bond paper was anything but random; it was as neat and orderly as a librarian's kitchen. I wondered, *What is the difference between polish and varnish?*

I tore out the page with the final entry, opened the main hatch— *good thing this paper is biodegradable*—and tossed the journal overboard. For me it was a consummate act of honesty. I was not even fond of the woman who had left North Carolina with me. It seemed perfectly reasonable to throw her overboard.

LOUISVILLE COLLEGIATE GAVE ME a fresh start. I would be described as an "enigmatic" teenager. Where other young women indulged in schoolgirl fantasies about musicians and movie actors, I had the names Thomas Jefferson and John Quincy Adams written across the toes of my basketball shoes. One day before gym class, Kim O'Callaghan pointed to the names on my high-tops and asked, "What? Did you cheat on a history test at your old school?" It was a question that other classmates must have been curious about, because every one of them paused to hear my response.

The situation triggered well-worn defense mechanisms. I didn't say a word. I stepped to where my back would be protected by a wall. Then I raised my fists and delivered a glare that sent a message: *The first person who touches me is going to die.* Kim took three steps back, and the other girls exchanged looks of shock and puzzlement. No one moved. After a tense silence, Kim said, "I'm not going to fight you; you're a tree." I relaxed my guard and smiled at Kim's description of me. The room itself seemed to breathe a sign of relief. Until that moment, I did not understand that I'd entered an idyllic world where physical violence was anathema.

In the years I'd served as Lamar's protector, I'd encountered my share of sticks and stones and heard many names that hurt me. Collegiate was different: never a stick, never a stone, and after that tense moment in the locker room my nickname would become "Tree."

At Collegiate, I found a world that was gracious enough to meet my awkward teenage feet. Mrs. Longley's history class was a world unto itself. In three years, she took us from the beginning of the universe through ancient China, Egypt, and Greece. On we went through Europe (both ancient and modern), and then we visited the history of the Americas. It was a stroll through a spacious realm of the mind: a walk with statesmen, inventors, artists, poets, scientists, and leaders. Mrs. Longley wove the voices of the past together with the articulate voices of the present and demanded that her students participate in the dialogue.

Other teachers introduced me to Homer, Plato, Shakespeare, and modern literature. In geometry, it was not enough to know the

Pythagorean theorem ($A^2 + B^2 = C^2$); one needed to learn the history of Pythagoras. Chemistry and biology opened new worlds for me to explore. There was art, music, and, uh, well, um . . . dance. Okay, so while Collegiate was idyllic, it was not perfect. One needed two years of dance to graduate from the school. All of my classmates had fulfilled this requirement many times over, leaving me as the sole student who needed to pay heed to the instructor of dance.

The first challenge was for me to locate ladies' dancing slippers in a size twelve. The man at the dance store explained that there wasn't much call for ballerinas who were my size. He all but advised me to give up the quest. I smiled stupidly in the man's direction and daydreamed about placing my size-twelve foot in the middle of the man's chest. He babbled on, "Your only option really is to use men's shoes. I have a pair right here."

"Fine," I responded dully. I knew Gracia Huntington would find the whole concept terribly amusing. She was not alone: there were giggles all around. The only person who didn't laugh at my shoes was the dance teacher, Miss Starr.

She was a profoundly kind soul. Some star-crossed deity brought the two of us together. I needed the dance credit. She needed a student who was required to take her seriously. We both rose to the challenge. After one particularly worthy effort on my part, Miss Starr called me "elegant."

From one of my classmates seated in the bleachers came the comment, "Yeah, gritty elegance, maybe." Miss Starr was not amused, but I wasn't offended. The phrase "gritty elegance" fit me better than those silly shoes.

While I felt inept in dance class, I was at ease on the athletic fields. When choosing sides for a field hockey game, Kim O'Callaghan picked me first. I was aghast. "But Kim, I don't know how to play field hockey."

"It doesn't matter," Kim responded, undeterred. Once the teams were complete, Kim gave us her plan for our offense. "Tori, I want you to run at the person who has the ball. Make as much noise as you possibly can. Be terrifying. I'll be right behind you, and I'll steal the ball." This offensive strategy worked like a charm.

Life at Grandmother's house was difficult. When I moved in, the doctor told me, "She has about three weeks to live." Her condition never improved, but she lived for another three years. One afternoon as I returned from school I heard Grandmother calling, "Help me. I'm lost." I followed the sounds to the living room. There I found grandmother's feet turning circles in the fireplace. She'd tried to clean the flue, stood up, and become lost in the darkness of the chimney.

At night, Grandmother would rattle the high sides of her hospital bed and shout things like, "Come push this car around the corner, I'm stuck." Or "Service, I want service, there's a man in my cabin." My room was at the top of the stairs, and Grandmother's groans would keep me awake. Soon Grandmother required full-time nursing care. With the night nurse downstairs, I could sleep in the closet, where Grandmother's moans were less audible.

About this time, my brother Duke, who was in his early twenties, began to experience medical problems. He lost some of his sight and had difficulty controlling his limbs. One morning as I was leaving to ride my bicycle to school, Duke fell down the stairs. Not long after that, he was diagnosed with multiple sclerosis.

I missed my brother Lamar intensely. His hearing was so poor that I couldn't really talk to him on the phone. When I saw him at Thanksgiving, I learned how unhappy he had been without me.

"You come home?" Lamar asked, his eyes full of hope.

"Just for a few days," I answered.

Lamar cried.

I felt an immense guilt. It wasn't as if life with the old bear (our name for Grandmother Neblett) was enjoyable, but it was safe. I wanted to tell Lamar that I didn't get bloody noses anymore, but I feared that he might be getting more than bloody noses.

My mind wrestled with my conscience. *I could flunk out of Collegiate; no one would know the difference. Well,* she *would know—Mrs. Longley would know. Why did she let me stay?* I couldn't turn my back on the faith Mrs. Longley had invested in me, not even for Lamar. How I wished he could have followed me into the sunlit safety of Collegiate, but he couldn't. I left him behind, and it felt abominably selfish.

Mrs. Longley would meet me before school to address any questions I might have about my homework. In English, we were reading the ancient Greek playwright Euripides. It was not enough for Mrs. Longley that I'd read the assigned text. She insisted that I learn the context in which Euripides wrote. "You cannot understand what he was trying to say unless you know something about the world in which he lived."

Over time, Mrs. Longley learned more and more about the world in which I lived. Mrs. Longley did not accept excuses. She explained, "It would be a simple thing for a young woman with your history to adopt the role of victim. Have you ever heard of a successful victim?"

I shrugged. "No, ma'am."

"You will not achieve anything of merit by proving that you have been more victimized than someone else. It's silly."

"Yes, ma'am."

"You cannot control what goes on at home, but you can do your homework. Come to school early, stay late, study at a friend's house, go to the public library, but get your work done."

"Yes, ma'am."

Had Mrs. Longley accepted excuses, helplessness might have retained a foothold in my life. *Why is it the words* helpless *and* victim *always go together?*

CHAPTER 10

Theodore Roosevelt's
Burial at Sea

July 24, 1998
latitude north 43:05, longitude west 51:09
days at sea: 40
progress: 1,594 miles

THERE WAS A WIND FROM THE NORTHEAST AND THE FOG was thick. The GPS gave me several false readings. In the overcast conditions, my sextant was useless. I noted my location as "the tail of the Grand Banks." As I was writing, a beaked whale swam up to the edge of the boat and spouted in my direction. It was dark gray with white scars along its back. Its small dorsal fin was about two-thirds of the way back on its body. The whale's head was melon-shaped, and its body was the length of my boat. It was too big to be a dolphin, but smaller than most of the whales I'd seen. He seemed a happy fellow.

On July 25, I caught a break. A tail wind out of the west-southwest helped me to cover forty-four miles. The fog was so thick it was as if the air and sea were swathed in gauze. My voice reverberated in the mist. When it wasn't raining, the water droplets stuck to the hair on my arms, legs, and eyelids. I hadn't shaved my legs in more than forty days, and I smiled to see them covered in a forest of water droplet trees.

That evening, as I was lashing down my oars, I felt a cool breeze and heard a growling sound like the creaking of old hinges on a heavy gate. Pops and groans followed. I checked my position. I was ninety miles north of where the *Titanic* had gone down. *Could those creaks and groans be from an iceberg? It would not be unheard of for the Labrador Current to push a big berg this far south.* It was dark. I couldn't see anything through the fog. *It's not as if I'm steaming across the North Atlantic at twenty-two knots. If the* American Pearl *drifts into an iceberg, it will bounce off. Experts built the* Titanic; *amateurs built the ark. Amateurs built the* American Pearl; *the* Pearl *will be fine.* I decided not to worry about the creaks and pops from an unseen something out in the fog.

On Sunday, July 26, I woke up feeling an unnatural vibration. I opened the main hatch and heard the thrum of engines. *Propellers, very close!* I scrambled on deck to see a large fishing vessel fifty yards away. It was moving slowly, and to my relief it clearly had the *American Pearl* in view. I tried to raise the crew on the VHF, but the helmsman turned hard to port, and in less than a minute the fishing boat disappeared into the fog. *They must have thought this was an abandoned lifeboat. They were probably thinking salvage until I popped out to spoil the fun.*

July 27 began with a northeast wind at twenty miles per hour and a loss of twelve miles. I rowed for a while, but when the headwind reached thirty-five miles per hour I threw out a sea anchor and crawled inside to ride out the building storm. By dawn of July 28 I'd lost well over fifty miles. The boat rolled on its side a dozen times, but it didn't turn completely upside down. Heavy waves drove cold ocean water through the seal on my stern hatch.

Wet and shivering inside my fleece bag, I thought about the last vestige of comfort that remained: a dry sleeping bag. I was reluctant to pull it out, because it would be drenched in a matter of minutes. I tried to convince myself that the psychological comfort of knowing I had a dry bag aboard was more valuable than actually using it. When my teeth began to chatter, mere psychological comfort was no longer enough for me. I pulled out the dry bag and slid into it. I slept soundly until a near capsize tossed me high up the cabin wall. When the boat righted itself, sloshing water ran through my bag like a cold chill.

Hungry, shivering, and desperate for amusement, I pulled out the books on tape. My rule was that I could listen to music or books on tape only while I was rowing, but the seas were so rough I couldn't hold on to a book, let alone read one. I was about to put a tape into my Sony Walkman when I remembered that it had an AM/FM radio. The radio would not draw as much power as the tape player. I turned the radio on and ran the dial up and down the FM band. Nothing. I switched to the AM band, ran the dial through the channels, and picked up a scratchy signal from St. John's, Newfoundland. I got a minute or two of a talk show with Dr. Laura Schlessinger. She seemed extremely sure of herself, if a little rude to her guests.

This was followed by a commercial for the telecommunications company Sprint with Candice Bergen. I laughed. "What I wouldn't give for a telephone that works!" After a commercial for cosmetic dentistry, I lost the signal. I was so starved for news of humanity that I would have traded a bag of dry cashews to hear just one more commercial, no matter how inane. *From this latitude it would be easy for me to row north, make a stop in Newfoundland, and have my phone repaired.* I imagined what the headlines would be if I made such a stop: "Woman Abandons Attempt to Row Across Ocean Because She Cannot Phone Home."

MY FRIENDS FROM COLLEGE *would never forgive me.* By my senior year at Louisville Collegiate, an outside observer might have thought that I had been born into the school. I was president of the student government, chair of the Honor Board, and captain of the basketball team. I went to school early and stayed late. My teachers and classmates filled my head with a rainbow of ideas. Life with Lamar had taught me the necessity of rising to physical challenges, but Collegiate taught me the delight of rising to intellectual challenges. If junior high had been Dante's Inferno, Louisville Collegiate was the Paradiso, only there were no romantic associations. There was no Dante for my Beatrice. I remained a solitary "tree."

I delighted in science and math because for every puzzle there was a solution. History was just a different sort of puzzle. Applying Mrs. Longley's GERMS theory, if one understood the government (G), economy (E), religion (R), military (M), and social (S) interests in a historical situation, one could make sense of the outcomes. I adore puzzles.

I did not like English literature. English literature was not a puzzle; it was a problem. Problems demand emotional engagement, and not all problems have solutions. With problems there are no right answers, only right reactions. I didn't react as others did; I didn't feel what others felt. Poems such as Edgar Allan Poe's "Alone" locked up my jets.

> *From childhood's hour I have not been*
> *As others were—I have not seen*
> *As others saw—I could not bring*
> *My passions from a common spring.*
> *From the same source I have not taken*
> *My sorrow; I could not awaken*
> *My heart to joy at the same tone;*
> *And all I lov'd, I lov'd alone.*

Growing up with Lamar, I'd been an outcast. The view from the margin doesn't match that of the mainstream. When I recalled my faint and girlish love, I didn't remember my innocence. I remembered only the outcome: my failure. The memory was a pain, a problem I could not solve. If ever I loved again, I would love alone. I would love from a distance.

The safest distance was time. John Quincy Adams would not love me back. I could spend the night with Galen, Pasteur, and Lister without danger of my contracting an affection. Copernicus, Galileo, and Tyco could put stars in my eyes, but they wouldn't blur my vision. I would not be blinded by love. I would not allow helplessness to sneak up on me.

THE HEADMISTRESS AT LOUISVILLE Collegiate served as the college counselor. I was not Miss Kussrow's favorite student. When I was new to the school, I asked Miss Kussrow why all the kitchen and custodial staff at the school were black but all the teachers and students were white. During our second encounter, I told Miss Kussrow that firing the physical education teacher after nine years of service and providing her with only a nine-word recommendation was "inexcusable." That was a big word for me in those days.

When the time came for me to discuss potential colleges with Miss Kussrow, she did all the talking. "You shall not apply to Harvard, Princeton, or Yale, but any other school would be acceptable. You might wish to consider a small liberal arts college where your proclivities toward social justice might be indulged." This was the sum total of my college counseling; it was a short meeting.

A few weeks later, my father visited Kentucky for the weekend. He asked where I intended to apply for college. I couldn't tell my father that I was deemed unfit for Harvard, Princeton, or Yale. Nor could I tell him that I planned never to fall in love. To evade these issues, I insisted that I would like to go to a women's college. The next morning, I woke early to find my father at the kitchen table surrounded by stacks of college directories. Adopting the guise of the average teenager, I retreated back to bed.

A few hours later, I emerged to find a pristine chart on the kitchen table. In the left column I read the names of thirteen colleges. Along the top of the chart, each column was labeled with some variable such as the student-faculty ratio, how many books were in the library, or whether or not they offered intercollegiate basketball.

Father explained that I should pick four schools and apply. I did, and thanks to the reputation of the Louisville Collegiate School, I was accepted for admission at all four.

In the end, I chose Smith College. When my parents dropped me off at Smith, father told me, "I hope you will be a B student." I was shocked. My father, a lifelong teacher, had never been happy with anything less than an A. He explained that at an institution such as Smith, much of the learning takes place outside the classroom. He said, "I know that you can get an A in any course that you put your mind to, but you should shoot for B's and use your time to get the most out of the experience." For once, I heeded my father's advice.

ON JULY 29, THE wind dropped to fifteen miles per hour and shifted to come out of the southeast. I'd lost a full degree of longitude to the storm, and I was itching to begin getting it back. Above the main hatch, I had taped a sign: To Live and to Serve. The sign had a water line running through the middle of it, tangible evidence that most of the boat had been underwater during the storm.

The seas were challenging, but I was able to claw and crawl fifteen miles through cross swells and unruly winds. On July 30, I took up the oars before dawn, but the boat felt sluggish and refused to go straight. When I investigated, I found a long section of driftwood wedged under the boat against the rudder. I climbed out through the stern hatch, hung upside down by my knees, and wrestled the log loose. As I returned to my rowing seat, I gashed my heel on a worm clamp in the cockpit. The cut was very deep. *Blood . . . blood is good.*

The conditions were no better on July 31, but dolphins kept me company. I told the video camera, "It's difficult to explain how much fun it is to observe wild creatures in their own habitat so closely. To be a part of their world even if it's just for fifteen minutes. It makes the calculating of food and distance, and how far did I make it last hour, all worthwhile." I rowed thirty-three miles and cooked a large dinner to celebrate the end of July.

Checking my deck log, I determined that the only full day that I had enjoyed favorable winds was July 18. The nearly constant struggle against adverse winds threatened to tatter my spirit. To stay motivated I'd convinced myself that if I labored through July and made it into August the wind would turn in my favor. *Tomorrow is another day. August is another month. I'll be able to move faster in August.*

When dawn brought still more wind from the east, I was furious. *The universe has betrayed me.*

THIS IS ALL RITA *Benson's fault.* I met Rita Benson in 1981 during my first year at Smith College. I was strolling though the athletic complex when this grande dame who'd taught at the college for more than forty years placed herself directly in my path and said, "Hello."

I straightened my back, squared my shoulders, and answered, "Yes, ma'am." This response was not unusual. Generations of Smith women had snapped to attention at Miss Benson's feet.

Her steely blue eyes looked through me. When the measuring stick of her mind had finished sizing me up, she said, "You will row."

I answered, "Yes, ma'am."

The spring of 1982, I learned to row on Paradise Pond, in the center of the Smith campus. Under Miss Benson's tutelage, I progressed quickly. As I was shoving off the dock my first day in a racing single, Miss Benson explained what was going to happen. "I know you," she said. "You will row up and down in front of the dock here, you'll row easy, and you'll do just fine."

"Yes, Miss Benson."

"Then you'll decide to row around the island, where no one can see you, and you'll take three hard strokes, and the boat will turn over."

"No, Miss Benson. I'll take it very gently."

"Right," said Miss Benson with only a hint of sarcasm.

True to Miss Benson's words, I rowed up and down in front of the dock for about forty-five minutes. The boat was twenty-six feet long but only twelve inches wide at the waterline. If I sneezed in the wrong direction, I would turn it over. Still, I felt I was getting the hang of it. Then Miss Benson went inside the boathouse to take a phone call, and I rowed around behind Paradise Island. I took three hard strokes. The boat turned over. It was early March in New England, and the water was so cold that when I surfaced I had to talk myself into breathing. By the time I managed to get back into the boat and row it back around the island, Miss Benson was standing on the dock. Water dripped from my hair and clothing.

Seeing me, Miss Benson smiled knowingly and said, "And *now* what are you going to do?"

"I'm going to do whatever you tell me to do, Miss Benson."

AUGUST 2 REDUCED ME to babbling at the video camera, "I need a valet. This morning it was cold. So I put on all of my clothes (except my fleece). I was still cold. So I said all right, it's time for fleece. I go in and find my fleece jacket. I take off my raincoat, take off my life vest. Put on my fleece jacket on top of my Capilene shirt, and I put my life vest back on; then I put on my raincoat. And I have my trousers on. I've got my Gore-Tex socks on. I go back out. I row for about fifteen minutes. Then I'm hot.

"Okay, I have to take off the fleece jacket. So I take off the jacket, take off the life vest, take off the fleece. I put on the life vest, put on the raincoat, and then it starts to rain. I can't leave the fleece jacket just sitting there on deck. I stop rowing, put the fleece jacket in its little baggy, and put it away in the cabin. Now it's sunny and it's raining. That's been the story all day. It's either raining, or it's sunny, or it's doing both at the same time. I can't decide what to wear. I put it on, take it off, put it on, take it off."

August 3 was my fiftieth day at sea. I was only two hundred miles short of halfway. This meant that I was only a week behind schedule. The predawn hours were cold, but blue moonlight wafted gently through the fog. In the pink of the sunrise, I noticed a dorsal fin circling the boat. Several feet behind the sharp dorsal, the tip of a tail peeked out of the water and swung from side to side. *The tails of dolphins go up and down, not side to side.* The presence of a large fish wasn't news to me. I'd observed a large gray-blue streak traveling under and around the boat for more than two weeks. I thought it was a big marlin or a swordfish, but this was wasn't any marlin. *It is a shark, and a big one.* I estimated the shark to be twelve or fifteen feet long.

I went to the cabin and pulled out my *Field Guide to Saltwater Fishes*. After the shark made a few more passes, I was able to compare it to all the shark pictures in the guide. I decided that my visitor was a tiger shark. It was shaped like a great white shark, but great whites are supposed to have slightly pointed snouts, and the snout on my visitor didn't look very pointed. At the time I neglected to notice that tiger sharks prefer warm water, while I was in water affected by the cold Labrador Current. Temperatures ranged between the high forties and the low fifties. Great white sharks prefer cold water. Not knowing any better, I settled into thinking the shark next to my boat was a tiger shark. The shark slithered through the water, always keeping its distance. Only rarely did it come close enough to let me get a good look at it. I shook my safety tether. *You're just waiting for me to fall overboard.*

Around noon the fog lifted, and for the first time in weeks the sun came out in full view. Everything in my world was soggy. I didn't know when the fog would descend again. So it was with a sense of urgency that I pulled out my sleeping bag and draped it over the cabin roof. With the sleeping bag covering the solar panels, I wouldn't be able to make fresh water. I would gladly hand-pump water in exchange for a dry sleeping bag.

With the constant dampness in my cabin, the stern wall was beginning to look like a science experiment. Black mold had taken over the back half of the cabin, and it was creeping forward. I wanted to open both hatches and both portholes, but this was dangerous. If a rogue wave surprised me, the cabin would flood, and if the boat capsized, I might not be able to right it again. It was a calm day. I decided to accept the risk. Still, I kept a vigilant weather eye on the ocean as I rowed.

After I dried my sleeping bag and my sleeping pad, I dried the pillow. Bringing along a pillow seemed almost as decadent as bringing along a library, but the pillow proved its usefulness by protecting my head in rough weather (and the library protected my head the rest of the time). By late afternoon, everything was dry and I'd made enough water to soap down the cabin walls and get ahead of the mold. To my regret, Theodore Roosevelt had a serious case of black mold growing under his plastic lamination. *I guess that's what happens when someone throws up on you.*

Theodore Roosevelt is one of my favorite presidents. An advocate of the "strenuous life," he was the sort of man who could have happily rowed across an ocean. The inspiration of his words had moved me to try any number of things. "Far better it is to dare mighty things, to win glorious triumphs, even though checkered by failure, than to rank with those poor spirits who neither enjoy much nor suffer much, because they live in the gray twilight that knows neither victory nor defeat." That afternoon I felt like a liberated prisoner, having escaped from the gray twilight of the Grand Banks fog.

Sadly, with Theodore's mold condition I could no longer keep him in the cabin, nor could I bring myself to place his picture unceremoniously in my garbage bin. Instead, I held the little portrait over the stove until it was well in flame, then placed it gently on the crest of a passing wave. *Sorry, old fellow. I shall miss having you on my cabin wall.* Theodore Roosevelt was both a scholar and an athlete. Had he not been genetically impaired, he would have gone to Smith.

MY EDUCATION AT COLLEGIATE opened a door for me to move from the margin to the mainstream. Smith College taught me to navigate the mainstream and to claim it as my own. I still felt different, but at Smith, this didn't make me an outcast. The witty princess from the Middle East shared a dining table with the razor-sharp woman from the Alabama trailer park and the insightful daughter of an Iowa farmer. Each of us was smart, but we were smart in different ways. We were united in our distinctiveness. For my first three years in college, I was pre-med, but toward the end of my junior year a friend from another school committed suicide. I began to think that the life of a physician might not leave room for the many things I wanted to explore beyond the sciences. While pathogens and cures were puzzles that demanded solutions, they would not quench the helplessness I felt when I looked into the face of human suffering. I shifted majors to study physiological psychology. (Neuroscience as a separate discipline had not yet come into its own.) At the same time, I began a more serious exploration of world religions. When the roads of science run out, we must move forward with faith.

The president of Smith College was Jill Ker Conway. She was poised, elegant, and fashion-model thin. The fact that her intelligence seemed to spill out all over everywhere made her a terrific role model for Smith women. She had been raised on a sheep station in the Australian outback, which made her just distinctive enough to fit in at Smith. One evening after she'd delivered a remarkable lecture at the Helen Hills Chapel, President Conway took questions. I leapt at the chance to ask, "Why would a woman like you, who wasn't raised in any particular religious tradition, choose to become a Catholic?"

Mrs. Conway smiled. She looked down for a moment, as if examining a chess board for the correct move. I was prepared to recite a litany of wrongs done to women in the history of Catholicism, and I fully expected to have an opportunity to demonstrate that knowledge. However, that evening President Conway didn't dabble with the pawns of history. Her answer was simple and direct. "Power is never given. Power must be taken."

These words passed through me like a bolt of lightning. I'd never heard anything so audacious in all my life. I was awestruck. The friend seated next to me waited a moment before whispering in my ear, "Have you any more questions?"

CHAPTER 11

Where's the Rest of It,
and What Ate It?

August 3, 1998
latitude north 44:42, longitude west 48:23
days at sea: 50
progress: 1,765 miles

THE EVENING OF AUGUST 3, I CLIMBED INTO A CLEAN cabin and folded myself into a dry sleeping bag. That night, whales sang me to sleep. They were close; I could feel the vibration of clicks and trumpets. Dolphin clicks sounded like a pencil tapping on a table. Whale clicks were like the deep rap of a drum beat. Patterns repeated. Low moans reverberated like a deep string bass. *This is bliss.*

The morning of August 4, the alarm went off at 5:00 A.M. A heavy rain drummed on the cabin roof and flashes of lightning lit up the cabin. *Argggh, I just got everything dry!* I switched off the alarm, pulled my knees to my chest, and rubbed my face in my dry sleeping bag. *No, no, no, no, I am dry, the cabin is dry, and I want to keep it that way.* It was several hours before my will prevailed over my want and I forced myself to crawl out into the driving rain. By that time, the worst of the lightning had passed. I could see thunderheads in the distance. It rained all day, but I made nineteen miles.

August 5 brought a strong wind out of the northeast. I wasn't able to drag the boat more than a few miles into the wind. At 3:00 A.M. on August 6, I woke up with what I had come to term "sea anchor psychosis." When the boat was on a sea anchor in steep seas, it was like trying to sleep inside a basketball. Even my small storm anchor jerked the boat off the tops of waves in a way that made the hull bounce.

The skin rubbed off my elbows and my heels. Strong winds wobbled the boat with a speed that was mind-numbing. It could go left and right fifty or sixty times a minute. *Every cut I have reopens. Every bruise gets redoubled. If my knee is up, it slams into the wall. If my knee is down, then the cut I have on my heel gets chafed back and forth.*

I longed to be still. Even on the calmest days, my soup did not stay on the spoon, but when the boat was on the sea anchor, the soup wouldn't even stay in the cup. When I was able to nab a little sleep, my brain rewarded me with lucid dreams. Aware that I was dreaming, I went for long walks in shady green forests. I relished beautifully prepared meals surrounded by friends. I sank into the cushions of a soft chair. I turned on the faucet and watched water run down the drain. In one lucid dream, I imagined I was sleeping in a bed that didn't move. *What a great dream that was!*

AT SMITH, I'D DREAMT of setting new records in the sport of basketball. The first women's basketball game in history was played at Smith College in 1893. By the spring of my first year, I was the starting center. As a sophomore, my skills improved and I continued to distinguish myself. After my sophomore season, I severely injured my left wrist in a bicycling accident. I took the words "It's not broken" to mean there was nothing wrong. I didn't slow down and, between torn ligaments and bone rubbing on bone, the wrist went from bad to worse. In December of my junior year, my basketball coach called me into his office. "How's the wrist?" he asked.

"Oh, it's fine," I said.

"Really?" he asked. "Then why are you playing ball with only one hand?"

Coach Babyak turned toward his television and cued game video. In the tape, I watched myself catch, dribble, and shoot without using my left hand. I didn't think it looked all that bad, but then Coach played two scenes in slow motion. In the first scene, I went up against an opposing player for a rebound. As my opponent went for the ball, she grabbed my left wrist and pushed. Holding a perfect Statue of Liberty pose on the way down, I crumbled backward. In the second scene, I went up for a rebound and another player knocked my legs out from under me. I spun in the air and fell head first toward the floor. On the way down, I reached out with my left hand and then pulled it back. I landed on my face. Coach rewound the tape and played the final segment three times.

Then he told me, "I've got to sit you down."

Coach Babyak wanted to keep me on the bench for my own good, but he couldn't do it. I kept showing up, and he kept letting me play. I didn't set any new records, but I played. As a senior, I co-captained the team with Veronica Blette.

At the end of the year, I went to the annual banquet for the athletes. Because I was the president of the athletic association, I was asked to hand out many of the awards. When the time came to announce the highest honor of the evening, the associate athletic director, Linda Moulton, quietly asked me to sit down. She stepped to the podium and explained that each year the coaches and the team captains selected the student who best represented the ideals of the scholar-athlete at Smith College. I was confident the honor would go to either Margaret Broenniman or Maura FitzPatrick, who had capped off their summer vacation by swimming across the English Channel.

When Linda Moulton read the name of the honoree, I was horrified. *Me? I'm not the best student. I'm not the best athlete. I'm certainly not the best scholar-athlete at Smith.* When Linda handed me the silver platter, I examined the engraving, expecting to read someone else's name and to have a chance to correct the mistake. The name on the platter was Victoria E. Murden. The athletes stood, applauding.

The next day, with the platter in my book bag, I went to Linda Moulton's office. I'd never returned an award before, and I wasn't sure of the etiquette. As I stood at the edge of Linda's desk, all the words in my carefully rehearsed speech vanished from my head. I must have looked like a lost puppy. Linda walked over to her small conference table and invited me to sit. Linda was a marathon runner who exercised unending patience with everyone but herself. She asked what she could do for me, but the words didn't come. After giving me a few seconds, Linda began to name various athletes. All were athletes who'd been injured at one time or another.

I knew each of them. In my four years at Smith, I'd earned my spending money by working as a student athletic trainer. Most student trainers didn't progress much beyond taping ankles and filling ice buckets, but that wasn't enough for me. When a player went down, I could never be content to stand on the sidelines feeling helpless. In my time at Smith, the head athletic trainer taught me as much as the law would allow.

Linda seemed to be trying to explain that it was the injured athletes who'd put my name forward as a scholar-athlete. This only made me feel worse.

"Standing on a sideline in the rain to clean mud out of a cut doesn't make me a scholar. Carrying a woman down a flight of stairs because she's torn a ligament in her ankle doesn't make me an athlete."

Linda didn't attempt to argue with me. She thought for a moment and said, "Most Valuable Players come and go. Being the best only lasts for a few seasons." She reminded me about how offended I'd been to see female athletes at other schools treated like second-class citizens. She called me an "idealist," but the softness in her voice made it clear that she meant it as a compliment. "You believe in the ideals of the scholar-athlete. No one can live up to that in four years. That may take a lifetime."

ON AUGUST 6, AT 8:00 A.M., the wind was from the northeast at thirty miles per hour. Conditions were difficult. My left wrist still bothered me. Whenever a wave caught my starboard oar and I had to arm-wrestle with the ocean to free it, I could hear the bones pop and grind. After several hours of arm-wrestling with the ocean, I had to concede that I was losing.

By midafternoon I was back in the cabin bouncing and wobbling on the sea anchor. The evening of August 6, I picked up an AM radio signal out of WCBS in New York City. "Traffic is backed up on the Tappan Zee Bridge, expect long delays there . . . The news will follow in two minutes." I hadn't heard news from the outside world in almost two months. One minute and fifty seconds later, I lost the signal. "No!" I ran on deck and held the radio as high as I could reach. Nothing. I often wondered what was happening in the world beyond my boat. The possibility of hearing the news of the day had been so tantalizing that when I lost the signal it seemed a cruel joke.

On August 7, the seas calmed. The big shark was still with me. It swam languid circles around the boat with its first dorsal and tail fins just breaking the surface of the water. Occasionally as it turned I could see the second dorsal fin near the tail. I tried to catch it on video and instead filmed a five-gallon paint can that was floating by. "I expected to see floating garbage every day, but I've seen very little," I narrated. Minutes later, an immense tentacle floated by. It was a yellowish tan, eight or ten feet long and six or eight inches in diameter at its widest point. The tentacle contained dish-shaped circles that I took to be suction cups. *Octopus or giant squid?* I spoke two questions out loud: "Where's the rest of it?" and "What ate it?" I watched the tentacle until it drifted out of sight and then returned to rowing.

AFTER SMITH, I NEEDED to stretch my legs. I signed up to do a semester course in Alaska with the National Outdoor Leadership School. In my first few weeks with NOLS, we paddled a few hundred miles of Prince William Sound traveling in sea kayaks. We

camped on the black pebble beaches, shaded by spruce. We kayaked
with seals, sea lions, and whales. We watched black bears, mountain
goats, and bald eagles. One evening, on Applegate Island, I watched
a killer whale take a seal from the beach. There was nothing repul-
sive about it. It was neither good nor evil. To the whale, the seal was
merely dinner.

After we left Prince William Sound, we backpacked through the
tundra of the northern Talkeetna Mountains. There we studied the
flora and fauna, learned to navigate with map and compass through
the backcountry, and endeavored to camp in such a way as to leave no
trace. My favorite section of the semester came at the end, when we
went into Denali National Park to study glacier mountaineering.

High on the Muldrow and Brooks glaciers, we practiced the
skills of mountaineering on snow and ice. We belayed one another
over crevasses, set anchors, managed rope systems, learned the skills
of crevasse rescue, and honed our ability to climb ice in all its forms.
We lugged heavy packs through deep snow up the sides of Mount
Silverthrone. A snowstorm pinned us down for almost a week on Silverthrone Col. Our tent blew down, so we built an igloo. I couldn't
remember a time when I'd been happier.

High in the mountains of the Alaska Range, I was filled with a
profound sense of awe and reverence. The rampaging mustangs of
my mind stood quiet. The sorrows and limitations of my "civilized"
life fell away. There in the cathedral of those mountains I felt a sense
of peace, whole and complete. I couldn't stand before the perfection
of those mountains without feeling that this kind of splendor did not
happen by accident. The dichotomy of good and evil that I relied
upon in civilization didn't exist in nature. *Good and evil are creations
of mankind; in our image, we created them.*

AUGUST 7, LATE IN the day, my shark disappeared for a while.
Soon I found myself surrounded by an immense school of striped

dolphins. After I'd counted three hundred, I gave up trying to estimate their number. I'd guess there were more than five hundred, but I couldn't be sure. In the early evening, the ocean was black as coal. The moon crept with the softness of kitten paws to the edge of the horizon. At first it appeared as a sliver of light, not much bigger than my fingernail. Then inch by inch the moon grew into an immense luminescent pearl filling the space between lacy clouds and lumpy sea. The water sparkled like quicksilver. Gazing into the patterns of light and dark was like watching a campfire in black and white.

In my civilized life, I have not always appreciated the blending of light and shadow. In the wilderness, I do not require the certainty of black or white. My mind is free to wander in the gray areas of uncertainty. The books I've packed are heavy. They provide an endless feast of the mind. Will my brain grow flabby with ambiguity? Will intellectual gluttony dull the stiletto of my wit? Out here, I shun the brightness of high noon and darkness of the new moon. Here I am learning to wallow in the richness of messy doubt.

A jellyfish the size of a golf umbrella floated alongside. Its octagonal bell pulsed with shades purple and red. Something about it was hypnotic, attractive, inviting. In the moonlight, its tentacles were not visible to me. Tranquility laced with terror. *Nothing in life is all light or all dark.*

THE SUMMER OF 1986, I traveled to Kenya with NOLS. We climbed Mount Kenya, sailed up the coast in traditional Arabian dhows, snorkeled in the Indian Ocean, and hiked the edges of the Serengeti Plain with Masai elders at our sides. Kenya was a magical place; I came to understand why every American who spends more than two weeks in Kenya feels she must write a book about it. It is also a tragic place. We visited Kiwayu, an island in the Indian Ocean. While we were there, we met a number of native children who suffered from significant medical problems. One boy had been burned on a cooking fire. The family had treated his burns with toothpaste. The tube had been left behind by some European visitors; the family thought it was medicine.

A woman in our group enlisted my assistance to teach a first-aid class at the island school. I was a reluctant recruit. I worried that we would come across as patronizing. Using an inventive mixture of Swahili, English, and hand gestures, I delivered the American Red Cross version of how to treat cuts, fractures, infections, severe bleeding, head injuries, shock, and respiratory emergencies.

When I had finished, Lynn asked if there were any questions. One of the teachers at the school mumbled something. Lynn asked him to repeat himself. After the third repetition, Lynn finally understood the question. "Could you please explain the woman's menstrual cycle?" I gave Lynn a crooked smile, walked across the room, and sat down. I figured she got us into this, she could get us out. I let Lynn struggle with the subject for about two minutes before I took pity on her and joined in the conversation.

Our little first-aid class had turned into sex education à la carte. There were questions about venereal disease and female sterility. When we suggested that male sterility might be an issue, we were all but laughed out of the hut. Following the lead of the local teachers, we talked at length about sexually transmitted diseases and the use of contraceptives. Once we got over our initial embarrassment, we discussed all sorts of things. I was surprised how much information the native population had about AIDS. It was 1986. The United States was only beginning to recognize the AIDS epidemic. On a remote island where toothpaste could be confused with medicine, they knew a good deal about AIDS.

Away from the madness and squalor of Nairobi and Mombasa, Kenya was a place of captivating landscapes, breathtaking wildlife, and enchanting people. I was mesmerized by the Masai. We hiked with Masai about a hundred miles through the Nguruman Escarpment at the edge of the Serengeti Plain. As a people, the Masai are undaunted. They are a proud, sable race. To be a Masai is to be a part of the greatest tribe on the planet, and if you don't understand that, then you are just stupid. Helplessness had no place in their presence.

I spent much of my time with two Masai junior elders: one named Moses, the other named Daniel. Yes, Christian missionaries had frequented their region of Kenya. One afternoon I had the honor of spending a few hours with a Masai *liabon*. I asked this healer and spiritual leader many questions. We spoke about faith. Masai have one God with two personalities: black and red, benevolent and avenging.

The *liabon* asked, "If Christianity is such a great religion, why is it the missionaries are always trying to have one another thrown out of the country?"

"Good question." I laughed.

He asked if I knew my animal ancestor. When I told him no, he collected colored stones the size of marbles, poured them into a calabash, spit into the calabash, and then emptied the stones onto a leather mat. He did this several times, looking very serious. "You are a snow leopard."

"A white leopard?" I asked.

"No, a snow leopard," he said sternly.

I was skeptical. "Are all *wazungu* [white people] snow leopards?"

If my question offended him, he didn't show it. "No, you are the first snow leopard for me. High mountain leopards are rare, and lonely." He emphasized the word *lonely*.

Even in the private corridors of my mind, I refused to admit the truth of this word. I wanted to push it back to the *liabon*. I wanted to ask, "How does a mystic in East Africa know about snow leopards in the high Himalayas?" But the time for questioning was past. He and I had fallen into a comfortable silence. It was an African silence, a quiet stillness that runs into the marrow of one's bones.

The experience of sacred awe that I'd felt during my wilderness travels in Alaska and Kenya made me want to wrestle with questions of faith, religious experience, and the ever-present problem of evil. I decided to go to divinity school. Remembering Miss Kussrow's college counseling, I applied for admission to Harvard, Princeton, and Yale and was accepted for admission by all three. I chose Harvard. I didn't know many women in the ordained ministry, but I didn't let that slow me down. After all, power is never given. Power must be taken.

ON AUGUST 8, I TOOK a 3:30 P.M. snack break. I opened one of my three bags of Triscuits. Most of my snacks were bagged as single servings, but I didn't want the crackers to become stale, so I'd left them in the bag that came inside the Triscuit box. I expected to get seven servings out of each bag. As I ate the crackers, I became utterly fixated on the sound and sensation of the crunch. I'd not eaten anything crispy in well over a month. Before I knew what I was doing, I'd consumed a week's rations of Triscuits, thoroughly enthralled by the crunch. *There's a new definition of boredom.*

On August 9, with the aid of the favorable wind, I rowed sixty-eight miles. August 10 and August 11, a gale forced me inside. The gale subsided on August 12. As I took up the oars and slid my feet into my rowing shoes, something cold and slimy touched my foot, and I jumped out of my seat. *Yuck, there's a dead fish in my shoe.* I pulled the fish out by its tail and flipped it over the side. On August 13, I rowed through great rafts of seaweed, and the water temperature rose into the low sixties. I hoped it was a sign that I might be near the northern edge of the Gulf Stream.

That evening, I tried to take a picture of a passing whale. To get a better vantage point, I climbed up onto the cabin roof. Before I could stabilize the camera, the boat lurched, and I fell off the roof and into the cockpit. I landed hard and heard a grinding pop from my right foot. The next morning, both sides of the ankle were purple, black, and swollen. The outside of my foot was tender; I wondered whether I'd broken the fifth metatarsal. *Fortunately, I am not walking anywhere.* I eased my sore foot into my shoe and started rowing at 5:45 A.M.

That afternoon, I found a Hershey bar mixed in with my food bars. Originally, I'd had eighteen Hershey bars on board. Unfortunately, between the heat and the salt water, all the bars I'd come across in my rations were inedible, but this one looked salvageable. Only half the bar was covered with the white crud that indicated it had been in salt water. I placed the bad half in my garbage bag and slowly savored the edible half. *Chocolate: humanity's greatest invention.*

I filmed myself eating the Hershey bar. "So at this point it is my sixty-first day at sea. I am well past halfway. I have about one thousand six hundred fifty miles left between here and France. Actually, ever since I passed [mile] nineteen ninety-eight, I have been thinking about history as I go backward, and thinking about going backward in time. So the eighteen hundreds and seventeen hundreds were really neat. The sixteen hundreds had a lot going on. There is a little gap in my memory between Charlemagne and Julius Caesar; so I may be lost for something to think about, but until then I will have plenty to ponder."

Oh, I remember. Imperial Rome ruled the West: Julius, then Anthony, Augustus, Tiberius . . . who's after Tiberius? Caligula, Nero, Claudius— it's all a muddle. Plutarch could tell me, but he is at home on the shelf. Hadrian and Marcus Aurelius came later, with the rise of Christianity. In the East, the Han Dynasty was in decline and Confucianism was beginning to bump into Buddhism. In between were the Mongol tribes; they had not yet become hordes. It's so hard to remember. If only I could talk to someone.

JOE CURRAN COULD HAVE sorted me out. It was the fall of 1986; the Master of Divinity program at Harvard was a three-year program that took the majority of students four years to complete. In addition to three full years of academic work, two years of field education were required. The school discouraged first-year students from beginning their field education, but I was in a rush. I went to the field education coordinator, Sister Mary Hennessey, and demanded a field assignment. "Give me the toughest placement in the city." She gave me Boston City Hospital, and she made the prediction, "You will not last three weeks."

I'm not sure which was more pivotal: the difficult assignment or the dire prediction. Either way, I was determined to finish the year at Boston City Hospital. BCH was a grubby place where the vast majority of the patients were uninsured. Bill Loesch, the supervisor of chaplaincy at BCH, explained, "The way you tell the doctors from the visitors is that the doctors never make eye contact." Other students from Harvard came and went, but, endeavoring to prove Sister Hennessey wrong, I stayed.

Bill Loesch assigned me to cover three wards: an oncology ward, a psycho-geriatric ward, and an orthopedic ward that soon became the first unit in Massachusetts for patients with AIDS. Brimming with youth and enthusiasm, I managed to get thrown up on twice in my first week. I lost the white tab to my clerical collar in the washing machine. Unwilling to admit my error, I resorted to using a folded three-by-five index card in my collar. As it turned out, the three-by-five cards came in handy for taking notes between patients.

On the oncology ward, a nurse introduced me to a patient named Joseph Curran. Joe was a perfectly rational, highly educated Jesuit priest who had lost many essential organs to cancer. I felt like a pretender as I stood at the foot of Joe's bed. The bright-eyed skeleton before me spoke: "I want to die." I stood there dancing on the verge of panic until the skeleton spoke again: "I'd like some water." I bolted from the room, filled a glass with water, and stall-walked back to Joe's bedside. Later, the nurses would give me trouble for having taken water to a patient without permission. Joe was grateful.

Joe would return that favor a thousand times over. His body had betrayed him, but his vibrant mind was ever faithful. He had been a teacher, and the fountain of his wisdom flowed freely for me. We both knew that I would be his last student. Joe was my Merlin. In our several months together, Joe transformed a wobbly-kneed young woman into a passable hospital chaplain. When I doubted my adequacy, Joe would chide, "You can't travel the road to wisdom in a feather bed." When I needed advice, Joe would close his eyes and recite long passages from Shakespeare, or this one from George Bernard Shaw: "This is the true joy in life, the being used for a purpose recognized by yourself as a mighty one; being thoroughly worn out before you are thrown on the scrap heap; being a force of nature instead of a feverish, selfish little clod of ailments and grievances complaining that the world will not devote itself to making you happy."

One afternoon Joe asked, "What is it that drives you?"

Without thinking I answered, "My brother Lamar." I explained that my brother was developmentally disabled. "Mother said that I got all his brains."

"And you feel guilty about that?" Joe asked.

"No, I feel guilty because I wasn't always able to protect him."

Joe smiled. "Guilt, the gift that keeps on giving. Your brother isn't here, so you find others who need protection. Who protects you?"

I wanted to say that I didn't need protection, but this wasn't true. If I told him that I didn't deserve protection, he would ask more questions. I turned to the books. "What shall it be today?"

"*Richard II*, Act III, Scene II. Skip to where Scroope enters."

Withered and grizzled by illness, Joe wasn't much to look at, but the tenderness in his eyes provided safe refuge. As time went by, Joe taught me to see beyond myself. He challenged me to venture unrehearsed into rooms of pain. *There were so many rooms.* I watched a three-year-old boy die from diarrhea. I told shattered parents that their teenage children were dead. They heard only solitary words: *alcohol, car, accident, truck . . . dead.* That last word always had an echo. I stayed with geriatric patients, watching them drool away the last of themselves. I stood vigil over the corpse of the homeless man who froze on a street corner during rush hour. The smell of gangrene became familiar as it seeped from gunshot wound after gunshot wound after gunshot wound.

At the end of one unendurable day, I fled to Joe's room. He was asleep. I sat quietly in the chair by his bed. Minutes later, about the time tears began to roll into my collar, Joe's eyes fluttered open. Turning toward me, he whispered, "Come here." I leaned my face closer to his. "Close your eyes." With eyes closed, I felt Joe's bony fingers brush the hair past my ear. When his hand eased lower to cradle my jaw, I became uneasy and shot him a sharp and wary glare. Joe responded with a light chuckle. "Steady now." As his other hand emerged with a tissue, I closed my eyes again and felt Joe wiping away my tears. "You must let your heart be broken by the things that break the heart of God."

I was a dutiful student, but this lesson was too advanced for me. I thought I understood; having perfect faith in my own understanding was the chief folly of my youth. My heart was breaking. God's heart was breaking. These things anyone could understand. But being at ease with this brokenness, being okay with it, seemed like surrendering to helplessness. This I could not do. The lesson was too advanced for me.

CHAPTER 12

Bad Breath

August 15, 1998
latitude north 46:12, longitude west 39:32
days at sea: 62
progress: 2,308 miles

THE MORNING OF THE FIFTEENTH BROUGHT A SQUALL
out of the northeast. The clouds were dark and menacing. They were
the kind of clouds you see in the movies right before the ship goes
down. I rowed off and on, retreating inside when the lightning came
too close, popping back out when the sky lightened from wrought
iron to pewter.

On August 16 I caught sight of a merchant ship with a tall gantry
crane. I'd not spoken to another human being in a month. It had been
sixty-three days since I had spoken to anyone on land. I switched on
the radio. "This is the rowing vessel *American Pearl, American Pearl.*
I've lost long-range communications . . ." For a solid ten minutes, I
repeated my usual plea. The ship passed without a word, but I kept
calling.

When the ship was perhaps a mile beyond me, the captain of the
ship, Scott Bainbridge, responded. "What can we do for you?"

Knowing that I had very little time before the ship passed out
of range, I asked the captain to relay a simple message. "I have been
disappointed by my progress, but I am rationing my food for a mid-
October landfall."

AFTER MY YEAR AT Boston City Hospital, Sister Mary Hennessey assigned me to work in an experimental program designed to assist homeless people. For the first month, I was to—as my supervisor phrased it—"hang out" in back alleys, underpasses, and other places frequented by homeless individuals. Once I had gotten to know various characters on the street, I was to match individuals with appropriate programs.

I'd been on the job maybe four days when a brute of a woman named Kim Fitzgerald took me into her confidence. Kim had been a drug dealer, and she'd done jail time for first-degree murder. Like any other group of human beings, the homeless population maintains a certain hierarchy. In the land that was Somerville and Cambridge, the rough side of the streets belonged to Kim Fitzgerald.

As Kim introduced me to people, I learned that she used a dozen names. Some people knew her as "Kim Dana." Others called her "Spike." The best story was associated with the nickname "Moonie." Kim had been arrested. She told me, "I didn't want to go back to Framingham [a women's prison]. It wasn't any fun after they fixed the fence so's you couldn't go into town and steal booze to sell inside," Kim said with a gap-toothed grin. "No, I wanted to go to the Cracker Barrel." The Cracker Barrel was the street name for McLean Psychiatric Hospital in Belmont. "So's when they hauled my backside into court, I dropped trou and mooned the judge. It's not so easy to do that in full-body bracelets [ankle cuffs, waist chains, and handcuffs]. The bracelets was fun when the bailiffs tried to get them pants back up!"

Kim showed me where to go and, more important, where not to go. Kim kept watch over those who were legitimately "crackers"; she made sure they stayed warm, and she saw that they always had a share of what there was to eat. "I steal from the rich and give to the poor; someone should write a book about me." When I offered to buy food for her, Kim looked insulted and explained, "Stolen food tastes better!"

Kim taught me how the cycle of money and drugs worked on the street. "The SSI and welfare checks come out the first week of the month. When the heads have money, you steer clear of them. Second week, the money is gone, but they'll still be flyin' high. Third week, that's when you might get 'em to listen. Fourth week, they's strung out and desperate. Stay away. Third week of the month is the only time you can reach 'em with any sense."

Kim was as valuable a guide for me on the street as Joe Curran had been at the hospital. Under her left armpit, Kim carried a knife with a twelve-inch blade. I never saw her use it except to divide portions of stolen food. Kim was the least selfish person I'd ever met. She led with compassion and always looked out for the best interests of her community. Kim made it possible for me to accomplish things I never would have considered on my own.

Not everything I learned from Kim was a blessing. I played basketball for the Divinity School in the intramural league at Harvard. It was a coed league, but I didn't see any other women playing. One night, in a game against a team from the Law School, I dislocated my left wrist. A string of expletives flew from my mouth.

A gentleman from the law school said, "Hey, watch your mouth. There's a lady on the court."

A gentleman from my team responded, "That *was* the lady."

A few weeks later, the Divinity School team was thrown out of the Harvard intramural league for fighting. I missed that game.

ON THE NORTH ATLANTIC some days are louder than others, and August 17 was a loud day. A crosswind blew up whitecaps that slapped the sides of the boat. In the afternoon, I flipped through my selection of CDs in the hope of listening to something other than the wind and waves. Almost all the CDs I had onboard were classical music: Mozart, Berlioz, Beethoven, Handel, Bach, Chopin. Toward the end of my collection, I came across a CD titled *Higher Ground* by Barbra Streisand.

A friend had given it to me, saying, "You're going to want some kind of high ground out there." I popped the anthology of faith and inspiration into my waterproof Discman. One song, a medley of "The Water Is Wide" and "Deep River," seemed to fit my situation perfectly, but for the most beautiful song on the CD, Barbra Streisand sings in Hebrew. The melody was enchanting, but I didn't understand a word.

I COULD HAVE STUDIED Hebrew at Harvard, but I was too busy trying to save the world. More than once, Kim Fitzgerald had to rescue me from my own stupidity. One afternoon, as I was on my way home from visiting a group of homeless men who lived in a shipping container, I took a shortcut and blundered into a drug deal. Before I knew what was happening, a massive hand grabbed me by the hair and pinned my face to a concrete wall. I couldn't see the man who had me, but he smelled of liquor and sweat.

Other hands pushed against my back and searched through my pockets. The only thing I had with me was a book, *Gandhi's Truth* by Erik Erikson. When I heard the sound of tearing pages, I knew that Gandhi's message of nonviolence was lost on these men. *If these guys decide to beat me senseless, will I stand and take it with nonviolent humility, as Gandhi suggests?*

Just then I heard the distant voice of Kim Fitzgerald. "Hey, leave her alone, she's a retard. She didn't see nothin'. She doesn't know nothin'. She's a retard, I'm telling you, a retard." Kim jogged up, grabbed me from behind, and slapped me harder than I imagined possible. Then she threw me out of the circle. I tripped over an outstretched foot and landed on my face. Kim helped me up and then nearly knocked me down again with a backhand across the jaw. After this, she punched and kicked me all the way down the street. All the while she yelled back at the bewildered gaggle of men, "I'll take care of her. Leave her to me. She's a retard."

As we ducked around the corner out of sight, Kim spun me around. Her eyes flashed, and she growled with a low guttural snarl. Her arm swung. Then her fist caught the left side of my head with astonishing force. As if to prove her earlier blows had been for show, this final punch was harder than the others. This one was just between us. All I could say was, "Thank you, thank you, thank you, thank you." I'd never imagined I could hear the word *retard* without wanting to rip someone's throat out. Nor could I imagine that I'd ever thank someone for giving me a beating.

Kim scoffed, "You're lucky. Those guys work the shallow end of the street. They wouldn't hurt you bad. They'd just mess you up a bit. You're lucky I was around." Then she grabbed my shirt to be sure she had my attention. "It better not happen again." Kim was a tolerant instructor; when I'd get fired up about wanting to rescue people Kim would say, "Who do you think you are? You're not going to save the world. All you can do is pray for the dead and fight like hell for the living."

In this, I discerned an echo of Joe Curran's "Let your heart be broken by the things that break the heart of God." My rational mind, steeped in educational privilege, started to rebel. Why study Lao Tzu, Confucius, or Augustine? Why learn about Muhammad, Aquinas, or Calvin? Why read Elie Wiesel, William James, or Thomas Merton? Is life nothing more than a sterile intellectual exercise? I might learn all that there is to know, but if I do not do something with that knowledge, what purpose will it serve?

The good and the evil around us are perfectly clear, yet we choose not to see. We moralize. We rationalize. We shield ourselves behind our incompetent helplessness. If we are competent, if we are not helpless, if we are not blind, then we are responsible.

Harvard University has an endowment larger than the gross

domestic product of many nations, and yet the university is also the largest slum landlord in Cambridge. The university symbolizes brains, talent, money, and power. All the while, in the shadows of its ivy-covered walls, people live an existence that can only be described as aboriginal.

This reality spun my reason and turned my stomach. I took it as a reproach to Harvard, and I took it as a condemnation of the church and my concept of faith. Despite my position as a lowly divinity student, I felt responsible. *How could I let this happen?* My frustration unleashed itself in the classroom; I picked intellectual battles with my professors. Attempting to bridge the gap between the tidy world of the academy and the not-so-tidy world outside brought me to a crisis of conscience. I needed to get away, far away.

I applied for a summer job working with troubled teenagers in the wilderness of eastern Kentucky. The organization was called Life Adventure Camp. I supervised health services, which meant that I carried the first-aid kit and dispensed the many drugs prescribed for the young people in our charge. My National Outdoor Leadership School experience proved invaluable. As the most competent navigator among the staff, I was usually the person sent to track down "campers" who attempted to run away. One young man gave me a merry chase.

It was midnight. I had been tracking Mike for more than seven hours. I had expected him to stop at sundown. It had been my experience that raging bundles of teenage anger transformed into frightened children when the sun went down. I'd never met an adjudicated youth who was not afraid of the dark, particularly when they were lost and alone in unfamiliar surroundings. Mike had endurance, but he didn't have any sense of direction. Like many people, when he came to an obstacle he tended to turn toward the right. This caused him to travel in sweeping clockwise circles. When he finally wore himself out we were only a few miles from camp.

Mike collapsed in a heap at the base of a tree. He shouted insults and obscenities in my direction. I rested at the base of my own tree about fifty yards away and waited. A half an hour passed, and I heard the sound that connects far too many of these young people: "Phhha, phhha, phhha, phhha, phhhha, huuua." The crying of a child alone in the dark.

I plucked some fern leaves for him to use as a Kleenex, and I moved close enough to hand him the ferns. Then I gave him a water bottle and a spare jacket out of my backpack. He threw the leaves on the ground and wiped his nose on my jacket. I sat down a few feet away. The young man was quiet for a while, and then the stories of monsters and demons began to pour out of him. These were not television characters. They were real people shaped like family or foster caretakers who understood the taking part but not the caring part.

This young man had called me every name in the book and added a few chapters of his own, but the stories he told that night went well beyond anything I had experienced. His insults toward me had merely been an attempt to build walls in the wilderness. There had been so many walls, but none that he could trust. I wanted to hold him, to tell him that all would be well, but that would be a lie. I didn't touch him. I didn't speak. I didn't promise aid that I knew I couldn't deliver. I sat silent, staring into his pain, feeling the cold breath of helplessness on my neck.

At dawn, Mike and I walked back to camp together. As we walked Mike asked, "Will you write to me?"

"Of course I'll write to you. I just need your address."

"I don't know my address."

"What do you mean, you don't know your address?"

"I'm a foster kid. Why should I know my address?"

I didn't respond; helplessness had me on that one. I just kept walking. When we returned to civilization, Mike pointed me out and, in a voice I was not meant to hear, he said, "That be Tori. She be bad-ass cool." After the insults he'd hurled at me, this compliment came as an unexpected treasure.

AUGUST 17, ABOARD THE *American Pearl*, Barbra Streisand was singing in Hebrew: "Avinu malkeinu sh'ma kolenu" (hear our prayer; we have sinned before thee). Just then a foul odor caught my attention. It was a sour, fishy smell. "Phew, I need a bath." A minute or two passed, and the smell assaulted my nose again. It was as acrid as a stink bomb. "I *really* need a bath." At that instant, out of the corner of my left eye I saw a patch of gray large enough to be a parking lot surface next to my boat. I stopped rowing and stood up. A fifty- or sixty-foot sperm whale surfaced six inches from my starboard gunwale. The sour fishy smell crossed the deck again. *Whale breath.*

I pulled off my headphones, and the sound of my own heartbeat pounded out a mixture of fear and surprise. The whale didn't move. I pulled my starboard oar in across the deck. Just when it appeared that my boat would drift into the whale, the creature let out a sigh, and with the slightest twitch it put a few more inches between itself and my boat. The grace of this motion was breathtaking. The creature was the size of a tractor-trailer truck. I was close enough that I might have stepped onto its back and taken a stroll.

I'd read about sperm whales, but I had no concept of just how colossal one would seem floating next to a twenty-three-foot rowboat. It was truly a leviathan worthy of legend. The whale hovered for a moment or two, and then with another twitch it began to drift away. I reached toward it. *Stay, please stay, just a bit longer.* The whale was not more than a few feet from the boat when it blew a bushy cloud of mist that wafted over the deck.

I launched myself toward the cabin to grab the video camera. In my haste, I knocked the battery off the camera. By the time I got everything back together, the whale was thirty yards away, and I was only able capture the arch of a long gray back before it disappeared under the surface.

When I returned to the oars, I kept a better lookout. My Chiricahua Apache ancestors would have been embarrassed that I allowed a whale to sneak up on me. By early evening, the noisy waves that had allowed the sperm whale to sneak up on me had shifted from uncomfortable to dangerous. I stopped rowing and filled the ballast tanks. Just as I was about to enter the cabin, a large swell struck from the port side. The boat tipped, and the starboard gunwale dipped into the water. I threw my body against the port gunwale. The boat teetered on edge for several perilous seconds before the weight of the seawater in the ballast tanks pulled the boat upright again. I wasted no time in capping the tanks and climbing into the cabin.

I turned on the video camera and lectured myself. "Today I have to recognize that I pushed it too far. I was rowing and taking waves over the side and kind of thinking it was fun, until the point at which I thought, 'Okay, this isn't fun anymore. It's dangerous.' There is a lot to do between deciding that it is too rough to row and actually climbing into the cabin." I talked about the time it took to fill the ballast tanks, move my gear inside, and lash down the oars. "All of these tasks, individually, they are thirty seconds, but added all together from the moment you decide, 'Okay, it is too rough to row' and the time you actually get inside is fifteen or twenty minutes." I pledged to be more careful.

On August 18, the rough weather continued. To make progress I had to row a course almost parallel to the swells (beam to the sea), which meant that every few minutes a wave would splash over the gunwale and drench me. After ten straight hours of getting slapped and sloshed by the ocean, I could take no more. I leapt out of my rowing seat, picked up my red bucket, scooped up water, and threw it at the ocean. I filled bucket after bucket: "Take that! Take that! Take that!" Breathing heavily with the exertion of my frenzy, I started to laugh.

That evening, I stared up from my mat into the eyes of Thomas Jefferson. Jefferson asked, "What did you do today?"

"I went rowing, just as I did yesterday, and the day before, and the day before that. But today I threw water at the ocean, and I feel very silly about it."

Jefferson answered, "My dear, we all throw water at the ocean. Some of us think it is very serious business."

August 19. The pattern of rough weather was unrelenting. The sideways rocking of rowing parallel to the swells put extra stress on my rowing seat. The aluminum seat frame fractured down both sides, and it gave way. If I couldn't fix the seat, I wouldn't be able to use my legs to move the boat. I would be reduced to rowing with just my back and my arms.

I rebuilt the seat using my spare seat axles as stabilizers. The tricky part was that I needed to drill four holes through the aluminum. My hand-crank drill didn't have a large enough bit, so I had to expand the holes using the awl on my Swiss Army knife. It was slow work, but once it was complete, the rebuilt seat was stronger and more stable than the original.

Conditions in the following days continued to deteriorate. I rowed on August 20 and August 21, but on August 22 I retreated to the cabin for what conditions told me would be a long stay. "August 23, two P.M. I just had a capsize. Fortunately, stayed pretty dry in the cabin. Wearing my life vest. Um, it's pretty big out there. Pretty nasty. Pretty scary. Large rolling waves. I have a cockpit full of water from the roll." I paused as a big wave came through. "That was just a little one. So I'm sitting here—" Another pause as another wave passed. "—doing a fair amount of praying, good old-fashioned praying."

I rode out a gale for the next four days. Every storm seemed to push me north, toward Iceland and the bowling alley of North Atlantic storms. I tried to row south-southeast whenever conditions allowed, but I wasn't able to hold my latitude. The afternoon of August 26, I returned to rowing. For the next several days, I made good progress rowing toward the southeast.

The evening of August 28, I fished two food bars out of a water-soaked compartment and collapsed into my cabin. The end of one of the food bars was covered in a green slime. I couldn't afford to waste food. I scraped away the green film and ate the bar. Within two hours, I had stomach cramps, and I threw up over the side. *I hate food poisoning.*

WORKING AT LIFE ADVENTURE Camp, I'd earned enough money to join a climb of Nevado Sajama, a mountain in the Bolivian Andes. I arrived to find that I was the only climber. The American who had invited me had sprained his ankle just before his departure, and he'd elected not to come. The four British climbers had been doing some acclimatization hikes with their wives and daughters when one of the women developed high-altitude cerebral edema. She died. Understandably, they'd returned to Britain.

On the way into the mountain, I did a few acclimatization hikes of my own with a guide, Juan Carlos, and a French woman named Anne Baron. Anne was an excellent climber, but she did not have time to make the Sajama climb. We were supposed to rendezvous with our driver, Fernando, in a tiny village near the base of Sajama. When the Land Rover finally arrived, a Bolivian soldier was driving with a second soldier in the passenger seat. The windshield of the truck had been smashed. The man lying in the back seat was so badly beaten that I didn't recognize him until Juan Carlos told me, "It is Fernando." He had been attacked by bandits.

Fernando's face was so badly swollen that he looked more like a caricature than a man. Anne Baron turned away from the sight looking perfectly green. "I cannot stand the sight of blood," she whispered to me. I'd been responsible for assembling the first-aid kit for the expedition team. Fortunately, I'd not yet pared down the kit for an expedition team of two. With Juan Carlos serving as a translator, I climbed into the vehicle and began to assess Fernando's injuries. One eye was bleeding, and the other was swollen shut. There were cuts all over his face and head. He complained of loose teeth. Fernando groaned loudly as I palpated his ribs. I felt gravel-like creaking in at least three places: possible fractures. His collarbone appeared to be broken.

Fernando wanted me to know that "the blood on my face is not only my blood."

Anne was a good sport. She sat with her back to us, handing me gauze and other items from the med kit. I cleaned a deep cut near Fernando's right eye. It needed stitches. I had a suture kit, but I hadn't the nerve to stitch a wound so close to the eye. The best I could do was to close the cut with Steri-Strips. I tried to pad Fernando's ribs, and I splinted his arm and shoulder to stabilize his collarbone. I was able to wash the contact lens out of his left eye with saline solution, but Fernando was in too much pain to allow me to wash the lens out of his right eye. The eye continued to bleed. Attempting to limit further damage, I placed a gauze "doughnut" around his right eye and bandaged both his eyes.

Then all six of us piled into the Land Rover. Juan Carlos and the army captain were in the front seats, Anne sat between them straddling a center console, Fernando was in the backseat with his head in my lap, and the other soldier sat in the rear atop our gear. I did my best to cradle Fernando's head in my arms as we crashed, bounced, and grunted our way driving cross-country toward La Paz.

Fernando was a tough fellow, but when we would hit a particularly large hole that would jar us all out of our seats, he would let out a little whimper or moan. I hadn't realized how much I depend upon being able to see a person's eyes to know how someone is doing. I was terrified that Fernando might die. Responsibility weighed heavily on me. Not only was I responsible for Fernando's care, but it was my fault that he'd been out on the road in the first place. I had the ghastly fear that this man would die in my lap, and I would never know more about him than his name. Two days later, we reached the hospital in La Paz. Fernando was expected to make a full recovery.

A couple of days later, I was supposed to leave for a climb of Huayna Potosí, an easier mountain close to La Paz. Instead, I suffered through a bout of food poisoning. I spent the day on the bathroom floor. The tiles felt cool against my face.

CHAPTER 13

The Weather Is Weird

September 2, 1998
latitude north 47:33, longitude west 30:14
days at sea: 80
progress: 3,122 miles

THE OCEAN WAS WRONG.

By all appearances, the weather was lovely. A bright blue sky stretched above me. There were no ominous storm clouds on the horizon, but something wasn't right. Rowing through ocean swells was like dancing to different tunes. Now the timing was off, and a sense of discord made me uneasy. I checked the barometer. It was steady.

As I rowed, long crested swells rolled in from the direction of the United States. I paused for breakfast. As I sat in the cockpit with my back to the cabin bulkhead, an unusually large wave washed over the top of the boat and landed in my granola. With a cold waterfall running down my body, I shouted, "That was rude!" I stood to look out over the cabin. Nothing. The ocean looked as it had a few minutes before except for the big angry wave stomping off toward Europe. I tossed out my sodden granola and went back to rowing.

A few hours later, I heard the distant sound of rolling surf. *Shoal water? Can't be. I'm well beyond the shallows of the Grand Banks. A row of dolphins preparing for a cavalry charge? Not so lucky.* Behind the boat I saw a wave towering over all the others. It was moving fast, overtaking the smaller swells that stood between me and it. I wanted to run. *Nowhere to run. Nowhere to hide.* The wave was thirty feet high or better. I pulled in my oars, fearing the wave would shear them off at the oarlocks. The boat dropped into the trough at the base of the wave. Then the water grabbed the stern and yanked it skyward. The angle of the wave was so steep I worried the boat would topple stern over bow and land on top of me.

An instant later, the water under the back of the boat disappeared. For a split second the boat seesawed on the brink. Then, as if the person on the other end of the seesaw had jumped off, the stern fell and the bow flew up. The boat and I slid down the backside of the wave like a log down a waterslide. When we hit bottom, a loud crack came from the rudder, and the boat spun in a half circle. *Two rogue waves in the same day? What is* that *about?*

A minute passed, and the mighty wave was gone. The uneasy rhythm of the ocean returned. I shoved out my oars and returned to rowing. Big waves from the west came every few hours. A set of large corrugated swells would precede the big breakers. Initially, the sets contained just one big wave, but as time passed the sets contained two or three giants. Throughout the night, the frequency of these waves increased and they tossed me around the cabin. Even strapped down by the makeshift seat belt, I had to brace myself to avoid injury. Sleep was impossible.

On September 3, dawn broke with brilliant red mare's tails across the sky. The air was damp, and it felt warm. As the sun came up, the barometer went down. Clouds marched in rolling battalions. Ranks of fluffy white cumulus clouds filled the sky with cauliflower caps. Before long those clouds darkened and grew heavy. By midafternoon, black swirling thunderheads started to drop rain. The seas became even more confused, and the air itself grew fickle. One minute there would be barely a breeze, and the next the wind would blast through at better than forty-five miles per hour. At 2:00 P.M., I made a quick notation in my deck log, "The weather is weird."

In the two and a half months since I'd left shore, I'd enjoyed precisely six minutes of human conversation. *I haven't talked to anyone on land in well over seventy days. I don't miss people, but I could sure use a weather report.*

WHILE I WAS AT Harvard, I went ice climbing with a couple of graduate students in psychology. There were other women on the trip, but I was the only woman who spent the weekend climbing. After that, I became a popular test subject for psychological research. I was probed, scanned, studied, and analyzed. It came as no surprise that I scored exceptionally high in tests of "resilience," "resourcefulness," and "comfort with uncertainty." Nor did it surprise me that I scored poorly in "social expressiveness" and "interpersonal dependence." Apparently, my approach to problem solving, while described as "highly effective," was uncommon.

One researcher accused me of corrupting his data when my scores graphed as the inverse of the standard bell-shaped curve. "Most people," he explained, "score low on pure analytical thinking. They do better at organizational, social, and structural thinking, and the scores tend to go down again with purely conceptual or purely creative thinking." When confronted with my test scores, the researcher was reduced to sputtering. On the left side of his graph I scored at the top of the chart with analytical thinking. At the right side I scored at the top of the chart with conceptual or creative thinking. In the middle, my bell curve was upside down. "Clearly you do not rely on social thinking to solve problems," said the researcher, pointing to a deep trench in the middle of my graph. "You combine styles of thought that are diametrically opposed. The analytical thinker is coldly logical, while the conceptual thinker is highly imaginative."

In his written report the researcher tried to make the best of it. "You are the sort of person who could solve the problems of the world, but you might not notice if the world ceased to exist in the meantime." He went on to write that while I tended not to depend on other people, "your quest for understanding (analytical) and your ability to see the possibilities in everything (conceptual) combine to make you an asset in any group."

After all the tests and all the scrutiny, all that can be said about me with certainty is that I am an introvert. The notion of spending months alone in a seemingly hostile wilderness is entirely appealing. The thought of attending a cocktail party with unfamiliar people elicits abject terror. I would rather pry a thousand dead squid off the deck of my boat than enter a room full of strangers for the purpose of engaging in small talk. It is my firm belief that unscripted social engagements should come with distress beacons.

I like to imagine that others interpret my social indifference as shyness or reserve, but I know better. At best, I might seem distracted or withdrawn. At worst, people see me as arrogant, unapproachable, or even intimidating. Sometimes I am not indifferent. Sometimes I'm just plain scared. Crowded places frighten me. Being in the center of a circle sets off warning bells in my head. Lamar understands this fear, but others see only an edgy social awkwardness. While I care deeply about social justice, I am not always very sociable.

THE EVENING OF SEPTEMBER 3, I put out my sea anchor and rigged for the storm I knew was coming. I slept in my life vest, or rather, I tried to sleep. The *American Pearl* groaned and creaked under an hourly barrage. At about 4:00 A.M., the boat tumbled down the face of a steep swell and dipped her roof into the sea. As gravity pulled me away from one wall and threw me into the other, I heard the sea anchor tear loose from its fittings.

The morning of September 4, at 5:30 A.M., I reeled in the tattered sea anchor. The heavy fabric was torn from stem to stern. The anchor's one-inch tubular webbing had parted like rotten shoestrings.

I placed the damaged parachute anchor in the compartment with my garbage and took up my oars. At 9:00 A.M. I pulled out my video camera. Sitting at my rowing station, I thrust both arms into the air and shouted, "I'm outside, and I'm alive."

The skies were a dark gray for 360 degrees of the compass, and the seas were too rough for comfortable rowing. Still, I was determined. I rowed. It was difficult to manage the boat. I rowed. At 11:30 A.M. a hard rain began to fall. I rowed. The winds shifted directions every few minutes. I rowed. At 12:30 P.M. the clouds turned black. I rowed. By 3:00 P.M. I was losing ground.

I checked my position at 3:30 P.M. and calculated that winds were driving my boat toward the United States at a rate of three miles an hour. The barometer continued to fall. Rowing as hard as I could, I couldn't move the boat into the wind. Unwilling to believe that the weather might get worse, I deployed my largest sea anchor. When I lashed down my oars, I doubled the lashings before crawling into my cabin.

At 2:00 A.M., the noise from the storm rose to a dull roar. The large sea anchor kept the boat perpendicular to the swells, but it held so firmly that I worried it would tear the cleats off the roof and rip a gaping hole in my cabin. I had to go on deck to reel in the large sea anchor and send out the smaller storm anchor that would allow the boat to move with the waves a little more.

I pulled on my life vest, secured one end of my tether to the vest's harness, and climbed out the main hatch. I clipped in and levered the hatch closed. As I stood to look out over the back of the cabin, the top of a swell crashed over the roof and hit me squarely in the chest. The surge of green water knocked me down. I scrambled to my feet, coughing water from my nose and mouth. *Work fast.*

Usually, hauling in the sea anchor was a simple task. I pulled in the anchor line, and the boat and anchor moved toward each other. The rope bit into my fingers as I wrestled in the line inch by inch.

The boat's gunwale was about eighteen inches above the surface of the water. Under normal conditions reaching over the side and pulling in the parachute was a simple maneuver. This time, dragging in the anchor felt like playing tug-of-war with a rhinoceros.

Once I had it aboard, I made quick work of tying in the small sea anchor. When I tossed the small anchor into the water, the two hundred feet of line played out so quickly that I dared not touch it for fear of burning my hands. I stood clear and watched it zip over the side. When the line ran out and snapped taut, I felt the boat slow.

With the next wave, the boat moved a few feet forward, but then the anchor tugged the boat lightly over the top, and it rode gently down the other side. *Perfect.* The rain was coming down in buckets. Lightning cracked like a whip in all directions. It was too dangerous to cross the deck and stow the big anchor in its compartment near the bow. Instead, I rolled it up and lashed it securely in the well of the cockpit. I didn't want the anchor to get washed overboard, so I took off my safety tether and clipped the sea anchor to the safety cable. *That should keep it with the boat.* Satisfied that I'd done all I could, I ducked back into my cabin.

As the storm descended in earnest, every piece of equipment mounted to the exterior of the boat began to whistle. The cleats hummed. The oarlocks warbled. When the lines from the sea anchor harness slapped the sides of the cabin it sounded like firecrackers going off. The most strident shrieks came from the wind crossing over and under the solar panels. Taken together, it sounded like a symphony of screeching car tires.

I couldn't guess the wind speed. The strongest winds I'd gauged from deck with my handheld anemometer were almost sixty miles per hour. Nothing could compel me to go back on deck to measure the wind speed. It was enough to know the winds were stronger than anything I'd experienced. *It didn't even blow this hard in the Antarctic.*

IN 1988, I NEEDED to think of a good excuse for taking two and a half months off in the middle of my last academic year at Harvard. I went to Professor David Eckle, my thesis advisor, and knocked on his door.

"Excuse me, Professor Eckle. My name is Tori Murden."

"I know who you are, Tori."

Then with polished earnestness I explained, "Well, sir, I was wondering if it might be possible to take some time off during my last year here, to do some field research for my thesis."

"What is your thesis topic?" asked this wise professor.

"The theology of adventure." I smiled.

"Ms. Murden, where are you planning on doing this field research?"

"Antarctica."

"Ms. Murden, there are no theological libraries in the Antarctic. What are you up to?"

I explained that I had been accepted as a member of the International South Pole Overland Expedition. We planned to ski 750 miles across Antarctica to the geographical South Pole. Our plan was to traverse a side of the continent that had not been crossed before. I would literally put my foot down where no one else had ever walked, at least not in the last million years. We would leave just before Thanksgiving and return in mid-January. "I'm a few credits ahead in my coursework—I'm sure I'll be able to make up the work. I might even manage to graduate in three years. My biggest concern is the time I will miss in your thesis seminar."

The sheer audacity of my proposal brought a smile to David Eckle's face. He thought for a moment, then with half a laugh he said, "If you can get permission from the dean, it's fine with me."

As a co-president of the student government, I already had an appointment to see the dean of the Divinity School, Ronald Thiemann. At the time, my arm was bandaged from elbow to wrist.

"What on earth did you do to your arm?" asked the dean when I sat down at his conference table.

"I fell down," I said, trying to brush off the inquiry.

Terry Mulry, the other co-president, who knew the entire story, chimed in. "Ask her how she fell."

"How did you fall?" asked the dean.

"I was roller-skiing," I said, shooting Terry a warning glare, which he ignored.

"Ask her where," said Terry.

"Whitehorse, Yukon," I offered.

"Ask her why she was roller-skiing in Whitehorse, Yukon."

The story spilled out. "I was training for an expedition to the South Pole. First, they took us Rollerblading down a gravel road. I'd never been on Rollerblades before. Then we switched to roller skis. I liked the skis better, but maybe that's because we were on pavement instead of gravel. I was flying down a hill when a rock got caught in the front wheel of my ski. I did a first-class imitation of a superhero soaring through the air. The landing wasn't very graceful; I skinned my arm from elbow to wrist."

The dean looked from me to Terry and then back again toward me. He must have been thinking that we'd made up the story as a joke. Then, as if it was a perfectly reasonable request, I asked the dean for a two-and-a-half-month leave of absence so that I might ski across the highest, driest, coldest continent on the face of the planet.

The dean scanned the faces of the few other people in the room. "In the three hundred fifty years of Harvard University, students have gone to great lengths for thesis topics, but this has got to be a record." Then he told me that I could go.

It took us fifty days to ski the 750 miles to the South Pole. We skied nine hours a day, seven days a week. We skied on Christmas Day. We skied on New Year's Day. There were obstacles. Skiing over and through sastrugi, the waves and ridges in the ice, was like trying to ski around a living room. Ski over a coffee table, small sastrugi. Ski over the couch, medium-sized sastrugi. To simulate skiing through big sastrugi, try skiing over a bookcase or two. The average temperature was about -25°F. When it hit -40° our skis stopped sliding. There were mountains and crevasses to cross, but the greatest obstacle was the Antarctic wind.

The wind blows north off the polar plateau toward the ocean, so we were always skiing into the wind. It was a wind like pounding surf. Sometimes it blew seventy miles an hour. It could reduce us to crawling things. We had to shout to be heard only a few feet away.

On January 17, 1989, the other expedition members and I became the first Americans (there were six Americans) and first women (there were two women) in history to reach the South Pole by an overland route.

I returned to Cambridge just in time to begin the spring semester. I still needed to complete the coursework I'd started in the fall, and I had to write my thesis. By mid-semester, I'd pretty much come to terms with the fact that I'd need to finish some of the required work over the summer. Then I heard that faculty members were taking bets on whether it was humanly possible for me to finish in time for graduation in June. That was just the impetus I needed to buckle down.

In my thesis, I contrasted my backcountry explorations with what I believed to be the vastly more important, and more challenging, urban explorations. From the backcountry I learned endurance and resourcefulness. In the wilderness, the superior becomes the servant. In the expedition equation, what we expect from each person depends upon his or her abilities, and what we give to each person is related to his or her needs. The strongest member of the team carries the tent.

We carry very little, so we learn to use the tools we have at hand. We persevere over difficult terrain, and we make peace with uncertainty. Within the expedition team, success and failure are shared experiences. The summit is sweeter when no one is left behind.

I wanted to translate these ethics into my "civilized" life. I wanted to show that human beings are worth more than what they own or what they earn. We must not take jobs we don't enjoy, buy things we don't need, worry about impressing people we don't like. Intellectual gluttony is a virtue; material gluttony is not. We must make shared experience more than watching television together. We can no longer afford to draw imaginary lines on the earth and say, "Over there, lesser people live." We can no longer leave "those people" behind.

When it came time for me to defend my thesis, I waited in the long wood-paneled hallway with several of my classmates. The gentleman ahead of me came out of the room in tears. His thesis had not been accepted, and he'd been sent back to do more work. I had the exact same committee of faculty reviewers. I gulped. I was next.

I entered the room and closed the heavy wooden door behind me. As one might expect, there was one chair on the near side of the table and three stern-looking faces on the far side of the table. I must have looked particularly timid when I took my seat, because when I looked up, my thesis advisor, Professor David Eckle, couldn't suppress a broad smile.

He said softly, "Don't worry, we're going to pass you. We just have to keep you here for a while." The committee asked a few tough questions. When one of the reviewers said that I'd clearly drawn upon Henry David Thoreau's *Walden*, I insisted that I'd never read the book. There was a debate as to whether I should be allowed to graduate with such a serious omission in my education. I promised that I would read the book at my earliest convenience, and the committee took me at my word. Of the more than sixty students in our entering Master's in Divinity class, fewer than fifteen of us graduated in three years, but I was with them in June 1989.

SEPTEMBER 5. THE WIND generated by the storm was stronger than anything I'd ever experienced, and the waves were bigger than anything I had imagined. I'd been through some nasty gales, and I considered anything over twenty-five feet really big. These waves went well beyond really big. They were the size of buildings. Not that I could get a good look at them; my porthole was so small I saw the waves in segments: a black bottom, a turquoise middle, a white raging top.

Huddled in the dark, I reached for the video camera. "September the fifth, dawn. I'm in by far the most violent storm that I've been in so far. It sounds like a train whistle outside. I'm going to put on my dry suit now, and my life vest, and keep praying, because I'm not sure I'm going to make it through this one."

Cringing in the eerie light of a cloud-drenched dawn, my solitude crowded in on me. Again I pulled out the video camera. "Six-thirty A.M. I'm definitely in something big and bad and ugly. I have my dry suit on. I have my radio attached to me, life vest on. And, uh, I'm really hoping I live through this. And if I don't . . ." My voice cracked. I paused to regain composure. "I really love you guys."

By sunrise, the water in my cabin was several inches deep. The waves hit with so much force that pinhole leaks sprayed like fine water jets. Because I couldn't sit upright, the water sloshed around my back and shoulders. I switched on the camera and reported, "Quarter to seven. As the water leaks into my cabin back here, I've been thinking a lot about 'What if the camera is found and I'm not?' Now 'Why did I come out here?' Ultimately, I think life is about service. And I had this idea that if I could pull this off, I'd have a shot at serving at some higher level. Which maybe I'll do even if I don't pull this off.

"I didn't expect the Atlantic to make me a better person. But I did expect the Atlantic to make me a wiser person. To temper this shallow vessel into something that could better take food to the hungry, water to the thirsty, and hope to those who live in fear. Because during this journey, I've been thirsty, and I've been hungry, and God knows I'm scared."

My boat felt like a bathtub toy in the hands of an angry two-year-old. As much as the earsplitting wail of the wind terrified, the periodic silences were worse. The wind was quiet only when an approaching wave was tall enough to block it out. Like ghostly fingers, the quiet moments pointed to the walls of water that were about to hammer me. The lull never lasted more than a few seconds.

At around 7:00 A.M., I heard the rumble of an approaching breaker. An avalanche of white foam was followed by the slam of a wrecking ball. I clawed at the walls and ceiling trying to get a grip. The only things louder than the roar of that wave were the yelps of my pain and the growls of my protest. The boat rolled, and I flipped head over heels. Then the boat spun on its bottom and rolled again, tossing me heels over head. Wood, fiberglass, flesh, and bone interacted in unnatural ways. As the violent motion slowed, the boat came to rest on its roof.

The returning whistle of the wind told me that I had a few seconds to sort things out before the next onslaught. Splashing around in the dark, I felt my way blindly. *Am I on the ceiling or the floor? Ceiling.* "Roll, baby, roll. Please roll. Please, please roll!" Upside down, looking through the hatches, I was the fish in the tank. I inched toward the light. Half begging, half praying, I urged the boat to do the same. "Climb toward the light. Climb. *Climb!*"

Every bolt, every screw, no matter how well sealed with epoxy and urethane, shuddered with each passing swell. The churning water tore at the solar panels on the submerged roof. Inside, the ceiling creaked under my knees. As the bolts from the solar panels wobbled, I watched water seep in around them. Seawater trickled past the hardware that held the rudder to the transom.

The boat shook for a moment and then flipped upright so quickly I didn't have time to think about landing. My body spun in the air, and my twisted torso landed on the floor with a harsh thwack. It was my first capsize of the day, and this was just the beginning.

The mountainous waves whipped the ocean into a fury of foam. The color of the ocean shifted from dark blue to bright turquoise.

The change in hue was caused by bubbles, but in my mind it seemed as if the water had been infused with energy, potential energy in the chemical sense that might crackle out as kinetic energy and kill me. Never again will I see turquoise as a placid color. The wind knocked the tops off the swells, blurring with heavy spray any distinction between air and water. The waves came in cycles: five to seven regular ones followed by one or two giants.

I didn't think of Isaac Newton. I didn't estimate the dynamic fetch required to create waves of this magnitude. I didn't calculate wave front equations. I counted on my fingers like a kindergartner: *One, two, three, four, five, six.* Silence. *Oh, God.* I braced my hands on one wall and my feet on the other. A deep rumble shook the air. Foam surged past the boat. This was the mushy part, the soft outer skin of the wave that concealed a harder core of green water. The green water was malevolent. It inflicted pain. Attempting to brace myself was futile.

The boat stayed upright, but the green water came down with such force that the *American Pearl* became a submarine. My ears popped from the increased pressure. Water sprayed past the seals of my hatches. Beneath the surface, the water roiled and foamed. Then the boat bobbed up like a cork and did a little hop toward the sky. The wind continued its concerto.

I was lying facedown catching my breath from a violent spin when the second complete rollover of the day hurled me into the ceiling. There a three-inch mahogany joist supported the roof. When the joist and my lower back came together, a razor of pain sliced through my spine and flashed down the back of my right leg. I heard a cracking sound like bones breaking. Against my spine, I felt the joist splinter and give way. As the wood tore free, the fiberglass that encased the joist shattered and flew in all directions. Lying on the ceiling, I felt blood dripping down my back.

With gentle fingers, I felt gingerly for a tear in my dry suit. A painful welt crossed my lower back where the joist struck me, but the material of my suit was intact. There was no way to reach a hand into my bare back without taking off the suit. I expected the boat to break apart at any moment. Floating in my dry suit, I might last several days. Without it, it would only be a matter of hours before hypothermia would set in and I would drown. Under the circumstances, I dismissed the liquid on my back as a meaningless distraction.

For two or three minutes the boat wobbled on its roof. As the boat rolled upright, I tumbled to the floor, and the roof joist clattered down on top of me. When I landed, I had no feeling on the right side of my lower back. My right hip and the back of my right leg were numb. The numbness extended around my heel to the little toe. The damage to the boat was even more serious. I doubted whether the roof would hold without the supporting joist. It wasn't long before water began to dribble in through the crack where the joist had been. Soon it became a gush.

Can't do anything about my back, but I can plug that gash in the ceiling. I opened a compartment under the cabin floor and retrieved the tube of epoxy putty. Lying on my back, I mixed the putty between my palms and slowly worked it into the gap where the joist had been. After about fifteen minutes of working the putty into the crack the cascade became a trickle.

CHAPTER 14

Hurricane Danielle

September 5, 1998
latitude north 46:65, longitude west 29:24
days at sea: 83
progress: 3,200 miles

WITH SO MUCH WATER SLOSHING AROUND THE CABIN, I worried that my two large gel cell batteries might give me a shock. Pulling out my spare headlamp, I shone it through the clear hatch of the electrical box. I didn't see any water around the batteries. *This is probably the only compartment on the boat that doesn't have water in it.* I sponged the water away from the electrical hatch, opened it, reached in, and rotated the battery switch to the off position. *If the compartment stays dry, the batteries shouldn't zing me.*

My mind was racing. *Track the storm; I've got to track the storm. I have to figure out how long this is going to last.* Changes in wind direction and barometric pressure could help me gauge the path of the storm. I turned my attention to a notebook in which I'd been keeping track of these things. In the earliest hours of the morning, the sustained winds blew from the south and the barometric pressure was 970 mm Hg and falling. (When I reached the halfway point, I changed the batteries in my electronic barometer. Because I was unable to recalibrate the unit, the readings after that point are not scientifically reliable. However, NOAA records for September 5 and

6 indicate the barometric pressures in Hurricane Danielle were 967 mm Hg and 964 mm Hg, respectively.)

Over the last several hours, the wind had moved in quick succession from southwest to west-southwest, and the pressure continued to fall, reading 968 mm Hg and then 966 mm Hg. From this, I determined that the center of the eye would pass to my north. I drew imaginary storm paths in the condensation on the ceiling. I didn't like the first answer. So I drew the picture over and over again, hoping to find some mistake in my calculation. *The wind and the storm are traveling in the same direction. I must be in the dangerous semicircle.*

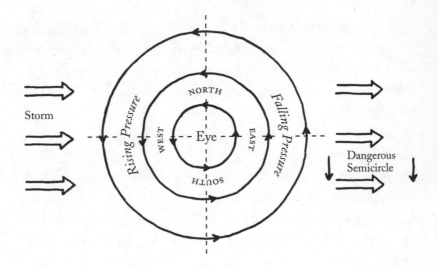

Bad weather on the North Atlantic typically moves from west to east. If I imagined the storm viewed from space, it would look like a circle with the winds moving counterclockwise. On the three o'clock side of the storm's eye, the winds would blow from the south (from the bottom of the clock). On the nine o'clock side, they would blow from the north (from the top of the clock). A vessel in a direct line with the center of the eye would experience winds from the south during the front half of the storm. A brief calm would descend as the eye passed over. On the backside of the eye the sustained winds would blow from the north.

If I'd had a choice, I would want to be twelve o'clock high, well north of the eye. There the winds would blow east to west (from 1:00 P.M. to 11:00 A.M.) while the storm traveled west to east (from 11:00 A.M. to 1:00 P.M.), but I was not so lucky. The fact that my winds were coming from a westerly direction indicated I was south of the center of the eye. Here the wind and the storm were moving in the same direction. In mariner's terms, this was the "dangerous semicircle": the side with the strongest winds, the heaviest rain, and the most damaging "wet fist."

Capsizes three, four, and five came so quickly I lost track of which way the boat went or which part of my body collided with what. One moment I was crushed against a bulkhead; the next I was flying through the air. Pain rolled itself into agony, and my brain rolled it back again. *Ignore it. What is pain, anyway? It's just a bunch of sensory neurons firing electrical impulses. More important things need attention.*

In the second half of the storm it was as if the giant spoon stirring the great soup pot of the ocean reversed direction. Wave trains collided with one another, forming immense pyramids. The boat took on so much water that it began to list toward starboard. My seat belt was on the starboard side. In an effort to balance the boat, I abandoned the restraint and sat on the port side. After the fifth capsize of the day, I began to think the next wave would be my last.

WHAT WILL HAPPEN TO *Lamar if I don't make it through this storm?* When I explained to Lamar that I was going to ski to the South Pole, I rolled out a large map of the Antarctic continent. Lamar studied the map. "No roads?"

"No, Lamar, no roads."

"Any buildings?" he asked, shaking his head.

"No, no buildings. We will stay in tents on the snow."

Lamar gave me a quizzical look, as if to say, "Let me get this straight." Then he said, "You gonna ski seven hundred fifty miles on snow, no roads, no buildings."

"Yes, that's right."

Lamar laughed, looked me straight in the eye, and said, "You crazy." As usual, Lamar spoke the truth.

When I told Lamar about my next adventure, his response had been equally memorable.

"Lamar, I'm going to row a boat across the ocean."

Lamar gave me the nod that meant, "Come again? I don't think I quite heard you."

"I'm going to row a boat across the Atlantic Ocean," I said a little louder.

Lamar furrowed his brow and said, "It take a long time row a boat across Atlantic Ocean."

"Yes, it will," I admitted.

"How long? How long it gonna take you row across ocean?"

"It could take as much as one hundred days."

Lamar looked over each shoulder as if he didn't want anyone to overhear the piece of advice that he was about to give his sister. "The QE2 only take five days!"

Leave it to my "mentally challenged" brother to put me in my place. *Silly woman—if you want to cross the ocean, take the QE2, not a rowboat. It would be much faster.*

IT'S TIME TO GET out of here. I'd deliberately mounted the distress beacon, the 406-megahertz EPIRB, on the bow bulkhead as far away from the cabin as possible. By positioning it there, I wouldn't be able to set it off in a panic. I'd have to think about it. As I moved toward the hatch to get the EPIRB, my right leg wasn't working. Anger coiled up in me, and I snarled, "I don't have time for this."

Dragging the leg behind me, I climbed out. Just as I closed the hatch, a searing bolt of pain shot through my back and down the injured leg. Hissing through clenched teeth, I nearly collapsed. To steady myself I leaned hard against the cabin bulkhead and clamped tight fists around the cleats mounted on the cabin roof. With eyes squeezed shut against the ambush, I stood with all my weight on my good leg. Slowly the pain subsided.

I opened my eyes and faced the storm. The windblown spray stung like blowing sand. I dared not lift my head to look for the top of the approaching wave. Then I remembered that the Argos tracking beacon was mounted on the cabin bulkhead. It was equipped with a distress switch. The EPIRB was an international distress beacon that would alert all the maritime authorities that I was in trouble. The Argos beacon would tell only my support team that I needed help.

With my left hand, I reached down and pulled the Argos beacon from its cloth holster. As I did this, I heard the rush of a wave about to hit. *I'm not tethered.* I dropped the Argos beacon and locked my hands around the roof cleats. The wave broke over the boat and foam swallowed me. For several seconds, I thought I would drown in the froth. Just as I was becoming desperate for air, the deck rose and lifted me clear of the ferment.

I was sure the Argos beacon had been washed away, but as the suds cleared and the turquoise water drained, I saw the beacon swimming around on the bench beside me. I lifted it out of the swirl. *I can't ask another human being to come out here and get me. I put myself out here. I chose my course. I must accept the consequences.* I tied the Argos beacon to my life vest and dragged myself back into the cabin.

Once inside, I glowered at my injured leg as if it were as useless as my salt-corroded telephone. I lifted my right knee with both hands and heaved the leg toward the back of the cabin. The right foot struck a rudder bolt. The metal gouged a flap of skin out of my middle toe, and blood bubbled up from the wound. *That hurt. I can feel my middle toe.*

Hours passed. The boat continued to list heavily toward starboard. Every wave bounced me down the hill, and with each lull I'd climb back up. After a rough spin landed me hard against the starboard wall, I gave in to gravity. I let the boat cradle me between the starboard wall and the cabin floor. Water covered my legs and torso. My hands relaxed their grips. My breathing grew shallow. *Running out of oxygen in here. Need to open the hatch for some fresh air.*

I lifted my right arm to open the hatch, but before I could grasp the handle the floor came up to meet my arm. My body felt heavy. The next thing I knew, the boat went vertical, and I was doing a crumpled headstand on the hatch handles that I'd thought of opening only a moment before. A second later, I seemed to free-fall to the back end of the boat. I must have touched the walls on the way down, but I didn't feel them go by. All I felt was a violent encounter with the transom as my six-foot frame crumpled into the two-by-two-foot space. I looked straight up through the main hatch and watched the bow draw a circle in the clouds. Then the boat tumbled backward onto its roof. The cabin went black.

Instead of rolling side to side, the boat had flipped end over end: a pitch-pole capsize. Pinned against the transom, I felt as if I were trapped in the jaws of an attacking beast. My mind rambled through a haze until a single message became clear: *Can't breathe.* It had nothing to do with the stale air; my lungs weren't moving. Seconds passed. *Can't breathe!* All thought concentrated on my chest until my lungs began to heave with short jerking gasps. "Ahhh, ahhh, ahhh." I cried the air out of my body with every exhalation. With progressive convulsions my lungs took in more and more air, until I could moan in complete sentences. "Dear God, that hurt. Dear God, that hurt. Please, don't do that again. Please, don't let it do that again."

The boat didn't turn upright. Instead, it lay on its side like a dead fish. Twisted under me, my right leg was no longer numb; a searing agony chewed up and down its length. Minutes passed; wave after wave slammed into the hull, but the boat didn't roll upright. *Why is the boat on its side? Why doesn't it right itself?*

Gradually, I shoved the pain into a corner of my mind, and I inched my shoulders along the cabin wall until my arms were free. I clawed forward, dragging my legs limp behind me, until I could see out the half-submerged main hatch. I looked for the American flag that usually waved from the starboard gunwale. The flag was several feet under water, but I could see red stripes flash in the boil of turquoise water. I could just make out the blue safety tether pointing into the depths. It was still attached to the steel deck cable, but the cable groaned under the stress of a heavy load.

The large sea anchor pulled out of its lashings. The pitch-pole carried the anchor over the side, and the safety tether caught it. The anchor is holding the boat sideways in the water. With the boat on its side, there were many leaks. If I did nothing, the cabin would fill with water, and I'd drown. Opening the hatch would flood the cabin. If a wave turned the boat upside down while the hatch was open, I'd drown. *Not much of a choice.* I pulled out my knife. *Death won't catch me cringing in a corner.*

As I hauled myself into a sitting position, pain stabbed my spine. *Silly neurons. If I die, I wonder which will go first, the pain or my consciousness of the pain.* As if on cue, my brain produced words from Hamlet: "If it be now, 'tis not to come. If it be not to come, it will be now. If it be not now, yet it will come. The readiness is all." Locking my battered knees against the edges of the hatch frame, I took several deep breaths. Then, pushing out and down with all my might, I opened the hatch. A gush of water entered the cabin.

With one last gulp of air I plunged my upper body into the waterfall. I dove down as far as I could reach without bringing my knees out of the hatch. *Dear God, let my legs be strong enough to hold if a wave hits.* I groped for the tether. Catching it in my left hand, I sawed on the thick webbing with the knife in my right. A minute passed. My lungs burned. My muscles screamed for oxygen. The tether was more durable than I expected. I sawed and sawed. Just as I was nearing panic, the knife cut through. The boat came upright, and the rising starboard gunwale lifted my face out of the water.

I gasped for air and rested my head on the gunwale. After a few seconds, the sound of an approaching wave spurred me back into action. I shoved myself back through the opening and slammed the hatch shut with so much force that I nearly stabbed myself with the open knife. The wave hit hard, but it didn't roll the boat. My hands shook so badly I had trouble closing the knife. I wasn't cold, but my teeth were chattering. The water in my cabin was waist deep. The line from my storm anchor was tangled around the bow of the boat. *The storm anchor is gone. Without a sea anchor, there is nothing to prevent the waves from spinning this boat like a yo-yo.*

The little flag waving on the gunwale caught my eye. I whispered "The Star-Spangled Banner" as if hearing the words for the first time: "O say, can you see, by the dawn's early light, what so proudly we hail'd at the twilight's last gleaming?" I squeezed back tears. I hadn't had anything to eat or drink in the last twenty-four hours. The rational, calculating part of my brain reasserted command. *Tears are a waste of water.* As callous as I tried to imagine myself to be, the national anthem took on new meaning in that storm.

The lightning became the "rocket's red glare." The explosive waves were the "bombs bursting in air." And, by God, that little flag on the gunwale was *still* there. *I am* still *here.* I decided that if that little rectangle of red, white, and blue could survive the storm, so could I. The presence of the flag was comforting. It was not as good as an arm around my wet shoulders, but it was close.

Before long, another wave torpedoed the boat. *There's too much water in the cabin. If I'm knocked unconscious, I'll drown. If the roof collapses, I'll drown. If the transom caves in, I'll drown.* My thoughts spun in divergent directions. *Can't lose control. Focus, have to focus.* The starboard porthole was under water. So I opened the porthole on the port side and started pumping out the water as fast as I could with the Beckson hand pump. The porthole was only open a crack, but for every two gallons I pumped out, one gallon sloshed back in.

I pumped and I pumped. My arms ached, but I kept pumping. I thought of my friends back home, and strength flowed in from some unknown part of me. I continued to bail until I'd reduced the water in the cabin to a couple of gallons. Still breathing hard from the exertion, I eased myself onto the floor and listened to the wind. I wondered if I could handle another capsize. I looked at the distress button on the Argos beacon. *Is now the time?* At that instant, the boat tossed me in the air, and I came down on top of the beacon.

"Get me out of here." I pulled the Argos beacon out from under me and tried to unscrew the cap over the distress switch. It wouldn't budge. I tried to pry it loose. I kept twisting until the tips of my fingers bled. *Find some pliers.* Opening the compartment under my left shoulder, I found it full of water. *I just bailed that out.* I pawed through the compartment until I could identify my tool kit. Using the pliers, I twisted the cap off the distress switch. In the time it took to do this, I'd gathered my wits.

I have come so far. It hasn't been easy—bad weather, no communications. From the moment I left shore, my life had been a series of challenges and crises. The fates tested me. They pushed until I didn't think I could stand anymore, and then they pushed harder. *Why is it so unrelenting? I can't just quit, give in. France is less than a thousand miles away.* As the proverbial crow flies, I'd made it 2,600 miles, but I had rowed nearly 3,400 miles. Another 1,000 miles seemed like nothing.

My thoughts tumbled in every direction. I no longer tried to catch them. I wanted to lose my senses, to flail, to rave like madness itself. I was a teapot tossing in a tempest. I wanted the wind to stop. I wanted the pain to stop. I . . . I wanted to stop. *No. Not here. Not alone. Not like this. Not alone, on the ocean, at night, in the dark.*

Just then I heard a crunching metallic sound like a car crash. *What was that?* I looked out the hatch just in time to see the last scrap of my metal radar reflector fall into the sea. *Oh, that's just great. I'm a thousand miles from shore with no running lights and no radar reflector, and two-thirds of the boat is underwater. I might as well be a contact lens on a rain-drenched football field. I'm a dead woman!*

A wave landed on the roof, and the boat made a sound like a human scream. The sound was so disturbing that it seemed my heart stopped to listen. *This is a tough little boat, but in a few hours it will be in pieces.* Triggering my beacon would only send, as my epitaph, the message that I was conscious and frightened, and that I passed my last hours in distress. *Haven't I tortured my friends enough?*

I reached for the video camera. "I've had about six capsizes now. The last one was a pitch-pole." I held Argos in front of the lens. "I have the Argos beacon with me. I would set off the distress signal, but I don't think it will work inside." I didn't honestly believe a sheet of plywood would block the signal, but I needed to provide some explanation as to why I held a distress beacon without setting it off. "I have it with me in case the boat breaks and I get forced outside and separated from the boat.

"I would try to get to the EPIRB to set it off, but quite frankly I don't want anybody else out in this. I got myself into this. I'm going to live or I'm going to die on the whim of nature, and that's that. I have no right to risk the lives of other people to come and get me out of this when I don't think they'd ever be able to find this little boat. It's so far under water right now the only thing that's showing pretty much is the cabin."

Thinking that this might be my last recording, I said, "I always hoped I'd have something eloquent to say at this point, but I am thinking about all my friends back home. I'm thinking about all the schoolkids who are thinking about me . . . and . . . Go ahead and chase your dreams. They don't always work out right, but go ahead and chase your dreams. You've got to do it." Frustrated by an inability to find the right words, I switched off the camera and tied it up in a corner.

I looked outside. The wind was coming from due north. *The eye has gone by, but here is where the cross seas will make things nasty.* As if to confirm this thought, a wave hit the port side like a freight train. The boat rolled. I banged into the starboard wall and did a backward somersault as the boat turned upside down. I landed heavily on my knees. I sat down on the ceiling, pulled up my soggy knees, and hugged them.

In the dark, I imagined I could see the faces of all the people I'd come to think of as the "pearls" in the *American Pearl* project. A chill climbed the ladder of my ribs as I pictured them at my funeral. I bristled, imagining that I might be described as "lost at sea." *I'm not lost! I know exactly where I am. Well, I knew exactly where I was before this storm started pushing me around.*

In the dark of an overturned hull, despair rode one wave, then hope surfed in on the next. The boat righted itself so slowly that I had time to slide gently down the wall. When I reached the floor I thought, *Perhaps someone* could *find me.* I began riffling through my storage compartment for a piece of sling webbing. Not only did I find an eight-foot length of nylon webbing, but I found a stainless-steel snap-clip carabiner. I yelled an instinctive "Thank you" at the ceiling. I tied one end of the webbing to my harness and the other end to the carabiner. *I am going for the EPIRB.*

Pausing just long enough to clip onto the safety cable and close the main hatch behind me, I staggered through knee-deep water across the rolling deck to the EPIRB. Kneeling, I pulled the EPIRB from its bracket and gripped the string that would remove the safety tab. I looked up and saw the flag waving on the gunwale. Nothing had changed. I couldn't set off the EPIRB any more than I could set off the Argos.

A great arm seemed to pull a velvet curtain across my mind. *I am tired, so tired. I don't want to fight anymore. Let me die.* The sounds of wind and wave became muted. I pulled the snap-clip on the strap that tethered me to the boat toward me and unclipped it. Time slowed to a halt. I clipped and unclipped the tether from the safety cable in a half-conscious game of roulette. Whether I did this for two minutes or twenty, I cannot recall.

I yelled into the storm, "You want me? I'm right here. Come and get me." I imagined my boat as a mouse in a room full of rampaging giants. Nothing happened for a long time. Then a colossal swell stomped the boat. In the torrent of the breaking wave, my thumb held the gate of the snap-clip open. The boat pivoted, and the clip pulled out of my hand. A second later, a jerk against my harness told me that I was still attached to the boat.

As the wave drove the boat far under the surface, I gripped the solar panel mounted on the port gunwale. The boat lurched and the panel tore away from its fittings. I let go and saw it disappear over the side. Just as I thought I would be swept out with the panel, the boat changed direction and the wooden frame of the gunwale drove into my rib cage. I felt a snap followed by a stabbing pain. The air bubbled out of my lungs. A second wave drove the boat further under the surface. My air was gone.

Here it is: the end. Pay attention. What does it feel like to take leave of yourself? I concentrated until I could feel my heartbeat and the aching stillness of breathless lungs. I watched my dying hands dance with the bubbles before my eyes. *Ah, now I hear it: the silence of the sea.*

Then I saw a flash of light. Not some glimmer from the world beyond. It looked like sky. The boat lifted me toward the light, but before my face cleared the surface of the water the boat stopped. My air was long gone, but the fingers of my brain clutched for a shred of control. *Sit up, you idiot. Sit up.* I lifted my shoulders, and to my astonishment, my head popped out of the water. I gasped, sputtered, and choked out the sea. For a few moments, I sat coughing and clutching my injured ribs with my elbow.

"Coward." The word flew from my mouth in a tone that was

shockingly crisp. *I didn't take the easy way onto the Atlantic; how can I justify taking the easy way out? If searchers find my body tethered to the deck with the cabin still intact, people are* really *going to think I was stupid.* Struck by the absurdity of my situation, I began to laugh. My tender ribs screamed in protest, but I kept right on laughing. *Why shouldn't I laugh?* I was tethered to the half-submerged deck of a rowboat a thousand miles from shore in a raging storm, worrying that someone might think I was stupid. *Could anything be more stupid?*

Half crawling, half swimming, I slogged back to the cabin. With my electrical system switched off, I wouldn't be able to turn on my running lights. *I could still change my mind.* Before going inside, I detached one of two rescue strobe lights from my life vest and tied it to a cleat on the roof. If I decided to trigger the Argos beacon, this light might help someone to find the boat. I paused, waiting for a lull. Then I opened the main hatch and tumbled headfirst through the opening, pulling my legs in behind me.

The eighth capsize hurt less than the others. Perhaps I'd reached the limit of my pain and I couldn't feel anymore. Perhaps, because I was too tired to brace for the impact, my body absorbed the force with less trauma. "Doesn't matter," I told myself.

I wondered if there were any conditions under which I would set off the EPIRB. *If the roof collapses, I would happily drown. If one of those monster waves crushes the boat into toothpicks, I wouldn't mind being crushed. If the* American Pearl *is torn apart but I survive, floating free in the water, then I will set off the EPIRB.*

Death by drowning or crushing I could accept, but I was afraid of being eaten. I was *barefoot*, for pity's sake. *A predator would probably eat me feet first. No, no, no, that would not do, would not do, simply would not* do! *Everybody knows I have delicate feet. I cannot be expected to depart from life feet first. That would be entirely unacceptable.*

The ninth capsize hurt. It was something between a regular capsize and a pitch-pole. One corner of the boat pitched me through the air like a baseball to the opposite corner. As I flew across the cabin my left arm struck the rib that supported the cabin wall. When I heard it hit, I was sure that the arm was broken. The boat rolled over several times, eventually coming to rest on its roof. It remained upside down for perhaps fifteen minutes. *The* American Pearl *is losing her ability to self-right.* I blew air into my inflatable life vest until it was half full in the hope that it might protect my ribs from further injury.

Even upside down, I could hear the roar of an approaching wave above. The side of my head struck the wall, and the edge of a porthole tore at the back of my left ear. Fireworks seemed to go off behind my eyes. The next thing I knew, the boat popped upright on the surface. *My ear's been torn off.* I touched the front of the ear and looked at my hand. It was clean. I touched the back of my ear, and my hand returned covered in blood.

The pain in my ribs was unbearable. I looked toward my chest and noticed that I'd landed on top of the video camera. *No wonder I can't breathe. Wonder if the thing still works.* I switched on the camera, and the familiar red light told me it was working. "I've lost track of the number of capsizes. I seem to capsize about every fifteen minutes. Last time it took it a great deal of time to come upright again. I've obviously filled up my life vest a little bit; in case I get pushed out of the boat at least I'll come right up. It might protect me a little bit from getting crashed around in the cabin. I think I may have broken my left arm."

Then I started laughing. "Oh, God, how did I get myself into this?" I switched off the camera. *I am so thirsty.* My water bottle was stowed in the compartment next to my head, but I didn't have the strength to get it. The fingers of my left hand were turning blue, and a massive lump was forming just below the elbow.

In the next capsize, the boat kicked me as hard as a Clydesdale. The rib that supported the port wall drilled into my left thigh, and I felt the lateral side of my quadriceps muscle give way. When the boat came upright, I was lying on my face.

The air is stale. Can't breathe. It had been a long time since I'd gone on deck for the EPIRB, and I had not opened the hatch since. A clap of thunder stung my ears. "Please stop!" I cried. Then, whispering, "Please make it stop. Oh, God, please make it stop. Or kill me now, just kill me now." With that, an extraordinary sensation washed over me. Light seemed to pour down through the clouds. For a time I no longer felt that I was by myself.

Instead of being alone in the universe, I felt one with it. I wanted my friends to know about this feeling, but I feared that I wouldn't survive to describe it myself. So I turned my head to the right and found my video camera. "I have a strange sense of peace at this point. I don't know what it means. Means I've come to terms with my imminent demise, or whether I've decided to live, or maybe I'm just running out of oxygen back here. I don't know. But there's something that's okay about this. I just wanted to make a note of it, in case it's okay that I die. I don't know. It's all right."

The brighter light gave me renewed energy. With my right hand, I lifted the camera over my head, trying to shoot video out the port holes. I said a few words attempting to describe the scene, but in the stale air my breathing was labored. I turned off the camera. In a few minutes, the sky grew dark again. The wind continued to howl. I breathed hard but couldn't get enough air. I felt dizzy and sick to my stomach. *I am so tired. I need to sleep.* I hadn't slept in days. Instead of rousing myself, I closed my eyes.

CHAPTER 15

I'm Alive!

September 6, 1998
latitude north 47:12, longitude west 28:23
days at sea: 84
progress: 3,340 miles

ENCLOSED IN MY WATERTIGHT CABIN, I WAS RUNNING low on oxygen. As if in a dream, I heard the voice of Diane Stege, a central person on my support team. Diane was swearing at me. *It must be a dream. Diane would* never *use such language. Maybe there is a boat outside? Is she on deck?* I opened the hatch to listen. Cool air rushed in along with the sound of wind and waves. I lifted my head to look out. *There aren't any boats out in this storm, Tori. You're delusional.* I was alone, but the fresh air smelled sweet. I counted to twenty and closed the hatch again.

If I fall asleep, will I run out of air and never wake up? I didn't think so, but I dug out my alarm clock and set it to wake me every half hour. The barometer was stowed next to the clock. The pressure was falling again, 963 mm Hg. *No!* I shook the instrument, trying to get the pressure to rise. *The eye of the storm has gone by; the pressure should be rising.* I checked the compass. *The last of the storm will bring wind from the north.* The wind had been from the north-northwest, but it was shifting back to come again from the west. I drew my theoretical storm on the ceiling again, but I couldn't make sense of the change in wind and drop in pressure. *Have I lost my mind?*

My theoretical storm formed a perfect circle. The front half passed in half a day, so the back half should pass in half a day. *But the storm outside is not behaving according my neat and tidy plan.* I racked my brain trying to remember every book I'd ever read about meteorology. I could picture each book in my mind. Their images were so clear I could almost turn the pages. I shook my barometer, trying to make the pressure rise, and I prayed for a north wind. Huddled in my little cabin, I had no way of knowing that a large portion of Danielle had broken off, swept east, then turned and crossed my position a second time.

It was nearing nightfall. I'd been in my dry suit since before dawn. Nature was calling. Extricating myself from the suit with a sore back and injured limbs proved to be a monumental undertaking. The hardest part was drawing my head through the rubber collar. The next problem was basic. The bucket was outside, and my pee bottle was insufficient to meet my particular needs. I looked in the compartment where I saved my garbage and found a zip-top bag. *Now* this *will be a challenge.*

When I managed to capture all that needed doing in the bag and snapped it closed, I took this as a sure sign that my luck was improving. With my dry suit still around my ankles, I started to open the main hatch to toss the bag out. Imagining what might happen if a wave hit, I decided against it. *Drowning with my dry suit down around my ankles would be undignified.*

I set the zip-top bag aside and wriggled back into my suit. Before opening the hatch to toss out the bag, I checked the barometer; it was definitely on the rise. *The worst must be over.* I picked up the zip-top bag and gazed out my porthole, looking for a good moment to open the hatch. Just then biggest wave I had ever seen eclipsed the sky. *This is not going to be good.*

The wave hit, and I watched helplessly as the zip-top bag flew out of my right hand and traveled unerringly toward my face. The bag broke on impact. The boat did a perfect 360-degree roll. The contents of the bag both solid and liquid went everywhere, and I laughed as hard as I have ever laughed in my life.

Still laughing, I cleaned the most offensive elements off my face. Peeking out that same porthole, I saw nothing was coming. I opened the main hatch, tossed out what remained of the bag, and washed my hands and face in the pool of water that filled the cockpit. I didn't have energy to do more. As I lay down in the smelly slosh, I thought, *At least I was wearing my dry suit.*

The night descended so quickly it was as if someone blew out the candles. To minimize complaints from my ribs and back, I breathed in short puffs. The alarm clock sounded, and I roused myself to open the hatch for twenty seconds. There were no stars to be seen. No moon shadows swirled around the deck. The air refreshed, I settled down again.

I was afraid to sleep. *What if something happens that needs my attention?* My eyelids felt heavy. *Stay awake!* I punched myself in my good thigh. *Stay awake. Is time passing?* I couldn't tell. Perhaps I slept a little. I felt disoriented. I couldn't see anything. *Am I dead? Is this what hell feels like to souls lost at sea? If I am dead, why does it hurt so much? Perhaps the pain is part of my eternal damnation. If I'm dead, why do I feel so tired?* I punched myself in the leg again. *No, I'm not dead. My stomach feels as if I've eaten a chain saw. Stay awake. The boat has kept me alive this far. I must stay alert and be ready to take care of the boat.*

The *American Pearl* creaked loudly as a large swell broke on the roof and a second wave rolled the boat upside down. *I'd willingly trade ten years of my life for one minute of stillness. Stop. Stop. Stop! No, don't stop—roll upright first, then stop.* I logged each passing hour in my mind until 4:00 A.M.

My eyes were crusted shut, but I could sense daylight. Rubbing the glaze of salt out of my lashes, I opened my eyes. The cabin ceiling came into gentle focus. *I'm alive?* I lifted my head and immediately regretted the movement. *Ouch. Yes, I'm definitely alive.* A passing swell jerked the boat, and I heard a groan. If I had groaned, I could ignore it, but the boat was groaning, and that required my attention.

There was only one problem: I couldn't move. *Take it slow.* I wiggled my toes. Then I shifted my legs. The front of my left thigh and back of my right thigh erupted with pain. I twisted my torso. Sharp twinges fired across my back, and zinged down the back of my right leg. Through the material of my dry suit, I felt ribs crackle under my delicately probing fingers. *I've broken ribs before. If I protect them, they'll heal.* I lifted my shoulders. *Sore, but they work.* A throbbing lump the size of half an orange just below my left elbow made it difficult to rotate my hand or flex my wrist. However, I could close the hand well enough to grip small items. *The arm's not broken; it's just a bad bruise. With a few days' rest, I might even be able to row.*

I surveyed the cabin. Salt water mopped the floor, but it didn't wash away the splatters of blood that covered the walls and ceiling. I couldn't find a tear in my dry suit, which told me that the blood was from my hands, feet, and head. A crust of blood from my abraded ear caked my neck. There were nicks and gouges all over my hands and feet.

Despite my battered body, my brain seemed as giddy as a child on Christmas morning. *I'm alive.* My entire being rose with elation. *Isn't breathing fabulous!* The boat groaned again. Slowly, I forced myself into a sitting position. The rowing deck looked like a child's wading pool. The only thing keeping the boat at the surface was the fact it was constructed of wood. If I'd had the money to build the boat out of fiberglass, carbon fiber, or Kevlar, it is likely that the boat would have gone down. These synthetic materials don't provide the natural buoyancy of wood.

Broken lines from the rudder and the sea anchors crisscrossed the deck. The starboard gunwale was underwater. The port gunwale had a crack a couple of feet long just above the deck. The rowing station rested at an odd angle, and all that remained of the deck compass were the screws that had once secured its bracket. Where the running lights had been there were pairs of exposed wires.

I licked dry lips and tasted salt. The skin on the back of my hand tented when I pinched it. *I'm dehydrated.* I opened a compartment and fished my two water bottles out of the soupy rubble. I opened the first bottle and drank greedily. Each swallow tasted better than the last. A wave broke over the boat, and my mouth lost contact with the bottle. I inhaled water. I coughed and bit my lip against the pain in my ribs. I counseled myself to drink more slowly and returned the bottle to my lips. Even taking a little at a time, the bottle drained quickly.

I unscrewed the lid on the second bottle. Then I paused, gazing toward the compartment on deck that held my water maker. Seawater burbled over its lid. I might not be able to get the water maker up and running again. The manual emergency water maker was in the bow compartment. With the force of the boat's capsizes I could expect to find it in several pieces. The only fresh water I was sure about was the one-liter bottle in my hand. It took a strong dose of discipline, but I screwed the lid back on the water bottle and put it away.

First the bad news. I am 980 miles from shore in a half-submerged boat without engine or sail. My body has been beaten to a bloody pulp. I have precisely one liter of fresh water.

The good news is that I am alive. My brain still maintains the illusion of control. It barks out orders that my body follows, however feebly. As long as the union between mind and body remains intact, I will cling to the idea that outcomes can be influenced, actions taken, and obstacles overcome. At least, I'll cling to that idea until I think of something better.

The skies were clearing, but the swells were mountainous. The boat could roll upside down at any moment. *The first task: bail as much water as possible out of the boat. The second task: make drinking water.* I considered several possibilities for a third priority, but I ran out of energy contemplating the first two.

Weak and hobbled by soreness, I set to work. It took me an hour and a half to bail the water out the cabin. Next, I stepped into the knee-deep water of the cockpit and clipped into the safety cable. The waves were no longer the size of buildings, but they could easily wash me out of the boat. As I opened the compartment that housed the water maker and my water tank, my heart sank. The fitting on the water tank was broken. *Salt water has mingled with the fresh.* When I'd bailed the water out of the cockpit, the water maker compartment, and out of the freshwater tank, the rowing deck just cleared the surface of the water.

When I stepped up out of the footwell onto the rowing deck a world-spinning agony crossed my lower back. Muscles seized. My knees buckled, and I fell forward. My battered arms did nothing to slow my descent as my face hit the deck. I ground my teeth, chewing on the pain, but I couldn't swallow it away. My cheek scraped softly along the rough surface of the deck. I knew this pain. It was familiar to me.

THE ORIGINAL INJURY TO my back occurred in 1992. On my way to the Olympic rowing trials, I was in an automobile accident. I was badly injured, but because I was in the best shape of my life, the worst of my injuries were not immediately apparent. My rowing shells had been on the top of the car, and they were destroyed. I arranged to borrow a scull from a Smith College friend, Karen Carpenter, but Karen didn't have any riggers. (Riggers, or outriggers, are the arms that extend from the sides of racing sculls and hold the oarlocks.) This was not a problem; I could use the undamaged riggers from my broken boat.

At the Olympic trials, I rowed poorly, but not so poorly as to be dismissed from competition. I would have one final chance to make the Olympic team. When I returned to prepare for my last-chance row, I ran into Michelle Knox. Michelle was one of the finest scullers in the country. There was no question she would make the Olympic team. Michelle seemed anxious, almost distraught. She'd broken a rigger on her boat and couldn't find a replacement. I knew my riggers would fit Michelle's hull. I took my riggers off the boat I'd borrowed, and walked over to Michelle.

"Here, take my riggers."

Michelle looked confused.

I explained, "You need riggers. Take mine."

"Don't you need them? Aren't you racing?" said Michelle, still looking puzzled.

"Michelle, I wrecked my car a few days ago. I can hardly walk, let alone row. I couldn't beat you on my best day, and this isn't my best day. Take my riggers."

A few minutes later, I went to withdraw from the competition. At that level, folks are curious about why someone would pull out. I explained, "I'm not feeling well—I totaled my car a few days ago." A local doctor convinced me to go and get some X-rays. I had two broken ribs and a chipped tibia. I'd also ruptured a disc in my lower back.

Michelle went on to make the Olympic team, and she raced in Barcelona. I have to believe that the gesture of giving her my riggers meant even more to me than it did to her. It gave validation to all the training and effort I put into getting that far. Michelle was a great sculler. She'd have made the team without my intervention. All I did was ease the path a little, but that's what matters. Isn't that how we beat helplessness?

In September 1992, I had surgery to remove the ruptured disc between the vertebrae at L5 and S1. One doctor told me I would never row again. Happily for me, my surgeon took a wait-and-see approach. Eight weeks after spinal surgery, I raced and won a bronze medal in a regatta in Atlanta, Georgia. It was not the Olympics, but I was pleased. I had the medal framed, and I sent it to my surgeon with a note that read, "I would have won gold, but I was taking it easy like you told me to."

SEPTEMBER 6. MY FACE was still rubbing against the deck. I focused my mind in a battle against the onslaught of pain from my lower back, trying to willfully smother the agony. Minutes passed. The sun peeked through the clouds and warmed the deck beneath my face. The muscle spasms began to ease. Out of the corner of my eye, I saw the shadow of a circling bird cross the deck. The shadow paused for a few seconds. The bird floated on the wind just above the boat. *It's a tropicbird. The Lone Ranger is watching.* After some time, the pain ebbed. I pushed myself up and went back to work.

Resting often, I pumped out the eleven compartments under the rowing deck and the bow storage space. When I finished bailing, I was exhausted beyond feeling, but I was pleased. If a wave rolled the boat, the *American Pearl* would pop back up quickly. I rested against the bow bulkhead and looked out at the ocean. It was here next to the EPIRB that I'd clipped and unclipped from the safety cable. Heads or tails? Live or die? To be or not to be? The coin landed on heads. Life went on. *Life is sweet, the world miraculous, and existence a treasure.*

I spent the next two hours dismantling the water maker, cleaning it, oiling it, and putting it back together. Then I went into the cabin, shifted the battery switch to the on position, and triggered the lever for the water maker. Nothing happened. "Of course not—that would be too easy," I muttered. Afraid to stand, I crawled to the bow compartment to retrieve my electrical tools. Water poured out of my "waterproof" repair bag. In the bag I found my voltmeter waterlogged, corroded, and useless. *How will I fix anything without a voltmeter?*

I pulled the EPIRB from its holster and took it with me back to the stern. Once in the cabin, I rested my cheek on the edge of the electrical box, closed my eyes, and went over the wiring in my head. I fancied the idea of being "the master of my fate . . . the captain of my soul." Now I was the captain, engineer, navigator, and deck swab.

I was even the boat's engine. *Wouldn't it be nice if I could just dial up the friendly neighborhood electrician? While I'm at it, I could ask the plumber to bring along fifty gallons of fresh water, and the cook could whip up a nice cup of cocoa.*

I thought about the engineering program at Smith College and wished that it had existed when I attended. *Stop it. Smithies don't whine. We rule. Figure this out. I just need to know where power is flowing. I could put my tongue across the contacts; that would be a thrill.* As I considered the wonders of my Smith education, the solution came to me. *Eureka, a light bulb!*

I rolled over and pulled out my headlamp. I opened my knife and cut the wires that ran between the headlamp and the battery at the back of the headband. Separating the positive and negative wires on the headlamp, I used them to check the power coming in from the solar panels. Both panels lit up the headlamp. A hoot of delight escaped my lips before my ribs could protest.

Next I touched the wires to each battery. The batteries had power. One of the batteries had broken from its tie-downs, and it had dislodged much of the wiring. Reattaching the wires was a slow process. The boat was rolling around, and my fine motor skills were nonexistent. At one point, my vise grips crossed a connection, which triggered a spray of sparks that spit into my face. I felt a sizzle on my eyebrow, but I was too sore to dodge out of the way. I merely waited for the sparks to subside and went back to work.

I was able to reconnect everything but the negative lead on my second battery. I spent a half an hour on it before giving up. I decided to try running the water maker from a single battery until I had the energy to fix the last negative lead. I set the battery switch to the appropriate battery, and the power system came to life. The giddiness of the morning returned, and I reached for the video camera.

"It's Sunday, September sixth. I'm alive! I'm delighted just to be alive." I talked about the pitch-pole, and about cutting loose the big sea anchor. Different capsizes ran together. Without sleep, my brain couldn't order the events of the day before. "I'm hoping I don't have any more storms like that. They were the biggest waves I have ever even imagined.

"I have brought the EPIRB, the 406-megahertz EPIRB, back to the cabin, because now, having gone through pretty big storms, I think I know when it's time to the push the button." I didn't want anyone to know how close I'd come to committing suicide by unclipping from the boat. I felt ashamed of myself, so I lied.

"I didn't have the option of pushing the EPIRB button because it was too far out on deck. And I had put it out there on purpose to make it hard to get to, because I figured if I were going to push the EPIRB button, I wanted to make sure that I thought about it and that I was truly desperate, and only desperation would have sent me out on deck yesterday." I had been every bit that desperate and more. The half-told story implied that I'd never been on deck. "So I have about forty bazillion other stories to tell you about yesterday, but I can't."

Struck by the absurdity of jabbering to a video camera to cover up for an event that no one had seen, that no one would ever know about, I felt ridiculous and laughed at myself. I wondered how this odd laughter would seem on the video. The line between laughter and hysteria is often a fine one. "Yesterday, I sort of giggled my way through, and that feels good, feels good, and I honestly believed that I was going to die. But I've spent enough time out here and had enough time in my head that I have good sense of what I'm all about, and what I've been about throughout my life, and what I hope to be if I make it through this adventure and I get back home, and it's not stuff to be sad about."

I remembered how it had felt to unclip my safety tether, and my emotions shifted from laughter to tears. "I'm about to burst into tears, but it's good stuff, and I'm real proud of myself, real proud of how far I've come. And even if I have to bail out or get killed after this, it hasn't been in vain." Then, without realizing it, I admitted that I'd been on deck during the storm. "I lost my strobe, which is another casualty. Thinking I might want to EPIRB out or SOS out, I tied my handy-dandy strobe light to the cleat on the roof, and I have a plastic clip from that light, and I have the rope from the light, but I don't have that light anymore. It's amazing, the force with which these things turn over and fly." I switched off the camera.

It was time to test the water maker. I went on deck, dropped the intake hose for the desalinator over the side, said a small prayer, and flipped the power switch to on. For a couple of seconds I heard nothing. Then a grinding sound gurgled up from the water maker. After a few more seconds, it sputtered to life.

The relief was so intense I thought the drop in psychological pressure would cause me to faint. I let the pump run for a few minutes and then drank the water straight from the output tube. It tasted great. I let the desalinator run. While it was working, I pulled the broken sea anchor out of the garbage and used an awl to sew up the torn seam. Then I cobbled together enough undamaged line to put it back into service. By that time the water maker had cranked out two liters of fresh water. The sun was too low in the sky for the solar panels to make more. I'd need a good day of sun to charge the batteries and refill the water tank.

I'd taken care of the boat. There was enough water to meet my immediate needs. *Now I can rest.* I crawled into the cabin, but I couldn't get comfortable. Every joint ached and every limb hurt. *I'm hot.* I decided to take off my dry suit. The ordeal of getting out of my suit sapped the last of my strength.

Once out of the suit, I'd hoped to examine my injuries more closely, but I was too exhausted even to sit up. I pulled my sleeping bag out for the first time in days and spread it over my legs. It was wet, but its fabric felt soft against my skin. I set the alarm to wake me in an hour and closed my eyes.

CHAPTER 16

Losing Consciousness

September 7, 1998
latitude north 48:00, longitude west 27:03
days at sea: 85
progress: 3,390 miles

IN WHAT SEEMED LIKE A FEW SECONDS THE ALARM went off. My watch reported that an hour had passed. I opened the main hatch for a full minute to let in fresh air. Having slept, I felt more composed. I thought I should make another attempt to record the events of the storm, and I reached again for the video camera.

"It's been a productive day." I talked about the water maker and making repairs. "It really hurts when I move. I'm feeling just a little puny—between being beat up pretty badly yesterday and not eating at all, it's understandable that I'm feeling a little puny. As long as the water stays out of my boat, things are pretty good. I'm hoping that I'll see a ship in the next couple of weeks so I can send a message to Gérard and Christophe asking for them to come out a little way to meet me with some lights, a couple of strobe lights maybe, and a radar reflector so I don't get run over by a freighter on its way into the [English] Channel or its way out.

"At this point, I am frightened enough that I'm just going to go for the nearest land. At this point that happens to be the Channel. So that's where I'm headed, or the western edge of France. Get me to land. If I can get there, I'll get there.

"Just had another thought. I was thinking about the large sea anchor and the time yesterday when I capsized and the boat didn't roll upright. I just remembered that Gérard had me lengthen that tether before I left. He said, 'I think this is a bit short—let me make it a bit longer.' So we made it about four feet longer. If we hadn't done that, I'd be dead right now. It was the extra length of the tether combined with the steel cable cutting through a piece of mahogany plywood . . . the boat had enough room between the tether and the sea anchor to right itself [halfway]. If I had been on a short tether, I'd still be upside down." With that, the camera ran out of tape.

Dark heavy clouds were approaching from the west. This made me nervous. I checked the barometer. *It's falling again.* I had planned to make soup, but the dark clouds stole my appetite. I didn't think anything would keep me awake that night, but fear is a powerful stimulant.

The winds regained strength with each passing hour. Just after midnight, the floor flew out from under me. The world lost itself. A blow of tremendous force hit, and the boat screeched with a sound like fingernails on a chalkboard. As the vessel went airborne, I forced myself to relax. Inertia threw me into the ceiling. Fighting against the impact only seemed to make things worse. My forehead hammered onto the wooden rib on the cabin's port wall. I heard the wood crack.

Then the world went quiet. My brain fell into a dark but merciful pit of confusion. I don't recall whether I lost consciousness. My thoughts tumbled away from me before I could collect them. Sensations came and went in a tangle of dreamlike images. When things began to make sense again, I was lying on my face. My neck felt stiff. I have a prominent chin, but the right side of my forehead stuck out farther than my chin or my nose. It was as if someone had cut a softball in half and pasted it to my forehead. I peered vacantly out the main hatch. The boat was upright. The deck was clear of water.

I tasted blood. *People say it tastes like salt water. It does a little, but it is not the same.* My face was covered in blood. There was a cut on my forehead. I tried to tell myself that I was fine, and the boat was all right, but I could feel my command of the situation slipping away. *Is this storm going to be as bad as the last? Will I die out here? Should I use the EPIRB while it is relatively calm?* The boat danced in the wind. It rattled, twitched, and jolted.

This isn't fair! I can't take another storm, not now, not so soon. A fury snarled out of me, too primeval to be confined by the coherent language of words. It poured out of my lungs in a wailing howl. The agony of my ribs pinned me down. My body refused to move. The tiny cabin closed in around me. A wave lifted the boat and spun the vessel on its bottom. My psyche spun out of control.

Pain and terror dragged me from the cave of myself, and it was as if my bleeding psyche lay naked and exposed. Then I felt the presence of the beast. Helplessness was sitting beside me. Pain and fear I could handle, but each passing swell gnawed away at my self-confidence. Thought lost its power to govern brain or body. The obstinate will, in which I'd placed so much faith, became impotent, and my spirit shrank like a leaky balloon. Helplessness had me by the throat, and there was no escape.

A massive swell lifted the boat. One second I felt crushed; the next I floated in midair. I might have enjoyed the feeling of weightlessness had I not anticipated the impact that would follow. I put my feet out to brace them against one wall, and I gripped the port rib as hard as I could with my right hand. The sea anchor jerked the boat so hard that it opened a crack in the roof. Water poured in. My feet slipped off the wall, and in sickeningly slow motion my body soared into the stern.

My body pivoted and levered my hand from its firm grip on the wooden rib. I felt a pop in my right shoulder. A white-hot pain raced down my arm and washed back up into my neck. The boat continued to spin and turn. When it finally came upright, the point of my shoulder curved inward. My arm sat at a grotesquely abnormal angle, and I couldn't bring the elbow into my side. My shoulder was dislocated. I roared more in anger than in pain.

Within seconds the ocean answered with a roar of its own. The boat spun and turned. My body and wounded shoulder collided with surface after surface until the wave released its brutal grip. The boat landed on its roof, and my shoulder crunched back into place. The white-hot pain remained, but the crater at the apex of my shoulder was gone. The shape of the shoulder seemed normal, and the arm pulled into its usual position at my side. The boat came upright. I felt faint. A spurt of vomit threatened to gag me, and I swallowed it back. I was nauseous, but it was the nausea of pain, not seasickness. My head felt as if it was in a vise. As each wave jarred my shoulder, my vision dimmed. Every movement pounded me like a heavy club.

The ocean seemed to be holding me in a recurring nightmare. Winds buffeted the boat from side to side, and the waves tossed my psyche one way and then another. The hoarse voice of my helplessness harangued me. *You thought you were so smart. You were going to cross the ocean and reach enlightenment. This ocean demands both gray matter and guts. At the moment, my dear, you're short of both. It's time to go.*

I looked outside. It was dark, but I could make out the waves enough to know they were half the size of the worst I'd seen. The winds were strong, but nothing like the roaring howlers of a day and a half before. *You can't make it alone. You need help. Call for help. Call for a rescue. You'll never make it without assistance.*

It was almost 4:00 A.M. It would be light in a few hours. *I'll feel better if I can just hold on for a few more hours.*

No, you've waited long enough. Send a signal now, and salvation might arrive by dawn. You've been alone for eighty-five days. Isn't that long enough? Call for help before it's too late.

I was losing command, and I knew it. If only I could sleep. Was now the time? Was it safe enough to ask for help? Push the button and live, or don't push the button and take my chances wrestling alone, on the ocean, at night, in the dark?

As I debated the question, the ocean lifted my boat stern first. My feet went into the air. My right shoulder hurt so badly that I bit down on the little finger of my left hand. The boat tumbled end over end. As I had with the first pitch-pole capsize, I ended in a crumpled heap wedged against the transom. The boat came upright quickly. I squirmed away from the back of the boat. My little finger dripped with blood. I looked at the wound and saw bone through the yawning hole. If I'd bitten down any harder, I might have chewed off my own finger.

The emotions of the last week jolted through my body, and helplessness flooded into all my hatches. My psychological buoyancy was gone. I couldn't roll with the storm anymore.

Losing control of my thoughts, I pulled out the EPIRB, tugged out its safety tab, and flipped the distress switch. The strobe light on the unit began to flash. The distress signal was being sent.

I felt ashamed. I wanted to turn off the distress signal, but that would be a violation of international protocol. By this time, rescuers would be trying to get a fix on my position. Turning off the EPIRB would make finding me more difficult, but they would still try. I pulled my dry suit back on. It smelled foul, but if I had to go overboard during the rescue, I would need it. I had lost. I'd given in to helplessness. Instead of dying on the ocean, I would have to live with the ignominy of my defeat. I turned my eyes inward and watched failure dance a tango with helplessness across the stage of my brain.

I worked a pair of Gore-Tex socks over my swollen feet. Dawn came with blue skies and the promise of a clear sunny day. I slipped my passport and my deck log into my dry suit. Then I collected items of sentimental importance: my grandfather's Bible, a teapot, the headlamp loaned to me by Molly Bingham, a card from some young men I'd coached, and the videos I'd shot while on board. I packed these items in a little bag, though I would leave them behind if taking them off the boat would be an inconvenience for my rescuers.

Around 9:00 A.M., I heard an engine. A minute later, a military green plane flew directly over the center of my boat. I pulled out my VHF radio and climbed out on deck to speak with the crew. They picked me up immediately. The gentleman on the other end of the radio explained they were from the Royal Air Force, based in Scotland. As the man on the radio told me his name, a swell crossed the boat drenching me along with the radio in my hand. It was a "submersible" radio, but it refused to work.

I grabbed my tools and took the radio apart to dry it more quickly. While I worked, the plane circled dropping flares. When the radio crackled back to life, I delivered what I could remember of the speech I'd been rehearsing for several hours. I explained that a few days ago, I'd been in a bad storm. I reported that I'd capsized fifteen or sixteen times in the last seventy-two hours. I'd hit my head. Last night had been a little rough, but seas were calmer now, and I was feeling better. I knew I was subject to their jurisdiction, and I would do whatever they asked of me, but if it was okay with them, I would like to carry on, on my own.

For the first time I considered how impossibly small my boat would look from the air. A sailboat might survive one capsize or two, but most oceangoing vessels are not designed to survive even one rollover. Here was a woman, alone, in a twenty-three-foot boat, saying she'd flipped fifteen or sixteen times as if she were reporting the score of a football game. The RAF crew must have thought me quite mad.

The voice from above explained that a container ship had altered course and would reach my position in a few hours. He'd like for them to have a look at me, and if I still wanted to continue, it would be up to the captain of that ship. The next time the plane circled, the voice from above explained that he'd been in touch with the U.S. Coast Guard and that they were reporting that a force 10 gale (winds fifty to sixty miles an hour and waves twenty-five to thirty feet) was on its way to my position. The radio operator said, "They strongly recommend that you quote, take the ride, end quote."

I am tired, haven't slept soundly in weeks. Can I survive another storm? I wasn't sure. I was nauseated. My head pounded like a kettle drum. The right side of my face and neck were a mass of blood. *Can they see me?* Using a wet sock, I wiped the blood and grime from my face. My right shoulder hurt, and my right arm was numb. My left arm worked, but below the elbow it was swollen to twice its normal size. My back was a battlefield of bruises, and my legs were barely recognizable as my own. *Those are excuses. The truth is, I no longer have the mental fortitude to weather another gale. If I let this chance go by and find myself in another storm, helplessness may consume me.*

At 12:00 P.M., the crew above asked if I could travel west to close the gap with the merchant ship. The request made me realize I hadn't told them that I didn't have an engine. I was too embarrassed to say no without at least attempting to row west. The winds were from the west at thirty to thirty-five miles per hour. Somehow I managed to get my oars into the oarlocks, and I began to row. After eighty-five days at sea, the rowing motion—while exquisitely painful—was as familiar as breathing. Still, I managed only twenty or thirty strokes into the wind before giving up.

The next time the plane flew over I explained that I didn't have an engine, and that while I was strong enough to move the boat with my oars, I would not be able to row it into the wind. The response from above was surprisingly detached and professional. "Thank you for trying," said the gentleman on the radio.

Around 1:00 P.M., the RAF plane asked if I could see a ship on the horizon. The plane was low on fuel and they needed to return to base. When my boat crested a large swell I caught a glimpse of what looked like a bulk cargo carrier way in the distance. I made contact with the ship's captain over the VHF radio. He couldn't see me at all, but I explained I had flares aboard and could help guide the ship to my location. The RAF plane departed.

Every few minutes, I reported my position to the captain of the approaching ship. When I could make out containers the size of tractor-trailer trucks stacked high on the deck of the ship, I set off a flare. The captain reported, "Yes, thank you, we see you now." A moment later he said that they had lost me in the swells. The swells averaged twelve to fifteen feet, but the top of my boat was only four feet high. Every few minutes a twenty-to-twenty-five-foot swell would wash over the boat and bury me. Because I'd lost my radar reflector, they couldn't pick me up on the ship's radar. As the ship continued to approach, I held up a second flare and then a third.

The captain explained, "We will not come in straight. I will circle you to starboard several times before trying to pick you up." This would bring the seas down and make it easier to come alongside. When I could clearly read the name *Independent Spirit* on the bow of the ship, the captain said, "We've lost sight of you. Do you have another flare?"

I triggered a red flare and held it as high as I could reach. The ship came close and circled like an elephant trying not to step on a grasshopper. The captain explained that he would make smaller and smaller circles until we reached each other. He also said, "When we are close enough to pick you up, we will not be able to see you from the bridge or the helm." The deck housing and bridge were located at the back end of the ship, and the center of the ship was stacked several layers high with shipping containers. Crewmen on the deck dropped a rope ladder over the side. The captain explained, "You must go for the ladder."

On the third pass the ship came so close, I thought we would collide. If my oar hit the ship it would shatter. I didn't want flying shards of carbon fiber to injure anyone, so I tossed my oars overboard. Just as the boarding ladder came into range the wind caught my boat, and I drifted away from the ship. On the radio, the captain asked, "Can you row in?"

I explained, "I just tossed my oars overboard—I was afraid they would hurt someone."

The captain said they would deploy a rescue boat.

The seas are too rough. Someone will get hurt. "Sir, I have another set of oars. I would like to try again, but it will take a few minutes for me to get the other oars out."

"Very well," said the captain. I cut the lines that tied my spare oars under the gunwale, and slid the oar handles made by Louisville Slugger into them. The captain continued to circle. When I was ready, I radioed the captain. "Sir, I missed the last time because the wind caught me just as I reached the ladder." The captain and I discussed the wind. My best chance to row in would be while I was on the leeward side of the ship, shielded from the wind.

The captain maneuvered his massive vessel with the precision of a runabout. He made a wide circle away from the wind, and as he turned, he put his ship between the *American Pearl* and the oncoming wind. The captain approached close enough to demonstrate his competence but far enough away that he would not collide with me. When I saw the bow of the ship pass, I rowed a diagonal course toward the bow, knowing this would bring me to the side of the faster-moving ship. As the boarding ladder came by, a member of the crew tossed me a line. I tied it to the bow cleat, and the crew pulled my boat up under the ladder.

I had a seventy-five-foot line attached to my little bag. I clipped the free end to my harness with a breakaway knot. If the line tangled or snagged, it would pull loose from my harness and the bag would stay behind. Two Filipino crewmen came down the sides of the ladder to assist, but apart from helping me to time my jump, there was little they could do. I watched the swells and synchronized my leap to correspond with the top of a wave. I made the jump without difficulty. As I started up the rope ladder, a surge of red-hot torment passed through my injured shoulder. My right arm threatened to drop me. I clenched my fist around the rung and paused for a few seconds.

This is no place to give in to pain. If I fall, I'll take one or both of these crewmen with me. If we are lucky, we'll land in a broken heap on the deck of my boat. If we aren't lucky, we'll fall into the ocean between the vessels and be crushed like pecans in a nutcracker. I stared at the side of the ship and pushed the rungs down one after another until I felt the hands of the men on deck above me. A small man grabbed my shoulder, I hissed, and before I could stop myself, I shot him a look that would have peeled the hide off an elephant. He let go, and I clambered up onto the deck. I locked my knees before they could betray me and took two or three steps to grip the rail and look down at the *American Pearl.*

CHAPTER 17

Independent Spirits

Aboard the Independent Spirit *heading west,*
bound for Philadelphia, Pennsylvania

MY BOAT LOOKED TINY, VIEWED FROM ABOVE. LIKE A cork bobbing on the waves. I tugged the rope off my harness and handed it to the man standing beside me. "Could you pull this up for me?" He didn't speak English. I tried to do it myself, but there was barely strength in my hands to grip the rope. The man beside me understood what I wanted, and he took the rope out of my hands. He heaved in the line until my small bag lifted from the deck, and he hauled it aboard with ease. I said, "Thank you," and hoped that he understood.

I looked down at my boat. A crewman had boarded the *American Pearl* and was tying lines to the port cleats. *They are trying to rescue the boat.* My attachment to my little vessel was nothing compared to the safety of the men who had come to my aid. The cabin roof was already cracked. The cleats would never support the weight of the boat. *If I'd known they would try to save the* American Pearl, *I would have prepared it properly. They were obligated to help me, not my boat.*

"Let it go," I shouted. "Let it go." No one seemed to understand. "Cast it off." I waved my hand, but the sudden movement sent such agony through me that I feared I would pass out. I turned to three men in turn. "Let it go. Let the boat go. Let it go!" A crewman signaled for me to follow him below.

Follow? For almost three months, I hadn't walked more than two or three steps at a time. I wasn't sure I remembered how to walk. The crewmen moved quickly toward the stern. I took a robotic step forward. The movement jarred my shoulder. I bit my lip and hooked my right thumb over the inflation nozzle on the left side of my life vest to steady my injured shoulder joint. Step after painful step, I followed the crewmen down the deck and over the threshold of a door. They went down a flight of stairs. *Stairs? You've got to be kidding me.* No one seemed to speak English. *Walk. Just keep moving.* My feet shuffled. I hobbled down one set of stairs.

The men ahead of me continued down. I stumbled on a landing near a doorway, and a man came through the door to steady me. With one hand he caught my right ribs, and with the other he grasped my swollen left elbow. I slammed my lips together, managing to stifle most of a groan. My mind screamed, *Don't touch me!* I raised my upper lip to growl but managed at the last second to turn it into a smile and said, "No, no, I'm okay." My voice shook with pain, but I hoped he didn't notice. The man was a foot shorter than I and looked Filipino. I straightened quickly, which pulled my arm out of his hand without my seeming to jerk it away. This sudden movement sent a lance of pain across my back and all the way down the back of my right leg. *I must keep moving.*

We continued down the stairs, and the men ahead of me passed through an open doorway. I entered the corridor just behind them and watched the men walk to the end of the hall. It was probably not more than twenty-five feet, but to me it looked like a football field. Placing one foot in front of the other, I limped to the end of the hall and turned left.

There I entered a pristine room that was the ship's sick bay. Seeing the immaculate white sheets on a hospital bed made me feel exceedingly dirty. I resolved to stay away from the bed. Men came and went, but a constant swarm of onlookers formed a horseshoe around me. One fellow told me he was the cook. Because I was still in my dry suit and socks, my only obvious injuries were the cut on my forehead and my battered hands. Realizing this, I relaxed. The pain in my shoulder eased, and I was able to move my right hand a little as I answered a few questions.

I asked, "In which direction is the ship headed?" "The United States," the cook told me. "Philadelphia," said another man. *Philadelphia, that's as good a port as any.* The ship had not yet resumed course, and in the steep seas even this large vessel rocked back and forth. When a tall man disappeared and returned with some gauze and antiseptic, I realized that there wasn't a doctor aboard. The man tried to clean the cut on my forehead. He might have had basic first-aid training, but he was too gentle, too uncomfortable with what he was doing, to be a medic. We were both wobbling. The man didn't want to hurt me, so he pointed to the mirror in the adjoining bathroom and handed me the gauze and antiseptic.

I went to the mirror and considered my reflection. My hair was wet. It had grown long during my journey. It hadn't seen a comb in weeks and had not been in a shower for eighty-five days. Blood dripped from a cut on the right side of my forehead, where a great lump ran from an inch above my hairline to just under my eyebrow. It still looked as if someone had slipped a half a grapefruit under the skin. The rubber gasket of my dry suit constricted my neck and made my face look swollen and puffy. I wet the gauze with antiseptic and wiped the blood and dirt from my face.

The deck beneath me began to vibrate with the propulsion of the ship's engines. *Engines—what a concept!* The *Independent Spirit* was getting back under way. Soon the ship's forward motion dampened the sway of the vessel, and the men around me regained their footing. I was moving away from the mirror when a crewman announced, "The captain." A dignified middle-aged man entered. In an instant, the room full of curious onlookers dispersed and only the captain, the chief mate, and the cook remained.

"I am Captain Lorenson." I would have recognized him as the captain without an introduction. His presence filled the room. The captain's blue eyes slapped me with a critical glare. This symbolic blow was almost a relief. I was so ashamed of needing to be rescued that some part of me wanted to be shackled and thrown into the bilge for the journey back to the United States.

The rescue itself had not been dramatic. The ship came alongside. I stepped off my boat onto the rope ladder and climbed aboard. The captain's experience and professionalism minimized the risk. Had I not tossed my first set of oars out of the way, they might have picked me up in as little as eight minutes. After the ship reached me, it picked me up and was back under way in less than a half an hour.

Still, a rescue at sea was the last thing I'd wanted. I was no innocent victim, no damsel in distress kidnapped against her will. My planning had been careful and deliberate. I'd gone to sea in a rowboat. No one would claim that the ocean had been kind to me, but the North Atlantic's reputation for brutality is hardly a secret.

Standing before the captain, I felt like a dog that had plunged into a fight with a much larger animal. The captain looked the part of an angry master who'd pulled a stray dog out of the fray. Now the fight was over, and I wanted to curl up in a hole and lick my wounds. Nonetheless, I forced my eyes to meet the captain's scolding gaze.

The captain asked, "Are you all right?"

I lied. "I'm fine—a bump on the head."

He said, "You should not have tried to do this. It is lucky that you are a woman. If you had been a man, I would not have stopped this ship to pick you up."

I nodded gently to acknowledge his comments. Even with this careful movement, the pain washed through me. A wave of dizziness disrupted my concentration. I leaned against the bathroom door to steady myself and fought to give the captain my full attention.

"I had to order your boat set adrift."

I didn't attempt to explain that I'd expected them to set the *American Pearl* adrift immediately. "Thank you for trying. I understand; it was too dangerous."

He went on to say that his was a cargo ship, that the worst kind of cargo was passengers, and that the worst kind of passengers were female passengers. It would take them a week to reach the United States. They had a room for me, but I should not expect any special treatment. "The cook will give you something to eat." The captain looked to the cook, who nodded his acknowledgment. With that, the captain turned on his heel and followed the cook out the door.

The air seemed to leave the room with the captain. It took a minute or two for me to catch my breath. Then two men led me to the guest room. After the months I'd spent in the cramped cabin aboard the *American Pearl*, the modest bed, table, and private shower looked like a stateroom. I dared not lie down for fear that I would not be able to get up again. The cook brought some soup, some yogurt, and an apple. I ate the soup but didn't have the stomach for more.

Sitting to eat hurt my back. I couldn't stand without wobbling, and I dared not lie down. Men hovered in the doorway watching me stagger around the room. I wanted to be alone; I turned to the men and explained that I would like to take a shower. They smiled and closed the door, leaving me in privacy. As soon as the door shut, I fell to my knees. Silent tears of devastation raced down my cheeks. *How did it come to this? All my work, all the work of my friends—how did it all come apart?*

This dry suit is strangling me. My mind roared, *Get this thing off!* If I'd had a knife, I would have cut the suit away from my aching limbs. I unzipped the waterproof seal that ran diagonally across my chest. *Get it off!* My left hand couldn't pull the rubber seal past my face without the help of my right hand. I lay down on the floor and forced my right hand to assist. After a squirming struggle that involved both hands and a table leg, I freed my head from the suit. I rested flat on the floor for several minutes. Then I slithered the rest of the way out of the suit like a snake shedding its skin.

Then, still wearing the stale long-sleeved athletic shirt and rowing shorts that I'd been wearing for over a month, I crawled to the shower. I turned on the water, but I didn't have the energy to stand. I sat in my shorts on the shower floor. I don't remember how long I remained there, crying and hugging my knees. When I became conscious of wasting water, I turned it off. Then I soaped one limb at a time and turned on the water only long enough to rinse off the grimy lather. I washed my hair four times, but it still felt dirty. When I could force a comb through it, I decided that was good enough.

There was a gentle knock at the bathroom door. "Yes?" I shouted without rising from the shower floor. It was the captain's steward. He wanted me to know that dinner would be in one hour. "Thank you," I replied, relieved that I'd taken the precaution of locking the bathroom door. I pulled myself to my feet, slid out of my clothes, and looked down at my battered body.

My torso looked as if I had been tattooed with ink blots. There were patches of black and blue as big around as a basketball. *I'm a walking Rorschach test.* In several places the skin had been abraded. Had it not been for the protection my dry suit provided, these abrasions might have been deep wounds.

I turned to the little bag that came off my boat. At the last minute, I'd remembered to pack my cleanest shirt and my Gore-Tex trousers. I slipped them on as gently as possible. The long-sleeved shirt and trousers hid the vast majority of my injuries. Where I'd bitten my little finger, I taped over the ugly gash with a piece of duct tape.

When I felt ready, I went to the door and propped it open. Within two minutes, the captain's steward popped his head in and asked if I needed anything. I pointed to my feet and asked sheepishly if he knew anyone who might loan me a pair of shoes. He looked down and giggled. In halting English, he explained that the crew was Filipino. "No one on board has feet that big, but I will ask."

After about fifteen minutes he returned with socks and a pair of sandals. "Brilliant," I said, and slipped them on. My feet hung off the backs of the sandals by almost an inch, but they would serve. Then the captain's steward escorted me to dinner. By this time the ship had reached the front edge of the force 10 gale. The seas were rough enough to make everyone stumble. My legs refused to cooperate, but as I crossed the room to the captain's table the weather disguised my staggering gait.

The captain stood to welcome me, and we exchanged pleasantries. He indicated that the empty seat to his right was intended for me. I stared at the chair, trying to imagine how I would lower myself into it with any modicum of dignity. I paused. Still standing, the captain introduced me to his officers. Each stood, and, because they were European, I was spared the American custom of shaking hands across the table. A polite nod to each seemed to suffice. *If anyone touches my right arm, I'll collapse in a heap.* The chief engineer was Romanian. His wife was visiting for the crossing from Antwerp to Philadelphia. As the only other woman on board, she looked happy to see me. The captain turned his back to get something from a table near the kitchen, and I seized on the opportunity to sag clumsily into my chair.

My first meal at the captain's table was awkward. I was relieved to be in the company of other human beings, but I could barely keep my eyes open. I hardly noticed that the captain spent most of the meal scolding me for attempting to row a boat across the ocean. "What possessed you to attempt such a thing?" The captain pointed out that my boat was unbelievably small. "Until we were within a few hundred meters, we couldn't even see it." He had been a professional mariner since the mid-1950s, he explained. "The weather on the North Atlantic is becoming more violent every year, and this year has been the worst summer season I have witnessed. The hurricanes came early." There had been Hurricane Bonnie, Hurricane Danielle, Hurricane Earl, and a number of other violent storms and gales. "What were you thinking? What were you trying to prove?"

The phone rang. It was the bridge—the British Broadcasting Company was on the satellite telephone, and they were requesting an interview with me. The captain explained that I would have to go to the bridge to take the call, and he sent one of his officers to guide me. From the galley, the bridge deck was up five flights of stairs. I cursed the BBC with every painful step.

Eventually I reached the communications room next to the bridge, but I can recall nothing of what I said. After the interview, I returned to dinner. I don't remember the meal because two other satellite calls came in from the press during dinner and two more came right after the meal. One of the calls came from Kenneth Crutchlow, executive director of the Ocean Rowing Society in London. The only blessing was that the stairs kept my joints from locking up.

An hour after dinner, the storm came on in full force, with sustained winds of sixty-five miles per hour and twenty-five-to-thirty-foot seas. The captain was on the bridge, and I knew enough to stay out of his way. After each telephone interview, I went below to my room. I'd stay there for ten or fifteen minutes. Then one officer or another would call down to ask me to return to the bridge deck for another satellite call. After the sixth or seventh trip upstairs, it was impossible for me to hide my soreness. I was moving gingerly past the captain toward the telephone when the ship lurched through a heavy swell. I staggered and collided with a bulkhead. My involuntary groan carried the unmistakable sound of pain. The captain's eyes met mine, and, for the first time, they conveyed sympathy. Without comment, I took the call and returned downstairs to the guest quarters.

Back in my room, I sat on a bench waiting for the next call. Aboard the *American Pearl* constant motion kept my muscles limber. Important tasks made it possible for me to disregard the pain. The *Independent Spirit* was not subject to every bump and swell. Muscles grew stiff, joints locked up, and there was nothing to occupy my mind except an ugly sense of failure. Helplessness had beaten me again.

I WONDER WHAT ADVICE Barry will have for me. We'd met in the fall of 1984, when I was a senior at Smith College. As I walked home from class one afternoon, Danielle Brian yelled down from the roof where she had been sunbathing, "Tori, there's a man rowing on Paradise Pond." *Impossible,* I thought. *The sun's gone to her head.* I looked for myself, and indeed, there was a man rowing on the pond. Worse, he was rowing in the sleek racing shell that I typically used. This was not to be tolerated. I marched down the hill to the boathouse and announced, "Miss Benson, there is a *man* rowing on the pond."

Rather than calling campus security to have the offender removed forthwith, Miss Benson replied, "Yes, I know. He's a sweetheart."

I was shocked. Clearly, this man had co-opted the mighty Benson in some way. I took it upon myself to remedy the situation. I went to the dock and watched scornfully as the man landed. Then, pulling myself to my full height, I asked with all the condescension I could muster, "Would you like some help with your boat?"

"Why, yes, I'd love some help."

As I gave him a hand, I treated this intruder with all the warmth of frozen asparagus. He was my height, but painfully thin and very pale. His hair was strawberry blond, his eyes blue, and perched on his upper lip was a perfectly ridiculous handlebar mustache. He looked to be in his early fifties. The man extended his hand in my direction. "My name is Barry Bingham. What's yours?"

"Tori," I replied, shaking his hand with the viselike grip of a lumberjack.

"I'm married to a student here," said the man with obvious glee. As if on cue, a stunningly beautiful older woman came into the boat bay. She was tall and slim, and moved with the grace of a dancer. "This is my wife, Edie," the man said. I nodded.

Edie Bingham was an Ada Comstock Scholar. The program brought a cadre of older women to the campus. The wisdom of their mature voices added immeasurable richness to my classroom experiences at Smith. When a young classmate babbled on and on in a class on adolescent psychology, an Ada Comstock Scholar in her seventies interrupted, saying, "Hon, let me tell you how it is."

Over the course of my senior year, I scrutinized this man, Barry Bingham. There was a sadness about him that made him seem trustworthy. It's important to say that he wasn't sad. Having a shelf of sadness in the library of one's experience and being sad are two entirely different things. Sad people are self-absorbed, which can make them untrustworthy. There was nothing self-absorbed about Barry Bingham, but his manner had an elusive quality: shy, reserved, and formal. The thing I liked most about him was that he adored his wife.

From time to time, I rowed with him in a double scull. This presented me with a problem: should I call him "Mr. Bingham" or "Barry"?

I consulted Miss Benson. "I think I should call him 'Mr. Bingham,'" I told her. "After all, he's old enough to be my father."

Miss Benson observed, "I think you should call him 'Barry.' He's from Kentucky, and rowers tend not to be so formal with one another."

The next time I spoke with my parents, I asked my father if he'd ever heard of a guy named Barry Bingham from Kentucky. My father said, "The Bingham family owns the *Courier-Journal* newspaper, along with a few television and radio stations."

This news did not sit well with me. I was going through that awkward phase of youth in which I thought anyone who had money was bad. I couldn't call him "Mr. Bingham" without seeming to curry favor, but calling him "Barry" would presume a familiarity that we did not share. In the end, I resolved not to call him anything, which often left me tongue-tied.

The year after Edie and I graduated, the fall of the Bingham empire became national news. Barry Bingham Jr. had been the publisher of the *Courier-Journal*. In the midst of rancorous family squabbles, Barry Bingham Sr. sold everything. At a time when most men are reaching the pinnacle of their career, Barry Bingham Jr. found himself out of a job.

I felt guilty for presuming that Barry and Edie Bingham enjoyed lives full of teacups and roses. I was embarrassed by my naiveté in thinking that wealthy people were insulated against helplessness. I regretted not having been more of a friend to them while we were at Smith. In April 1986, I wrote a mildly apologetic letter to the Binghams. It was Barry who responded.

This exchange of letters opened a correspondence that would span twenty years. In that time, Barry became my best friend. I would grow to love him as much as I loved my brother Lamar. It was easy to love Barry Bingham; he was an honorable man who loved his wife. Our relationship was impeccably Victorian. Loving Barry was as safe as loving John Quincy Adams. Barry's letters were contemplative, forthright, and full of sage advice. I don't imagine he valued my letters to him as much as I valued his letters to me, but I'm sure mine amused him. He cherished the spiritual clarity of idealistic youth, however erroneous it might have been.

When Barry wrote to Smith to tell Miss Benson that I was planning to row across the Atlantic Ocean, she wrote back imploring Barry to stop me. "What am I supposed to do about it?" Barry replied. "*You* Smith people taught her that she can do anything she puts her mind to!"

CHAPTER 18

Pain Settles In

September 7, 1998
days away from land: 85
aboard the Independent Spirit *heading*
westbound for Philadelphia, Pennsylvania

AFTER I COLLIDED WITH THE BULKHEAD AND THE CAP-
tain heard my involuntary groan, he saw to it that I received no more
messages to come to the bridge that evening. As I would find out the
next morning, he took every call, explaining that I had gone to bed
and that I needed to rest. No, he would not wake me up, not for CBS,
not for NBC, not for anyone else. When the ship's phone didn't ring,
I eased myself into bed. Because I expected more calls, I didn't take
off my clothes. I was asleep in seconds.

IT'S DAWN. GET UP, you lazy drone. It's time to row. The motion of
the boat felt wrong, and I could feel the thrum of engines. I opened
my eyes and remembered that I was no longer aboard the *American
Pearl. There will be no rowing today.* During the night, every joint
in my body had rusted into immobility. *I can't move.* My right arm
refused to work at all. I lifted my head and pain stabbed through my
shoulder and back. My legs were as lifeless as two rows of brick.

*This isn't good. At least I have my clothes on. That will make things
less embarrassing when someone comes looking for me.* I couldn't imagine

how I'd get out of bed and make my way down to the captain's mess. I focused on small movements. I inched my body toward the edge of the bed a little at a time. The bed was not tall, perhaps a foot and a half or two feet off the floor. There was a leeboard to keep the sleeper from being thrown from bed in a heavy sea. I flopped my right leg over the board and heard my foot hit the floor. The board dug into a bruise at the back of my thigh, but I couldn't reverse the movement.

Little by little I worked myself into a sitting position. My head throbbed with each beat of my pulse, and liquid dripped down my chin. *I am drooling. Lovely—if Smith College could see me now, they would expunge my name from their records.* Just then there was a knock on the door, and the captain's steward announced that breakfast would be in fifteen minutes. I said, "Okay," but made no effort to reach for the door.

It will take every bit of fifteen minutes for me to get down the stairs to the galley. My best hope for maintaining any dignity would be for me to leave at once and to trust that my aching joints would relax along the way. Slowly, gripping walls and railings for support, I made my way down the hall. I slipped and fell down a flight of stairs. No one was around. I pulled myself up and eased down the next set of stairs. When I finally reached the captain's mess, no one was there.

I looked into the galley. The cook appeared exhausted. Without really looking at me, he pointed toward the captain's table. The captain's steward came in and began to set the table. He looked perfectly green. I asked if he was okay. He shook his head and muttered, "My stomach." The rough weather had made him seasick. I looked out the window and assured him the weather was clearing. "I hope so. Last night . . . very bad."

I wanted to be comforting, but every gesture caused pain. I lowered myself into my chair and concentrated on sitting very still. In a few minutes the captain came briskly through the door. Despite our gruff introduction, I instinctively liked this man. He was West

German, of medium height and a strong build. I'd guess he was in his late fifties, but he moved with the agility of a much younger man. His hair was gray with a peppering of red. Untold storms showed in the weathered lines of his face, and his blue-green eyes were as deep as the ocean itself. His whole being conveyed wisdom and authority.

The captain spoke several languages, and his command of English was better than many Americans'. He took his place at the table and asked me how I'd slept. I replied, "I slept very well." He looked surprised, and paused to study my face. Satisfied that I had spoken the truth, he said, "Well, then, you were the only person on board who slept last night." The captain explained that the storm had sent gear and equipment flying in all directions. Waves had come over the bow and broken quarter-inch steel deck plates on the foredeck. "Crewmen were tossed from their bunks, but you slept through it?" This seemed to impress the captain more than the fact that I'd rowed a boat more than three thousand miles across the North Atlantic.

No one joined us for breakfast. I wondered if the rest of the officers were sick, exhausted, or too busy to eat. The captain's steward brought breakfast to the table. As we started to eat, Captain Lorenson explained that when he received my distress signal, he thought it was a mistake. "On the weather map, your position was centered in a small band of clear weather between two immense low-pressure systems, the hurricane and the gale." This was the first time I heard the word *hurricane* attached to the storm I'd experienced.

The captain went on to tell me that recreational sailors do not traverse this part of the North Atlantic so late in the season, and commercial vessels rarely request assistance, because it can subject the ship to the right of salvage. Until the RAF search plane confirmed that there was someone to rescue, the captain thought he had been asked to alter course to pick up a phantom.

The captain's tone was more cordial than it had been at dinner. "Such a small boat . . . the hurricane passed directly over your position." The captain wondered aloud about the timing of my distress signal. He put down his knife and fork, resting his hands on the table before him. His eyes held a question. No longer able to meet his gaze, I let my eyes fall to the table. I didn't wait for him to put the question into words. I spoke first. "I couldn't ask another human being to come out into that storm to get me."

By the time I'd worked up the courage to lift my eyes, the captain's face had softened. He leaned away from me and placed an elbow on the back of his chair. It was the captain's turn to stare off into space. I wondered: *Can he imagine me on deck, chest deep in water, holding the EPIRB? Or is he revisiting his own storms, recalling his own moments of doubt?* The cook appeared with more food. The captain cleared his throat loudly, and we both returned to our breakfast.

Regaining a little of his gruff façade, the captain told me it was lucky that I'd requested assistance during the lull between storms. "In last night's swells, we might never have gotten you off. That storm might have finished you."

"I was lucky to be on this ship last night," I concurred. Then, half joking, I said, "I would not have been able to sleep so well on my boat." The captain flashed a broad smile.

After this exchange, I felt a little more at ease with the captain. The day before, he'd seemed to think I'd treated the ocean, his ocean, with disrespect. I would not say I was in his good graces, but he looked at me differently. *I may be a fool, but at least I'm not a damn fool.* I ate slowly with my left hand, holding my right as still as possible in my lap. I was not ready for the captain to know the full extent of my injuries. I had a terrible headache. With the modest breakthrough between us, I thought about asking the captain for some aspirin, but before I could muster up the courage the chief engineer came stomping into the room.

He was red-faced with anger. Apparently he'd been having a fight with a member of his staff over a broken piston. The captain changed the subject briefly, asking about the chief engineer's wife. The chief engineer replied that she was extremely seasick. "Everyone is ill?"

questioned the chief engineer, pointing to the empty seats at the table. In response, the captain merely shrugged his shoulders. There was an exchange between the captain and chief engineer in German, not intended for my ears. The captain finished his breakfast quickly and left with the chief engineer to address whatever the fuss was about. I hobbled back to my room.

AFTER DIVINITY SCHOOL, I had an opportunity to take a job in Boston. It was Barry Bingham who convinced me to return to Kentucky. He argued that the Boston bureaucracy was so entrenched that I would spend decades working my way up through the ranks before I'd be able to make a genuine difference. Kentucky, he insisted, had all the same problems, but I could be of service more quickly. Is there a better way to bait the hook for youth and idealism than to say "You are needed here"?

In Louisville, the Bingham family was something close to royalty. Having Barry Bingham Jr. to act as a reference for potential employers should have been a good thing, but right away I managed to stick my foot squarely in what Barry delicately called the "goo-goo."

I was interviewing for a job to work with homeless drug dealers in what passed as Louisville's roughest neighborhood. I went to the interview wearing a neatly pressed navy blue suit, a white linen blouse, a new pair of hose, and well-polished black pumps. I presented the interviewer with a neat resumé on white linen paper.

"Hmm, Smith College," said Fred Banks, reading.

"Yes, sir," I said.

"Divinity school at Harvard."

"Yes, sir."

When he'd finished reading my resumé, Fred held it out, gestured toward my outfit, and said, "Well, obviously, I can't send someone of your background to work with homeless drug dealers in the West End."

"Oh, but I'd be great at working with homeless drug dealers—just ask Barry Bingham Jr.!"

Fred tried not to laugh.

It was probably the first time in the history of Louisville, Kentucky that the words *homeless* and *drug dealer* had been used in the same sentence with Barry's name. The interview was over.

Barry chuckled heartily when I confessed that I'd dropped his name in a job interview at the worst possible moment.

Eventually, I was able to find a job running a shelter for homeless women in the West End. The majority of the women in the shelter fell into one of three categories. Some were mentally ill, some had issues with substance abuse (often related to mental illness), and some were circumstantially homeless. Providing a safe, secure, sanitary environment usually allowed the women in the last category to stabilize their lives, find jobs, and return to a life outside the shelter system. For the women in the other two categories, the shelter system was a semipermanent arrangement. The mentally ill stayed mentally ill, and those addicted to alcohol and other drugs stayed addicted.

For these women, hospitals and jails provided the only means of escape from the shelter system. Housing people in hospitals and jails is vastly more expensive than creating affordable housing with appropriate treatment and support. I tried to lobby local politicians to construct more humane alternatives, but I had difficulty convincing anyone to take me seriously. When I realized that most of the people who were in positions to make these kinds of changes were or had been attorneys, I decided to go to law school.

Barry Bingham did not approve of this idea. "If you are in search of wisdom," he told me over lunch, "you aren't going to find it in law school." Barry always gave me good advice, but I didn't always take it.

At the University of Louisville, I was described as a "brilliant but erratic" student of the law. When I was supposed to be reading modern works by Prosser and Keeton on torts, I studied the oratory of Cicero and the systems of justice outlined by Justinian for ancient Rome. I skimmed through assigned works by Miller on civil procedure and McCormick on evidence but paid careful attention to William Blackstone's *Commentaries on the Laws of England*, which outlined natural rights and the rules of civil conduct. While studying constitutional law, I launched into a study of political philosophy consulting the intellectual trinity of Locke, Hobbes, and Rousseau.

Thomas Hobbes wrote that life in a state of nature was "solitary, poor, nasty, brutish, and short." He argued that in civilization, our "social contract" calls for rule by one strong and absolute sovereign. Jean-Jacques Rousseau, the long-haired hippie of the trio, believed in the natural goodness of humanity. He favored rural simplicity and group consensus, and he was more of a socialist. John Locke stood in the middle with a set of checks and balances that combined natural rights with contract theory.

As a law student, I didn't take notes in class. I didn't make course outlines. I didn't join study groups. I studied what I found useful and ignored the rest. After the first round of exams, my professor for property law was aggravated by what she took to be my poor performance.

"Look, you get it, right? You know that when we write essay questions with a set of facts where the little old lady loses her house to the big ugly corporation, the law will always be on the side of the bad guys. I can't give you any points if you insist on arguing what is right or what is just rather than what is legal."

"Did I give you a good argument?" I asked.

"Well, yes, but that's not how this works. I can't give you points for making a good argument. Arguing what the law should be won't get you anywhere; you have to stick to what the law is. You knew the correct answer when you took this test. Why didn't you just give it to me?"

She was right. I knew the answer that she'd wanted me to give. I'd been to Louisville Collegiate, to Smith College, to Harvard Divinity

School. These were excellent schools where I'd learned to play the academic game. My love of learning was as strong as ever, but by the time I reached law school I was no longer interested in learning on anyone's terms but my own. The letter of the law was not enough for me. Mrs. Longley had taught me to explore the text, the context, and the subtext.

My personal subtext hadn't changed. I wanted to understand the law for the same reason I wanted to understand a chain saw: competence trumps helplessness. If I couldn't make the law serve the weak, if I couldn't use it to care for the infirm, if I couldn't beat helplessness about the ears with it, then the law would be of no use to me. I refused to view the law as all-powerful or unchanging. Human beings make laws. When laws run counter to justice, then it is incumbent upon human beings to make better laws.

To the irritation of my professors, I would pull out arcane references from the Napoleonic Code or canon law as a means to argue that the hypothetical little old lady should keep the hypothetical house. I would not let helplessness win, not even in the hypothetical world of a law school exam.

I humored some professors. With others, I was willfully obstinate. As a result, there were several semesters in which I scored near the top of the class in one course and barely passed others. The only time I played the game with any seriousness was when I sat for the Kentucky bar exam. My reputation for being "brilliant but erratic" wouldn't hurt me so long as I passed the bar exam on the first try. I passed.

Barry had been right. I failed to find wisdom in law school.

A FEW MINUTES AFTER breakfast, the phone rang. The chief mate asked me to come to the bridge for a satellite call. Getting up the stairs was far more difficult than it had been the night before.

When I finally made it, I was relieved to note that the captain was not on the bridge. He had other duties that morning. The second mate explained that the phone had rung all night, but that the captain intercepted each call. *I do like that man.*

The second mate suggested that I remain on the bridge, as every incoming call would be for me. Rather than face the stairs again, I took his advice. As he predicted, the phone rang every few minutes. Most calls were from members of the press, but a few friends managed to get through. I did my best to sound chipper and upbeat.

When a news station called from my hometown, Louisville, I perked up a bit. They put one of my best friends, Beth Brown, on the line with me. Beth had been my racing partner; we rowed a women's double together for years. She asked, "How are you?" Knowing our comments were being recorded, I glossed over my injuries. Beth knew me well. We had raced in flat-water regattas for several years, and we almost always finished first. I was sure that Beth could hear the pain in my voice, but she didn't make an issue of it.

Tuesday, September 8, flew by in a blur of interviews. I asked my friends to circulate a message to stop calling the ship. It was disrupting operations. After Tuesday, my friends restricted their communications to the ship's fax. This was far less intrusive. After a very pleasant dinner with Captain Lorenson, I made it a point to tell him that I was a little tired and that I planned to go straight to bed. As I had hoped, the phone in my room did not ring. As I had the night before, I slept well.

On September 9 I managed to get out of bed without drooling. The seas were calmer, and my headache was less severe. I showered before breakfast, hoping that the hot water would relieve some of the stiffness, and then I put the same shirt and trousers back on. With the calm water, my limp was more obvious. Again, I had breakfast with the captain. With the better weather, we had a little more company at the breakfast table. At lunch the chief engineer's wife reappeared for the first time since the evening of my arrival. Her English was as nonexistent as my Romanian, but she asked me to visit the chief engineer's cabin after lunch.

When I arrived, she offered me cookies and some of her clothing. I'd been wearing the same shirt and trousers since my first shower. She didn't have anything long enough to cover my limbs, but she offered a pair of her shorts and a few T-shirts. I thanked her and returned to my room. Over the course of the day, calls from the outside dwindled to a trickle. After one of the calls I asked the mate who was on duty in the radio room if he would mind showing me the weather reports from September 4, 5, 6 and 7.

ON THE THIRD OF September, Hurricane Danielle passed south of Nova Scotia. According to a deep-water buoy, the height of ocean swells grew from five feet to fifty-two feet in a six-hour period. Danielle had been a small but powerful hurricane. The odd waves I encountered on September 3 and 4 were not unlike the waves that form when you throw a rock into the pond. Even a small hurricane is a *big* rock. Aboard the *American Pearl*, I hadn't guessed that the monster waves from the west were the harbingers of a hurricane.

On September 5, the day Danielle reached me, its average sustained winds were seventy-one miles per hour. This placed it at the high end of a force 11 tropical storm. Nearer the core of the storm, the sustained winds exceeded 125 miles an hour: hurricane force. As the hurricane lost its tight formation, the dynamic fetch of the storm increased dramatically. The dynamic fetch has to do with the distance that wave-generating winds travel over the surface of the water. The greater the distance, the longer the fetch; the longer the fetch, the more time the wind has to whip up larger and larger seas. The seas were unusually large where I had been, on the storm's south side. The mate showed me a report that indicated that the average wave height for the entire area of the storm was thirty-five or forty feet.

What I did not know at the time was that the *American Pearl* had gone through both eye walls of the hurricane. At the eye walls, the swells averaged sixty feet. The maximum waves generated in similar conditions with a similar dynamic fetch have been estimated at 126 feet. Months later, Dane Clark, a weather expert with the National Oceanic and Atmospheric Administration, would explain that as Hurricane Danielle broke up, a large portion of the storm swung around and crossed my position a second time. This was what had so confused me when the pressure fell on the backside of the storm.

While the American side of the Atlantic downgraded Hurricane Danielle to an extratropical cyclone late on September 4, forecasters in Scotland continued to describe it as a hurricane until well after it had passed my position. On September 6, the coast of Cornwall was evacuated as waves from Danielle passed over several houses. On the Isles of Scilly, Danielle swept an all-terrain vehicle into the ocean.

During the early morning hours of September 7, about the time one capsize was dislocating my shoulder and the next capsize was putting it back into place, Hurricane Earl was passing north of my position. In the last week of August, much of my stormy weather had been triggered by Hurricane Bonnie, passing to the south of my position.

THE CREWMAN WHO HAD shown me the weather reports said, "You are lucky to be alive." That afternoon I took a long nap. Not wanting to wear the same clothes to dinner for the third evening in a row, I put on the flowered short-sleeved shirt and the shorts loaned to me by the engineer's wife. I was walking better, and I could use my right arm a little more each day. It had been five days since Danielle. The massive lump on my forehead was down to the size of a golf ball. My left thigh still had a large purple knot on it, but much of the swelling on my arms and legs had gone down. Despite the rainbows of black, blue, and green that covered every patch of skin, I thought

I was looking much better. When I reached the captain's table and noted the shocked expressions of the captain and his men, I realized I'd miscalculated.

The instant the officers saw me, the room fell silent. They shared looks of surprise with one another. Without breaking the silence, the captain's eyes spoke. They were filled with compassion. I looked down at my battered limbs. In my cabin, the lights had been dim and muted. In the captain's galley, the lights were fluorescent. The bright orange and red flowers in my borrowed shirt seemed pale compared to the skin of my arms and legs. I didn't know what to do. Part of me wanted to back out of the room, never to return. Instead, I looked up and joked, "It's a nice shirt, isn't it?" The captain smiled and pulled out my chair for me.

There would be no surreptitious slide into the chair. Every eye in the room was on me as I eased into my seat, and the captain helped me to scoot the chair forward. Just then the chief engineer's wife sauntered into the room, and seeing me in her shirt, she began to laugh. Her contagious laugh quickly circled, and the room seemed to decompress. Dinner that evening lasted for several hours. At one point the phone rang, the captain answered it. "Tell whoever it is they will have to call back; she's eating her dinner."

None of the other officers had the captain's command of English. They departed one by one, but the captain stayed. Perhaps he guessed that the worst of my physical pain was behind me. He offered no anesthesia. Instead, he let me dwell in the shelter of his stories. Tales of the storms he'd weathered filled the air around us with spray and foam. He spoke of death and of sorrow. He admitted to carrying guilt that was not his own. He confessed to having dared a few mighty things in his time, and probed gently at the edges of my psyche. I tried to explain that my physical explorations were merely my attempt to balance an intellectual energy that my spirit seemed unable to master.

Not all of the captain's stories came from the sea. He had a life on shore, a home and a family. Like two old warriors, we compared battle scars but never acknowledged the suffering that came with them. In this, I had to concede the advantage brought to the captain by his years. We had more in common than either of us might readily acknowledge. We were both stubborn beyond measure. Too often we tried to bend the world to meet our will. The captain had tangled with his share of storms, but he had come to understand the peace brought by wisdom. He generously tried to share that peace with me, but I did not feel worthy of a gift so freely offered.

The phone rang again, I looked at my watch; it had been several hours since the last call down from the bridge. I nodded to the captain and said, "I better take that." He smiled and nodded back. We left the room together. Watching me limp up the stairs, the captain asked if I wanted some aspirin. "No, but thank you."

Once on the bridge, I took a call from a California radio station. The news anchor told me that over the course of the summer, "Americans have lost heart." They'd lost faith in their government. "You may not have succeeded, but you tried to make us proud." It had been three months since I'd seen a newspaper or heard a news report. I knew nothing about the hottest new story of that summer: President Clinton's affair with Monica Lewinsky. When I hung up the phone, I had a new sense of dread. That interviewer's call suggested that people beyond my immediate circle of friends had followed my story. I knew that I'd let my friends down, but if Americans had "lost heart," had I let other Americans down, too? This made me terribly uneasy.

When I left the communications room, everything was dark. The bridge was lit only by moonlight and the glimmer of the radar and navigational equipment. The ship that stretched out ahead of the bridge seemed the size of a city block. We were so high above the swells I couldn't judge their size. The vessel plowed through a cross sea without any notice.

On the *American Pearl*, I often heard the clicks and squeaks of dolphins or the echoing songs of passing whales. All I heard now was the hum of diesel engines. Even though the bridge was dark, I couldn't see even half the stars I had seen from my speck of a rowboat. While I rowed, I kept constant tabs on the weather and the direction of the wind. A headwind meant no progress and no food. Rowing in the rain, I had to take care not to become chilled. On this ship, a headwind merely reduced fuel efficiency, and rain was meaningless. The *American Pearl* and the *Independent Spirit* were on the same ocean, but they were from different worlds.

The next afternoon, I stood on the bridge looking out to sea. Sunlight danced across the surface of the swells. The seas were calm enough that I could barely feel the waves passing under the hull. A large shearwater flew over the ship. It circled the deck below the bridge and rested for a moment on one of the neatly stacked shipping containers. It was an easy afternoon.

The captain made his rounds. He looked over the shoulder of an officer who was reviewing the weather fax. Then he checked the helm and the radar. When the captain reached the end of the instrument console, he paused and studied the floor. "Hey, who's bleeding?" He looked in my direction. "Not me," I responded confidently.

The captain looked to the third mate, standing at the helm. "Not me," said the third mate. The captain stuck his head into the weather room. "Are you bleeding?" "No." Captain Lorenson began to follow the trail of blood. As he moved in my direction, I looked down. There were drops of blood all around me and along the windowsill where I'd been standing. I raised my hand and saw a trickle of red fluid dripping from the tape on my little finger. About this time, the captain's feet entered my peripheral vision. I lifted my eyes to his face. His eyes were leaving my hand and moving up my arm. As our eyes came together, I blurted out, "I'm sorry."

His eyes held mine. "There's no need to apologize." I could almost feel him willing me to be all right. The ship swayed gently, and I groped for the bulkhead to steady myself. The captain stepped toward me. I gave the captain a quick nod to assure him that I was fine. "Chief mate," Captain Lorenson barked. He must have noticed that I jumped a little, because he spoke more softly when the chief mate stepped up. "Take her downstairs. Take care of that hand and see that she gets whatever she needs." He stressed the word *whatever* in a way that seemed to convey permission for the chief mate to unlock the drug cabinet. I wrapped my hand in a tissue to catch the blood and followed the chief mate downstairs.

We went into the dispensary, which was a storage room next to the sickbay. Slowly I pulled the tape off my finger. The wound had reopened, but I could no longer see bone. It needed stitches, but after five days it was too late for sewing. Watching me remove the tape taxed the chief mate's tolerance for the sight of blood. The edges of the gash showed no sign of infection. The chief mate helped me find some antibiotic ointment and a proper bandage. He made sure I had some extra tape and clean dressings for the rest of the trip. He offered to open the drug cabinet, but I demurred, telling him, "There's no need."

Dinner that Thursday evening was very pleasant. The captain continued to regale me with stories. I enjoyed his company more and more. We talked about my boat and things I would change if I ever tried again. Of course, the captain hoped I would *never* do anything like that again; ours was merely a theoretical discussion between two seafarers. First, the boat should be smaller and lighter, designed to carry one person, not two. It would need to be exceedingly strong. A new boat that met the requirements of the North Atlantic would be expensive and would almost certainly require corporate sponsorship to build.

A faster boat would allow a person to leave from Cape Cod and shorten the journey. With favorable weather and some luck, that person might still be able to swing far enough south to pick up some assistance from the Gulf Stream. This person should leave in late April or early May, rather than in the middle of June. The captain thought the boat should be painted safety orange to make it more visible. I'd had a good communications system, but I let it get wet. Finding better ways to keep things dry would be essential. "When I lost communications, I lost the Gulf Stream, and when I lost the Gulf Stream, the boat just stopped," I commented. I figured staying with the Stream would have shaved a month off the trip.

Friday morning at breakfast, the captain asked if I needed any clothes and offered to lend me some of his. I thanked him for the offer but declined. That afternoon, the captain took me on a tour of the ship. In the captain's eyes his was not an impressive vessel as cargo ships go, but I was impressed. The cargo holds were immense, and the deck was stacked several layers high with containers. The captain spoke of his ship the way a workingman talks about an old pickup truck.

The *Independent Spirit* had seen better days, and the captain had mastered finer vessels, but it was a worthy ship on an expansive ocean. The captain explained that his crew's last performance inspection had been less than stellar, and this clearly annoyed him. Still, they had managed to pluck me from a churning sea without incident. That, the captain explained, is far more important than any supervisor's review of the ship's crew and paperwork.

As the ship powered west across the Atlantic, it gained six hours, but for me the closer we came to shore the more time seemed to fly. The moment I set off my distress signal, news of my failure was broadcast around the world. My defeat was public knowledge. I expected that a storm of reproach would greet me on shore. To prepare, I practiced by reproaching myself: "I quit." "I didn't make it." "I needed help." "I abandoned my vessel." I looked forward to seeing friends, but I feared that my failure would tarnish our reunion.

Saturday evening when I joined the captain for dinner, we knew it would be our last dinner together. I told him I would miss our conversations. He looked me over for a moment and said, "You know, when we first picked you up, I wasn't sure if you were a blue person, a purple person, or a black person. Then you became a green, yellow, and orange person. Now I am beginning to think that under all the bruises you might be a white person." He smiled. I laughed and looked down at my legs. It was true. They still looked bad, but they were much better than they had been.

CHAPTER 19

Philadelphia

September 13, 1998
days away from land: 91—one-quarter of a year
aboard the Independent Spirit, *nearing port*

SUNDAY MORNING I STOOD OUTSIDE ON THE WING OF the bridge deck. A strange cloud appeared on the horizon. I had rowed 3,400 miles toward France. The haze on the horizon was land. *This is the wrong shore, and I am standing on the wrong boat.* A few minutes later, the captain came out on the bridge wing. Behind the screen of my sunglasses, I struggled to compose myself. Captain Lorenson pointed out Cape May and asked me how long it had been since I last saw land. "Ninety-one days," I replied.

The captain shook his head and told me he'd never been out of the sight of land for that long. He meant it as a compliment, but I didn't take it as one. *If my boat had been lighter, if I had been more efficient, if I hadn't lost communications, I might have made a successful crossing in far less than ninety-one days.* The captain stood with me for some time without speaking.

After a long silence, the captain explained that soon the Delaware River pilot would come out to meet us. He would bring newspapers with him. I hadn't seen a newspaper since I left shore.

The pilot boat met us in Delaware Bay and pulled alongside. When the captain saw the pilot, he was very pleased. "This is a good pilot," the captain said, calling him "very experienced." Coming from Captain Lorenson, this was high praise. As promised, the pilot brought newspapers. After the captain and the pilot exchanged pleasantries, the captain handed me the *Philadelphia Inquirer.*

It was Sunday, September 13, 1998, and I held my first newspaper in ninety-two days with the reverence of a sacred text. I was hungry for news of the world and eager to learn about the things I'd missed, but that morning there was only one story. On Friday, September 11, the independent counsel, Ken Starr, had released an explicit report that included lurid details of an affair between the President and a White House intern, I may have been the only American on the planet for whom this news came as a complete shock. *No, no, no, this is not possible.*

I vaguely recalled a woman named Lewinsky. Before I left shore, Secretary of State Madeleine Albright had defended President Clinton. She said the allegations of presidential misconduct were "completely untrue." Now, it seemed that the secretary of state had been misled. The newspaper contained excerpts from the Starr Report. *The President said what? Monica Lewinsky said what? They did what?* Articles carried phrases such as "sorrow for a degraded presidency" and "high crimes." It was as if I'd left one country in June and I returned home to an entirely different place in September. I remembered the reporter who had told me over the phone that Americans had "lost heart." It had made me feel uneasy and now I understood why.

I set the paper aside and went out on the wing of the bridge to smell land and to admire the greenery of its trees. A few hours passed, and someone wanted to talk to me on the VHF radio. It was Diane Stege, one of my best friends and the anchor of the *American Pearl* support team.

She was in a boat alongside and requested permission to come aboard. The captain explained that we had not cleared U.S. Customs and that no one would be allowed to board until we did. Diane asked how I was. I told her, "I've just read the paper. It's very depressing." Diane responded that the news coverage about my trip had been overwhelmingly positive. I replied, "That's not the news I'm talking about!" Diane didn't understand. I keyed the radio and spouted, "The president."

"Oh," Diane responded. "We can talk about that later."

I left the radio and went out on deck so I could see Diane. A little boat pulled up below me. I saw Diane; Kenneth Crutchlow, who was the director of the Ocean Rowing Society; Christophe Hébert, who was a member of my French support team; Daniel Forster, a photographer; a videographer who had a camera running; and the boat's driver. The last person who came into view took my breath away. A lean Frenchman stepped out onto the bow.

It was Gérard d'Aboville.

He had traveled all the way from France to greet me. Diane and Christophe waved and Kenneth bellowed cheers, but I couldn't take my eyes off Gérard. "You did capsize?" he yelled up. I nodded, Yes. He rotated his hands past one another in a tight circle indicating a normal capsize. I nodded. He shrugged. Then Gérard rotated his hands in a larger elliptical pattern, as if to indicate the violent motion of a pitch-pole. I nodded again, and Gérard shrugged once more. His body language said, "Well, Tori, there was nothing you could do."

Gérard was the one man on the planet capable of understanding all that I had gone through without my having to utter a single word. For a few fleeting moments, my sense of failure lessened. No one would have faulted Gérard if he'd chosen not to travel to the wrong side of the Atlantic to welcome me. Yet here he was. *I might think of myself as a failure, but if Gérard shared that opinion, would he be standing on the boat beneath me?*

I walked up to the bow of the ship, and the cameraman continued to shoot video. They wanted me to hold my arms in the air in a victorious stance. I was in no mood for such things and settled for waving my hat with my left hand. My right shoulder still hurt, but I gestured enough with my right hand not to call attention to it. After about twenty minutes the boat headed off with a report that all was well. They would see me when the ship cleared customs.

The customs official in charge of checking our passports cleared me first. I was told to wait in my cabin with the door open until someone came for me. After what seemed an eternity, a crewman brought my friend Kathy Steward up the stairs. Kathy gave me several choices of things to wear. My sponsor wanted me to wear a Sector Sport Watches shirt. They hadn't sent any shirts with long sleeves, but the bruises on my forearms were barely noticeable. I didn't worry about it, but it would be several months before I allowed anyone to see my legs. Kathy had brought the American flag I'd asked for. With the presidential scandal, there would be people who thought my carrying a flag was silly, but I didn't care.

When I was dressed, Kathy and I went down to the lounge to meet the few friends who'd been allowed aboard. Gérard was there, along with a camera crew and two representatives from my sponsor. Barry Bingham gave me a dozen yellow roses. I laid the roses across my right arm. They were perfect camouflage to disguise the limited movement of my battered shoulder.

The captain had gone back upstairs to continue his work with the customs officials. I worried that I had not said goodbye. I've never been very adept at goodbyes, and I thought, *Perhaps the captain is no better at it than I.* We headed out the door to see members of the crew lining the deck. I didn't say goodbye; I just kept saying, "Thank you."

I was so busy trying not to limp that I didn't notice the transition from the boat to the shore. Had it not been for Gérard stopping me to point out that I was on land and to ask me how it felt, I might have missed the significance of the moment. For the first time in ninety-one days, I was standing on terra firma. The *Independent Spirit* had been such a stable vessel that I didn't have to search for my land legs. Had I stepped directly from my rowboat to the shore,

I'd have been wobbly for a few days. Other friends were waiting for me outside the fence. We piled into a small pickup truck that took us to the gate.

When I stepped out of the truck, I could see not only a group of my friends gathered at the gate but a cluster of children. They were children I'd never met. Seeing their curious faces, I stood a little straighter. I held up my head and walked as tall as my sore body would allow. Friends stepped forward one by one to welcome me home.

"Don't hug me too hard—I'm pretty sore."

"Oh, it's so good to see you," said one friend.

Lamar was there. My friend Ann Hassett had looked out for him in my absence. My brother Duke had come from St. Louis, and he brought greetings from my parents.

Once we'd exchanged our hellos, the curiosity of the children began to burst at the seams.

"Was it scary out there?" asked a girl with long blond hair sitting on a bicycle.

"Sometimes, yeah," I responded casually.

A shirtless boy beside me asked, "Did your boat flip?"

"Yeah, it did. It flipped hard too. It was kind of like having a bike wreck. Have you ever wrecked your bicycle?"

"What happened to your pinky?"

"I don't know; it could be broken." I felt my ribs and said, "I have all sorts of little things that could be broken." I laughed an easy laugh, and everyone seemed to join in with me. "But I'm upright and walking, and things are good." I spent several minutes answering questions for the children. The adults standing at the outside of the circle were patient, but before long they began to clamor for my attention. Someone indicated that we should head for our rented bus.

The crowd parted, and I saw Noreen Powers. Noreen had done the vast majority of the wiring aboard the *American Pearl*. I wanted her to know, "The electrical system worked great." She smiled.

I was told a man from the Associated Press wanted to interview me. The children still held my attention. I climbed onto the bus but talked to the kids out the window. The AP reporter started asking questions. The questions from the children outside were far more interesting.

A boy outside wanted to know if I ever had bad dreams. The AP reporter asked me if I had any hobbies besides ocean rowing. I answered the dream question.

A young girl outside asked, "Can I have your autograph?"

The AP reporter asked where I was born.

"Sure." I wrote my name on pieces of paper and passed them out the window. The children outside vied for position.

One little boy pushed his way to the front. "Did you see any whales or sharks?"

The AP reporter asked me how I got into rowing.

"Yeah, I saw lots of whales; a sperm whale came right up to my boat. It was six inches away from me; I could smell its breath. And sharks—I saw sharks all the time, big ones. A tiger shark followed me for a week when I was off the coast of Newfoundland."

A girl asked about dolphins. "Yeah, I saw dolphins, and turtles, and jellyfish. They were great."

The AP reporter gave up and started taking notes on the kids' questions.

Soon the bus pulled away, and I was stuck with the AP reporter. "Why did you do it?"

Ugh, what a bore. The children were way more fun.

The reporter's questions were shallow and seemed designed to make me feel stupid. "Why didn't you just sail across?"

I settled for the usual answers. "I wanted to row." As the bus bounced through the Philadelphia streets, every jolt hurt. The pain gnawed at my thin tolerance.

After one particularly banal question, I looked over the reporter's shoulder to my friends. *Am I the only one who doesn't appreciate this guy's line of questioning?* I caught the eye of Barry Bingham, who, after all, had been the publisher of one of the top ten newspapers in the country. Barry rolled his eyes. *That's a relief. I haven't lost all touch with reality; Barry thinks this guy's annoying too.*

When the bus reached the hotel, my friends rescued me from the reporter. They whisked me upstairs to where a room was being held for our dinner. Gérard sat to my right. After dinner there were toasts. Barry's toast boiled down to "Don't you ever do that again!" But he phrased it much more eloquently. Kenneth Crutchlow delivered his standard Russian salutation honoring the men and women of the sea. Then Gérard stood.

He read a passage from his book *Alone*, which is about his solo crossing of the Pacific.

> They say that with the passage of time the worst memories have a way of turning into positive memories. I know that these will never change; they were, and will always remain, terrible and terrifying. I'll never forget the many times the boat capsized, especially when it turned a complete somer-sault, throwing me against the bulkhead. Then, with my frayed nerves stretched to the breaking point, I kept wait-ing for the final blow, the blow that would end it all, and let out a primal scream, like some wild beast. Nor will I ever forget those other times when I battled for my life, feeling my strength waning minute by minute. And the taste of salt water in my mouth. In my lungs, the taste of death. And, all that alone, alone, alone.

As Gérard read this passage, tears of recognition filled my eyes and ran down my face. A video camera was rolling, but I didn't care. When Gérard finished, friends encouraged me to speak, but I wasn't able.

At that moment, my brother Lamar stood to give a toast. Had the room not been filled with understanding friends, the desire of a men-tally handicapped adult to address the room might have been met by a communal shudder. Lamar is usually a quiet fellow, but when he wants to tell you something, there is no stopping him. Lamar had a message for me. "I not have a [com]puter, I need a puter. People at church they have puters, they know about you. People at work have puters, they know about you, but I not have a puter. Duke have a puter, Tori have a puter, but I not have a puter." I stood and promised Lamar that I would get him a computer for Christmas. Satisfied, Lamar took his chair.

Well, I was standing, and every eye in the room was on me. Watching Lamar reminded me of the days when he used to compete in the Special Olympics. What could I say? "The oath of the Special Olympics is 'Let me win, but if I cannot win let me be brave in the attempt.' I didn't win this time, but I hope I was at least brave in the attempt." As I sat down, Gérard said quietly, "You were, Tori, you were."

PART II

THE JOURNEY HOME

God, whose law it is that all who learn must suffer.
And even in our sleep pain that cannot forget, falls
drop by drop upon the heart, and in our own despair,
against our will, comes wisdom to us by the awful
grace of god.

—Aeschylus

CHAPTER 20

The Tragedy of "Civilus"

September 14, 1998
Philadelphia, Pennsylvania
days on land: 1

WOULD I NOW WRITE THE STORY OF MY LIFE AS A COMEDY, a history, a tragedy, or a romance? My life was feeling like a tragedy. I knew that my uncle was right: anyone over the age of thirty can write the story of his or her life as a tear-soaked muddle. He had counseled, "There's no challenge in that," but when I awakened that first morning in Philadelphia, I felt perfectly tragic.

Aboard the *Independent Spirit*, Captain Lorenson had been the only person who was fluent enough in English to engage me in conversation. After our rocky introduction, he had taken care to shelter me from the weight of too many words. In Philadelphia there was no protection from the bombardment. Words flew at me from every direction. As Gertrude Stein might have phrased it, the words demanded "everything all at once and immediately."

Sector Sport Watches had organized a press conference at city hall. After the formal exchanges, I ran a gauntlet of individual interviews. Nothing felt right. I didn't fit. I couldn't reassemble the shattered pieces of my façade. Hurricane Danielle had unmade me, reduced my existence to raw materials. I felt like a rabbit in a room full of hungry hounds.

I can't keep up. There are too many parts to play, so much traffic, so much commotion, so many voices. I did what I often do when I am uncomfortable: I took shelter within the fortress of my mind and fired clever volleys over the castle wall. *Be clever, hide the pain.*

When the interviews were complete, I wanted to escape to someplace familiar, someplace safe, where I might find my land legs. I turned to the person coordinating the media. "Independence Hall. I have to go to Independence Hall."

"There's no time for that," was the response.

I turned toward two of my friends, Beth Brown and Luckett Davidson. "I need to go to Independence Hall."

They looked at me, looked at each other, and marched off like two women on a mission. Before long, I was in a van bound for the airport via Independence Hall. We had only a few minutes to spare. Beth and I entered the historic building through a back door. I was vaguely aware that other people had tickets. They were escorted by National Park Service guides, but no one disturbed us.

I led Beth to the rail of the assembly room. "This is where it all began. In this room the Second Continental Congress appointed George Washington to lead the Continental Army. It was in this room that they adopted and signed the Declaration of Independence. The Constitutional Convention met here." *If only I could step over the railing and stroll through the history of this room.* I told Beth stories about Benjamin Franklin, John Adams, and Thomas Jefferson until she said apologetically, "We have to go."

As we left the building, I paused to feel the earth beneath my feet. To me, it was hallowed ground. Our founders pledged their lives, their fortunes, and their sacred honor to establish a nation dedicated to the principles of liberty and justice. Standing in the shadow of Independence Hall, I felt the full weight of this inheritance.

As my ocean self struggled to find footing on land, it helped to remember that our founders knit a coalition out of disparate states, governed by men of different tastes, temperaments, and faith traditions. It was not an easy task, certainly not "self-evident." It took careful tending to cultivate common ground among the intellectuals of New England, the merchants of the Mid-Atlantic, the landed gentry of the South, and the sturdy frontiersmen of the West.

I was a product of this blending. The bulk of my postsecondary education came from New England. My love of the land sprouts from southern roots. From the Midwest, I learned to take pride in working with my hands, and I cherish the rugged lessons of Alaska and the western mountains.

Because our young nation had little history or literature of its own, we were free to adopt the history and literature of the Western world. We borrowed tactics from Alexander, Charlemagne, William the Conqueror, and Genghis Khan. We took Shakespeare for our own, but we also claimed Dante, Voltaire, Goethe, and Cervantes. To these, we added the restless spirit of the frontier as outlined by the historian Frederick Jackson Turner. The character of America is a crowd with one face: *e pluribus unum*, out of many, one.

Is it any wonder that in leaving the cocoon of my solitude, I feel so pulled in divergent directions? I am quintessentially American. My civilized self loves books, libraries, history, and all the advances that education represents. My wilderness self longs to be settled but refuses to be tamed. I enjoy solitude, but I cannot be alone and still fulfill the obligations of citizenship. Nothing great is built alone. There is no service in solitude. Solitude doesn't build schools, bridges, or hospitals. Solitude cannot link the life of the mind with a real-world struggle for justice and human dignity.

Beth Brown gently called me away from these thoughts. "You need to eat." She pointed to a bench in the courtyard where other friends were waiting. They handed me a sandwich. As I ate, no one spoke. It was a good sandwich.

I REMEMBER VERY LITTLE about the flight back to Kentucky or the press conference at the airport upon our arrival. The crowd was large, and I thought, *My friends must have gone to a great deal of trouble to recruit so many people to come out to welcome me.*

The following day, Kathy Steward and Diane Stege scheduled appointments with various physicians. I was not a willing patient. I refused to take off my clothes, insisted that I was "perfectly fine," and hid all evidence to the contrary. I consented to X-rays only in places where I didn't think anything was broken: my head, my shoulders, the little finger with the bite wound, and the ankle injury that was more than a month old. The doctors didn't find anything because I didn't want them to find anything. I didn't want anyone to know the extent of my injuries. I did not wish to be comforted. My shame and failure might be public knowledge, but my pain was private.

My friends took the no-news report as good news, and we went to a lovely party. The next morning, I returned to work. There was just enough money in my bank account to purchase groceries. My financial cushion was so thin I felt sure Kathy Steward and other friends had taken up a collection to spare me the indignity of receiving a foreclosure notice on my house.

Fortunately, my job with the Louisville Development Authority was waiting for me, and I launched myself into helping to draft a major grant application for the City of Louisville. It was an application for a $100 million federal Empowerment Zone grant. We planned to use the money to turn around distressed neighborhoods. The project had reached crunch time, which meant that for fourteen or sixteen hours a day I could bury myself in work. Not only did this all-consuming task provide a much-needed anchor against the desolation of my failure, but it also distanced me from the concern of friends.

It was difficult to be with friends. I felt that I'd let them down. They tried to insist that I hadn't, but I thought they were lying. "You did your best, people admire that." *Ugh.* The more friends came around, the more I avoided them. I'd left my emotional armor out on the ocean. I felt psychologically naked, as if my frailties were exposed for all to see. Even worse, I couldn't make any sense of my notoriety.

For a long time, I thought friends were bribing people to be kind to me. In the grocery store, ladies with wrinkled fingers would stand before me smiling, shaking my hand, touching my arm, speaking soft words of kindness. Perfect strangers would come up to congratulate me on my attempt to row across the Atlantic. *Has civilization gone mad? I failed. Failed, failed, failed! There is nothing laudable about failure.*

IN MID-OCTOBER THE INEVITABLE happened: the Empowerment Zone grant application was finished and we sent it to Washington, D.C. I looked at my boss, Barry Alberts, a brilliant, hardworking man whom I greatly admired, and asked, "What's next?" There wasn't anything. Because of a term limit, Mayor Abramson would leave office the end of December, and Mayor David Armstrong would take over. There wouldn't be any new projects. There was nothing to do but mop up and put our files in order for the transition.

"But I need something to *do*!" I insisted.

Barry understood my frustration. He shared it. Barry sounded confident when he said, "You'll find something to keep you busy." A few days later, an e-mail went out to all city employees saying that Mayor Abramson wanted a good turnout for the groundbreaking of Louisville Slugger Field. I had nothing else to do, so I went.

I was standing at the edge of a growing crowd when a tall, handsome gray-haired man walked up and stood beside me. "Have they found your boat yet?" he asked.

I looked at him but didn't answer.

"I'm Mac McClure," he said with an easy smile.

"Yes, I know. We met last year when I gave a speech to the Downtown Rotary Club."

The Rotary Club, in Louisville, tends to be populated by men and women in business suits. Mac had made an impression because he wore a tweed jacket, a pressed oxford cloth shirt, blue jeans, and green rubber garden clogs.

"They are going to find your boat pretty soon," said Mac.

"No, it will wash up on the coast of Africa, and some fisherman will chop it up for firewood." I didn't want to discuss it, and I hoped that the tone of my voice would make that clear.

"I think someone will find it and you'll get it back."

I just gave him a shrug.

He kept talking. "It may drift around for a few more weeks . . ."

I stopped listening.

Then, to my relief, the ceremony started. Various dignitaries walked out to where the mayor's podium had been placed in the middle of a bare field. The mayor's assistant, Monica Scheckles, was introduced to sing the national anthem. There was a flag. I hadn't noticed it. I stood a little straighter, and I placed my right hand over my heart. Monica started to sing:

"O say, can you see, by the dawn's early light . . ."

Suddenly, I was back aboard the *American Pearl*. I'd just cut loose the big sea anchor that had kept the boat from righting itself. I was in the cabin waist deep in water. My little flag was waving on the gunwale.

"Whose broad stripes and bright stars, through the perilous fight . . ."

Tears began to stream down my cheeks. *No, stop. Not here. Not now. For pity's sake, get hold of yourself.*

"And the rockets' red glare, the bombs bursting in air, gave proof through the night that our flag was still there . . ."

Watching the flag, I could hear thunder, feel wind, taste salt, smell fear. My hands started to shake. The tears kept coming. There was no holding them back. I tried to wipe them away.

Mac McClure whispered, "Are you okay?"

"I'm fine," I said, a little too gruffly.

Mac put his arm around my shoulder.

How dare he? Can't he see my Do Not Disturb sign? Nobody touches me. Not now, not ever! I wanted to hit him, but my mind balked. *I can't punch a man during "The Star-Spangled Banner."*

"O say, does that star-spangled banner yet wave, o'er the land of the free and the home of the brave?"

The song ended, but the arm around my shoulder remained. It was a strong arm, and it felt nice around my shoulder. The speeches started, but the arm remained. The arm stayed until I was able to stop crying.

Between speeches I offered Mac a feeble "Thank you," and I eased out from under his arm. "I'm okay, really. It's just that song . . . it made me remember something."

"It's all right. You're entitled," said Mac softly.

The ceremony ended. Mac said, "Give me a call when they find your boat. I'll help you rebuild it."

"Yeah, sure, thanks," I said.

I left as swiftly as I could manage without knocking anybody down. I went home and stumbled off the edge of my map.

I COULD NO LONGER fill my evenings and weekends with productive work, but I continued to shut out my friends. I didn't return telephone calls, didn't hang around with rowing buddies, and didn't go to lunch with colleagues. I made gestures to sanity. I went to work, showed up at the scheduled appearances, and delivered the obligatory speeches. Then I fled home to the seclusion of my library and to the tragedy of myself.

My books reminded me that I was not the first person to experience difficulty with reentry into civilization. After the Lewis and Clark expedition spent two and a half years charting a route from the Mississippi River across the middle of North America to the Pacific Ocean and back, Meriwether Lewis had difficulty making the transition back into "real life." Lewis was not alone in this; John Colter, one of the members, turned around before the expedition reached St. Louis on its return trip, and he retreated back into the wilderness. I envied Colter's choice.

What did John Colter miss? He missed hearing the news of the day: Thomas Jefferson had been reelected president, and the nation was about to go to war, either with the British or with the French, no one knew for certain. Colter missed gorging himself on the post-expedition food and liquor. He missed being bombarded by questions about what it is like "out there." He missed being treated like a conquering hero when he knew he was just a man. He missed telling people that you cannot conquer nature; it merely allows you to pass.

In 1809, three years after the expedition returned, Meriwether Lewis died from gunshot wounds. Some said the wounds were self-inflicted, that Lewis had committed suicide. Others preferred to think that the great explorer had been murdered. The man who probably knew Lewis best, the co-leader of the expedition, William Clark, wrote, "I fear O! I fear the weight of his mind has overcome him." Clark understood the weight of Lewis's mind. If Lewis did commit suicide, he would not have been the first explorer to have done so, nor the last.

I feared the weight of my own mind. My thoughts were ungainly. This wasn't the first time I'd had difficulty in making the transition back into civilization. I even had a name for the disorder: I called it "civilus." But this time the "civilus" was worse than usual. A surprising number of friends misinterpreted my social withdrawal as conceit and self-satisfaction. A few would remark that I had become too self-important after the "success" of my rowing adventure to associate with old friends. My older brother Duke telephoned to tell me that his wife thought that I considered myself too good to be bothered with them.

It wasn't self-importance that was cutting me off from the world;

it was depression. I wasn't good company for myself; how could I be good company for anyone else? Some psychologists insist that people who spend long periods in the wilderness experience a kind of postpartum depression upon our return to civilization. They surmise that we get depressed because we cannot control our world with the same certainty that characterizes our control of life in the backcountry. This is nonsense and drivel. Who is able to control the weather, the grizzly bear, or the avalanche? Our depression has nothing to do with a loss of control. It has everything to do with a tragic loss of clarity.

My backcountry experiences, especially my time with the National Outdoor Leadership School, had taught me that life in the wilderness has a transparency that is difficult to find in civilization. Just before NOLS students return home, the school briefs them on what to expect as they reenter the "harsher environment" of civilization. Life in the backcountry is reduced to the bare essentials: some equipment, some food, and, if you are lucky, a few friends with whom to share the experience. You don't carry much with you, so you take care of the things you have. You watch the weather and always know where to find your raincoat. You learn to take care of yourself and the people around you. You don't leave things half done, because a half-tied knot or a half-pitched tent can lead to serious consequences. You do things that are difficult. You take risks that may require you to trust your companions with your very life. When you ask another climber, "How are you?" you genuinely care about the answer.

Life in the "real" world is hazy, and it is piled full of superfluous things that have little bearing on survival. Modern conveniences equate with disposability. When things break, we throw them away. When friendships break, we throw them away. After all, there are so many people. We don't watch the weather; we change the thermostat. We don't take care of ourselves; we leave that to the doctors and the lawyers. We don't take care of the people around us; we pay taxes and expect the government to do the caretaking. We place our trust in our locks and alarm systems. People come and go at dizzying speeds, and most encounters are frustratingly superficial. When I remember to ask someone, "How are you?" I seldom slow my pace to listen to the response. Reality is sometimes difficult to find in the "real" world.

I was lost in this world. My compass, sextant, and charts were useless. I knew my location, but I had misplaced my sense of place. I reread Plato's allegory of the cave but had no way of knowing if I was inside the cave, confusing the shadows on the wall for reality, or outside of the cave in the light of day. In the hope of finding some escape from this existential void I revisited Kierkegaard and Kafka. Kierkegaard gave us a name for the void, Kafka made it literature, but it all gave me a cosmic headache. So I turned to books on astronomy and theoretical physics. I gave in to the gravity of massive compact halo objects and weakly interacting massive particles (aka "machos" and "wimps").

I buried myself in chemistry and vector mechanics. *If the speed of light isn't a constant, then we can't know for certain that the Doppler effect demonstrates the universe is expanding. If the universe isn't expanding, was there a big bang?* I went from string theory to fractal geometry and back again through chaos. Nothing helped. I couldn't outrun the wasps flying around my brain.

I failed.

I quit.

I set off my EPIRB.

I didn't make it.

I abandoned the American Pearl.

I allowed helplessness to win.

Somehow, the self-derision of my solitude was easier to tolerate than praise by strangers. *It's easy to live up to small. It's easy to give in to gravity. It's easy to be a tragedy.*

NOVEMBER 27, 1998, THE day after Thanksgiving, my telephone rang with the news that an American oil tanker had spotted the *American Pearl* floating about eighty miles off the coast of Portugal. A few minutes later, I spoke with the captain of that tanker. The captain told me, "We saw the large American flag decals on the stern of the boat. That made us curious, and we decided to investigate." They sent out a safety launch and a crewman pulled the EPIRB off the *American Pearl*. They called the U.S. Coast Guard with the registry number from the EPIRB. The Coast Guard relayed the story of my trip and rescue at sea. The captain asked, "Do you want us to pick up your boat?"

"Yes, but, please don't put anyone at any risk."

"No problem," said the captain.

I got the sense that he would log picking up the *American Pearl* as a "safety exercise."

About a half an hour later, the captain telephoned again. "Are there any lifting points on your boat?"

"No, sir, there aren't."

"How did you get it in the water?" asked the captain.

"I backed it off a trailer."

The captain laughed heartily. "Okay, we'll see what we can do."

Later that day, I received an e-mail with a picture of a tiny rowboat sitting on the deck of an immense oil tanker. The *American Pearl* had been rescued.

The ship's next port of call was Le Havre, France. When the captain tried to off-load the *American Pearl*, there was a glitch. French customs wanted the captain to pay a duty to bring the boat ashore. "But it's a rowboat—it's not worth anything," the captain insisted. The customs officials reasoned that if the boat wasn't worth anything, the tanker wouldn't have stopped to pick it up. Around and around they went.

Finally I sent word, via fax, to Gérard d'Aboville. The fax

explained that my boat had been rescued and that it was in Le Havre, but that there was some trouble with French customs. Not only was Gérard a member of the European Parliament, but his solo rows across the Atlantic and across the Pacific had made him a national hero in France. In a surprisingly short period of time Gérard telephoned. "Tori, there is no problem. Your boat will be off-loaded tomorrow."

United Parcel Service maintains an air hub in Louisville, and a friend was able to get the company to move the *American Pearl* from France to a UPS warehouse in Germany. As out of place as I still felt, it was comforting to know that the *American Pearl* was no longer lost at sea.

CHAPTER 21

A Comedic Flirtation

Love is the wisdom of the fool
and the folly of the wise.

—Samuel Johnson

THE LOCAL NEWSPAPER IN LOUISVILLE CARRIED A short story about the recovery of the *American Pearl*. The day the story ran, a man telephoned. As he said his name, there was a buzz of static on the line, and I didn't get the name. The fellow was nice enough. He offered to help me rebuild the *American Pearl*. I knew I'd heard the voice before, but I couldn't place it. He was full of ideas, but after about five minutes my telephone tolerance was nearing its end. I pretty much cut the guy off midsentence: "Thanks very much. Goodbye." It was only as I hung up that I realized that I'd been talking to Mac McClure.

Weeks passed; Christmas came and went. Mayor Abramson left office, and Mayor Armstrong came in. I wasn't sure that I wanted to work for Mayor Armstrong, but without any definite plans, I needed to hedge my bets. Everyone who was anyone in city government would attend Mayor Armstrong's inaugural ball, and as with the high school prom, no one would go alone. *I need a date*. I ran through a mental list of the men I'd dated over the course of the last few years.

My favorite was Eric Friedlander. We were friends. One evening, after a glass of wine had lowered my barbed wire, I asked Eric if we might ever become more than friends. Eric was thoughtful. He sat quietly for some time. Then he said, "You and I would have some fun, but sooner or later you'd get bored. Then you'd run me over like a bulldozer." I wanted to argue, but we both knew he was right.

So I had kept my teenage pledge to remain solitary and vigilant. I'd remained free of romantic entanglements. I'd been tempted. I'd toed the edge of love's pond on occasion, but I'd never gotten my feet wet. Men of the testosterone-and-gorilla-dust sort would test my ramparts from time to time. Some were amusing. Some were attractive. Some were devoted. But men need to be needed even more than they need to be loved, and I wasn't any good at either. *All I need is a date for one evening.*

I was scheduled to speak once again to the Downtown Rotary Club. I decided that if Mac McClure was at the meeting, with or without his garden clogs, I would ask him to go with me to the mayor's ball.

The day came. I walked up to Mac, who was in line at the salad bar. I asked, "Mac, what are you doing on January twenty-second?"

"I don't know. Why?"

"Well, there are no strings attached, but I need someone to go with me to this thing. The deal is, I'm tired of dating testosterone-and-gorilla-dust guys, and at least I know you can carry on a conversation." I handed him an invitation to the ball. "You don't have to answer now. You can wait until after my speech." Without giving him a chance to respond, I turned on my heel and left him standing with his salad in one hand and the invitation to the mayor's ball in the other.

At six foot four, Mac is a head taller than most Rotarians. It was easy to spot him in the audience. After I finished my speech, Mac didn't approach the podium immediately, but waited for the crowd to disperse.

"Well?" I asked.

"Okay, sure, I'll go with you," he said. "Do I need to get two tickets?"

The tickets were $250 apiece. I couldn't afford to buy two, but I certainly didn't want to give him the wrong impression. Sounding a little insulted, I said, "I'll buy my own."

IT WAS RAINING ON January 22, 1999, when Mac came to pick me up. I knew that a proper lady would wait for a gentleman to come to her door, but with the rain it seemed more practical to meet Mac halfway. I raced out of the house in a black evening gown, and Mac met me on the walk in his tuxedo. Together we hurried to his car.

The mayor's inaugural ball was in the Seelbach Hotel. When Mac and I entered the lobby together, heads began to turn. Ordinarily, attracting stares would put me ill at ease, but with my hand in the crook of Mac's arm I felt safe. People smiled and nodded as we passed. This made me feel quite special. We went to the registration table, I with my ticket and Mac with his. Then, to my horror, I learned that we'd been seated at different tables. *This isn't happening. What to do? Oh, what to do?* A mental picture of my inverted bell-shaped curve appeared in my mind: great conceptual ability on one side, great analytical ability on the other side, and in the middle almost no social skills.

I looked around the room and spotted Maura Temes. *I need help from a social genius.* Unlike me, Maura's social awareness scores would be in the top 1 percent. *Her bell curve would look like Everest.* I'd met Maura when I worked in Mayor Abramson's office. I had been a bounding puppy, but Maura did her best to keep me out of trouble. She'd had plenty of practice. She'd been keeping Jerry Abramson on the straight and narrow for decades.

I grabbed Mac's arm and yanked him toward Maura. "Maura, I need help. I'm here with Mac." Maura lifted her hand to indicate that she needed a moment to absorb this interesting combination.

Maura considered my gown. She turned to Mac, eyeing his tuxedo and his perfectly polished black patent leather dancing shoes. Then she turned back toward me with an approving smile.

"What can I do for you?" she asked.

With unrestrained desperation I blurted out, "We bought our tickets separately. They have us at different tables."

"Well, we can't have that, now can we?" said Maura with perfect assurance.

Maura entered the ballroom, selected an appropriate table, and removed two people.

"There seem to be two open seats right here."

"Thank you," I said.

"Happy to help," said Maura.

As we took our seats, I was relieved to find that I knew most of the people at the table. *Mac knows everyone. It wouldn't have mattered if Maura had seated him at the head table or in the kitchen; Mac would have found friends.* I didn't see any other table where I could have been more comfortable. If Maura Temes had delivered an impromptu lecture on drag coefficients, I would have been less impressed. *That woman is a genius!*

Mac and I exchanged an easy banter throughout dinner. After dinner, the dancing started.

"Would you like to dance?" asked Mac.

"Not really—I am not a very good dancer." I smiled, remembering my ballet slippers.

"That's okay with me. I'd probably step on your feet."

We sat talking.

The next thing I knew, we were sitting alone at the table in a near-empty room. I felt intoxicated, but I'd not had anything to drink. My mind was quietly attentive to Mac. He looked at his watch. I looked at mine. We looked at each other.

"I'll take you home."

MAC WALKED ME TO my door, and, surprising myself, I invited him in. We chatted for another hour. As he was leaving, Mac leaned in for a kiss goodnight. Having no experience in this arena, I employed an inappropriate vector for the approach. Our respective kisses missed. He laughed, and we settled for telling each other goodnight.

The week after the ball, I was slated to deliver seven speeches in six days. A strain of pneumonia had been working its way around the city, and I caught it. I was not accustomed to being sick, and I was certainly not going to let it stop me. *I get injured. I don't get sick.* Mac and I made plans to get together after an evening lecture I was to give at the community college. When I'd finished my scheduled time with the students, the professors offered to cancel the next class period if I would stay and continue talking with their students.

I knew this would make me late for Mac, but I agreed. I didn't own a cell phone, and I never considered leaving the classroom to place a call to Mac. By the time I reached home, I was nearing exhaustion, and I could barely speak.

I was relieved when I didn't find Mac waiting on my doorstep. He'd left some soup and a bottle of wine by the door. *He must have gone home. I'll apologize tomorrow.* I let myself in and was on my way to the couch when the telephone rang. It was Mac.

"Mac, I'm sorry about tonight." I was coughing and could only get out a few words a time. "I was talking to a roomful of young people." *Cough.* "The professors asked me to stay." *Cough, cough.* "I knew I'd miss you." *Cough.* "But I stayed." *Cough, cough, cough.*

"You sound awful. I'm coming over."

"No." *Cough.* "I'm okay." *Cough, cough.*

"I'll be there in a few minutes," said Mac.

The line went dead, and I stared at the receiver in my hand. *That didn't exactly go according to plan.* In the time it took me to put away my coat and go through the mail, Mac was at the door. *How did he do that?* I opened the door and invited him in.

"Mac, we need to talk." *Cough, cough.* "This is who I am." *Cough.* "I have things I need to do." *Cough.* "Tonight, when I had to choose between you and those students, I chose them." *Cough, cough, cough.* "I like you, but I don't really have time for a relationship." *Cough.*

Mac sat near me, but for once he wasn't talking. He let me tell him about the plans I had to change the world, and how he didn't really fit into those plans.

Then Mac said, "Let's go upstairs. You can get into bed where you belong, and I'll give you a back rub."

Mac was speaking English, but his words weren't making any sense. *Go upstairs? Him, with me, go upstairs?* My living room was filled with bookshelves, and my mind reached out to the books. *Hey, help me out here.* Nothing—they were silent. *I guess you're the wrong kind of books. Thomas Jefferson said everyone should read fiction.*

Mac knelt in front of me. He took my hands and lifted me to my feet. Then, with his hand on my back, he led me toward the stairs. We went up. I turned on the lights, and Mac sat in my bedroom as I went into the bathroom to change clothes. Rather than pajamas, I opted for a sweatshirt and sweatpants. *What's he thinking?*

Racked with a series of coughs, I fell onto the bed without bothering to pull back the covers. Mac perched on the edge of my twin bed and rubbed my back until the coughing subsided. He was gentle. His hands never wandered.

I AWAKENED IN A dark bedroom. I sat bolt upright. *That was a dream. It must have been a dream. I dreamed that!* I was covered with a quilt that Mac had taken from the far side of the room. I went downstairs. The wine was on the table. I checked the door. The deadbolt was unlocked, but Mac had turned the thumb lock in the door handle. He'd left, and locked the door behind him on the way out.

I walked over to my bookshelves. I remembered the question I'd posed to my uncle: "Shall I write the story of my life as a comedy, a history, a tragedy, or a romance?"

I could hear my uncle's voice. "A romance—it must be a romance."

Among the hundreds of books that lined my shelves, there was only one that could be called a romance. It was a biographical novel about John and Abigail Adams: *Those Who Love*, by Irving Stone. Historical fiction, not exactly helpful.

Somehow, I knew that reading about romance and engaging in romance are two very different things. The map is not the land. For me, love was an uncharted territory for which my books could not prepare me. There were no maps to serve as guide. Would I sail off the edge of the world and bump into sea monsters? Would the adventure be worth the peril?

I SPENT MOST OF the following weekend with Mac. We watched the Super Bowl together at his house. It was halftime; the Denver Broncos were leading the Atlanta Falcons by a large margin. This time it was I who suggested that we go upstairs. Mac had a queen-sized bed. I was thirty-five. *The map is not the land.*

LIFE AT WORK WAS slow. Louisville didn't receive a federal Empowerment Zone designation. The hundreds of millions of dollars went to cities with more political importance, not, we will always insist, to cities with better proposals. I was offered a position overseeing the redevelopment of brownfields and other environmentally compromised properties in the downtown area. It was a good job, the best my new supervisor had to offer. As a lawyer, I allegedly possessed the necessary skills, but I couldn't envision myself as a real-estate developer.

In late February, Barry Alberts, who had taken a position as the executive director of the Downtown Development Corporation, asked if I would be willing to assist with the development of the Muhammad Ali Center. There were risks. If fund-raising didn't go well or if the idea of the center didn't take root, I'd be out of a job. I jumped at the opportunity.

Barry explained that Robert Lipsyte, the well-known sports journalist, was coming to Louisville to write a story for the *New York Times* about the creation of the Muhammad Ali Center. Muhammad and his wife, Lonnie, would also be in town. "Can you join us for lunch?"

"Yes, I think I can work you into my empty schedule," I answered. I'd met Muhammad and Lonnie Ali during the time I'd worked in the mayor's office. Given the number of people they meet in the course of the year, they wouldn't have any reason to remember me.

The day of the luncheon, a number of local dignitaries joined the group. Being unsure of my place, I waited until the important people were seated before I approached. As it happened, the only chair left open was directly across the narrow table from Muhammad Ali.

Muhammad gave me nod as I sat down. I nodded back, expecting him to turn his attention elsewhere, but he kept looking at me. Significant people were seated to my left and right, but Muhammad didn't even glace in their directions.

When this monumental man locks his attention on you, it has a way of removing the oxygen from a room. *He can't possibly remember me from the mayor's office. He's just trying to figure out what a pedestrian like me is doing at his lunch table.*

His hands trembled with Parkinson's syndrome, but his large face was as handsome and gentle as ever. Then, leaning in my direction, he asked, "Were there times out on the ocean when you wondered, 'Why am I here?'"

My brain went into overdrive. *Muhammad Ali just asked me a*

question. And it was a good question. He didn't ask, "Why did you do it?"
He wouldn't need to.

I answered with a question of my own. "Muhammad, were there times in the boxing ring when you wondered, 'Why am I here?'"

Muhammad's eyes sparked with joy and understanding. He leaned back in his chair and started to laugh. I joined him. An ocean of unspoken truth filled the space between us. I didn't need to describe the taste of blood in my mouth, or the faith that fueled endurance. He already knew more about those things than I could say.

Muhammad Ali and I are from the same city, Louisville, Kentucky, and we are from different poles of existence: one male, the other female; one black, the other white; one educated by the world, the other educated by books; one Muslim, the other Christian; one world-famous, the other obscure. Despite our differences, the common ground we shared that afternoon was bigger than a boxing ring or a rowboat.

CHAPTER 22

The History of Muhammad Ali

Furthermore, we have not even to risk the adventure alone, for the heroes of all time have gone before us. The labyrinth is thoroughly known. We have only to follow the thread of the hero path, and where we had thought to find an abomination, we shall find a god. And where we had thought to slay another we shall slay ourselves. Where we had thought to travel outward, we shall come to the center of our own existence. And where we had thought to be alone we shall be with all the world.

—Joseph Campbell

MY JOB WAS TO STAFF A GROUP OF PEOPLE WHO WERE working to create a center to honor the legacy of Muhammad Ali. Muhammad and his wife, Lonnie, were adamant; they didn't want the Muhammad Ali Center to become a boxing museum. They wanted it to be an educational center modeled on the best elements of Muhammad's character: self-confidence, personal conviction, self-discipline, tolerance for diversity in all its forms, charity toward all, and a deep spirituality.

As I studied the life of Muhammad Ali I realized that our goal was to honor the myth of a man. Many people make up stories about themselves, but it is a rare individual who is able to grow into his legend. The myth of Muhammad's life is simpler than the history of that life. At age twelve the young Cassius Clay leaves home with a new bicycle. Someone steals it. Young Cassius wants to beat up the thief, but he doesn't know how to fight. A policeman takes him under his wing and teaches him how to box. Cassius Clay wins the Golden

Gloves. He goes on to win a gold medal in the 1960 Olympics. Eventually, he becomes the heavyweight champion of the world, and with this transformation he changes his name to Muhammad Ali.

There are other twists and turns. He begins his religious pilgrimage as a Christian but converts to Islam. As a conscientious objector, he refuses the draft for Vietnam. Muhammad could flee to Canada, but he doesn't. At the height of his physical prowess, he receives a felony conviction for draft evasion. He is stripped of his heavyweight title and banned from boxing. Ultimately, the United States Supreme Court overturns his conviction and upholds his status as a conscientious objector. Muhammad Ali fights Joe Frazier, George Foreman, Ken Norton, Larry Holmes, and dozens of other men. Then he becomes a champion for tolerance and healing. He marries, is divorced, marries again, is divorced again, marries yet again, is divorced yet again, and marries once more.

Studying Muhammad's life reminded me that a person who falls is not a failure. The failure is the person who falls and doesn't get up again. For Muhammad, getting up again was an act of faith. When there is no answer for helplessness, when competence is not enough, when knowledge comes up short, when action will not answer, it is natural to turn toward God. If there are no atheists in foxholes, there are also very few atheists who are willing to joust with helplessness. If we have faith in nothing else, we must have faith that we can improve the future.

One afternoon, I was walking down the street with Muhammad. As we passed a rumpled man who appeared to be homeless, Muhammad paused. Reaching for his wallet, he pulled out a twenty-dollar bill, signed his autograph, and handed it to the man, who said, "You're Muhammad Ali!" As we continued on our way, Muhammad chuckled lightly to himself. He'd given the man a puzzle. Would the man spend the twenty dollars, keep Muhammad's autograph, or sell the autograph for something more than twenty dollars?

This was classic Muhammad Ali.

OVER THE COURSE OF that winter and early spring, Mac lifted me out of my depression. He understood the territory. He'd navigated through those mountains himself. With patience and fortitude, he coaxed me back into the world. For twenty-four years, Mac had run Bernheim Arboretum and Research Forest. At heart he is and always will be a forester. He loves trees. I didn't tell Mac that my nickname had been "Tree," but he loved me just the same.

Mac is a man of unflinching honesty. He generously gives his opinions to others (whether those opinions are wanted or not). He owns a stately house and a fine car, but these things do not—and will not ever—own him. He is not a simple man, but he lives simply. Where most of us change our temperaments to match our wardrobes, Mac is always blue jeans. Next to Muhammad Ali, Mac is the freest man I know.

Mac is at his best when he is needed. Mac's mission in life is to "comfort the afflicted and afflict the comfortable." My brother Lamar approved of Mac without hesitation: "He a good man." Mac is entirely egalitarian in whom he helps. He knows every blue-collar person in the area. He knows the names of their children, and he knows their stories. If he thought he could help, he would carry on a twenty-minute telephone conversation with someone who dialed a wrong number. In afflicting the comfortable, Mac is much more selective. His favorite quarry seems to be politicians, wealthy people who don't share, and snobs. I couldn't help loving him.

IN LATE MARCH 1999, I received news that two other women were planning to attempt to row solo across the Atlantic. Each was planning to row east to west across the mid-Atlantic. In ocean rowing circles, this is known as the "easy way." It is the easy way because the trade winds, at that latitude, blow east to west, and they have blown east to west for all of recorded history. One can leave the coast of Africa in a barrel and still get to the Caribbean. If one's barrel is equipped with oars, one will arrive somewhat faster.

In late April, I traveled to meet Gérard d'Aboville in Paris. Sector Sport Watches had been the major sponsor for my first solo row. Sector had sponsored two other failed attempts by women, but Sector was willing to give the endeavor one last effort. It was Gérard d'Aboville who convinced Sector that I was the woman for the job. This must have put him in a difficult position. One of the other women who sought assistance from Sector was French. Her name was Peggy Bouchet. Gérard seemed sure that I would try again. For my own part, I was not at all certain.

There would be significant challenges. Sector was only willing to become a partial sponsor. I'd need to find other sponsors to help me build and outfit a boat. Sector would help with the trip itself, but I couldn't count on Sector unless I could raise at least half the money that would be needed. I'd need to build a boat and ship it to the Canary Islands, and because one of the women planned to leave in early September, I didn't have much time.

Gérard took me out to dinner to break the really bad news. He told me, "There is not enough time, nor will there be enough money, to build a new boat. You must rebuild the *American Pearl.*"

"It's too big, too heavy," I protested. "You called it a barge. It *is* a barge!"

Gérard argued that a big boat would be less of a detriment on the mid-Atlantic route because I could count on a push from the trade winds.

"The *American Pearl* is still in Germany. Do you have any idea how many holes it had in it before I left it? It can't be seaworthy."

"You will repair it," said Gérard firmly. Then he took a softer, more encouraging tone. "Tori, this route is the Champs-Élysées of the Atlantic." He took a dramatic pause before ending with the words, "This row is yours to do; you must go and do it."

SOON AFTER I RETURNED from Paris, Muhammad and Lonnie Ali paid a visit to Louisville. We spent much of the day together in a series of meetings about the Muhammad Ali Center. As the day wore on, Muhammad grew more tired and less attentive. Muhammad's friend and longtime photographer, Howard Bingham (no relation to Barry Bingham), was with Muhammad, and the two men were actively bored. Howard asked if they could leave, and Lonnie explained that she would stay and we could continue our work without the two gentlemen.

A few hours passed and I was dispatched to locate them. I found Muhammad devouring a plate of fried chicken. Howard made me promise not to tell Lonnie. Muhammad invited me to sit down, which annoyed Howard. "She's not my type," he said, glowering. I might have taken offense, except that I'd seen Howard's type. I sat down. Muhammad gave Howard a mischievous glance.

Muhammad asked, "What happened to your boat?"

"It was picked up near Portugal. It's in a UPS warehouse in Germany."

"Are you going to get it back?" he asked.

"Two other women are going to try to row across the mid-Atlantic. I've been thinking that if I could get the boat home and rebuild it, I could join them."

It was late in the day. Muhammad was tired. His speech was sometimes difficult to understand, but his next words were spoken with perfect clarity. "You don't want to go through life as the woman who almost rowed across the Atlantic."

He was right. I didn't.

THERE WAS SOMETHING UNFINISHED. Every classic work of Western literature that I admired was a retelling of the hero's journey. These stories were almost always about men, white men, white men who had some money, or white men who were on their way to getting some money. The structure of the monomyth is simple: a man leaves the world that he knows; he is tested usually by some villain or a fire-breathing dragon; he is assisted by guides, mentors, or "unseen hands"; the man is tested again and slays the dragon; after he slays the dragon the man is transformed in some way; the man returns home, ascends the throne, marries, and often lives happily ever after. Up to the last step, the myth of Muhammad Ali had followed the traditional path, except that Muhammad was neither white nor wealthy.

Had I been following the thread of the hero path? I'd gotten into a rowboat and launched it onto the ocean. I had been tested. I'd drawn upon the teachings of guides and mentors: Gérard d'Aboville, Helen Longley, Joe Curran, Barry Bingham, and others. Wind, rain, wave, and storm tested me. I'd tangled with Hurricane Danielle and lost. *Is this where I went awry? At the end of the journey, I was supposed to beat the dragon; I was supposed to kill helplessness, but the dragon defeated me. Did I lose because I am a woman? Why did the storm that kicked my butt have to have a woman's name?*

At the end of the story the hero is supposed to return home whole and complete. When I faced the dragon of my helplessness in Hurricane Danielle, I lost! I returned home with its hot breath still roasting my backside. I carried no treasure of wisdom to justify either my exertions or my wild deviation from the norms of feminine behavior. The deeper knowledge remained lost to me. I had to return to the ocean. I had to finish the journey. I had to go back to the edge of the map. I had to slay my dragon.

THE DAY AFTER MY conversation with Muhammad, I sent a letter to UPS explaining that a Norwegian woman and a French woman were going to attempt to row the east-to-west route across the Atlantic. If I could rebuild the *American Pearl* in time, I promised to place an American in the field of women who would row across the Atlantic Ocean. UPS agreed to put the *American Pearl* on the first plane with sufficient space that was bound for Louisville. Ten days later, the *American Pearl* arrived in Louisville aboard a UPS plane.

During the intervening period, I explained to friends that I wanted to try again. No one was pleased with the news. More than one friend argued against it, but the dream was too heavy for me to carry by myself. I couldn't afford to fail again. On my first solo trip, I had accepted help. On the second solo trip, I accepted that I needed help. The two women most crucial to the endeavor were Kathy Steward and Diane Stege. They were not happy about my plans, but each agreed to stand by me. They were the ones who kept the project organized and moving forward.

The *American Pearl* arrived home broken and battered. There were large holes in the bow compartment and in the stern cabin. The port gunwale was cracked nearly the full length of the deck. A thick layer of green slime in every compartment made me wonder how much of the boat had been above water when the American oil tanker had lifted it out of the ocean.

One stipulation made by my support team was that we would hire a marine architect to survey the *American Pearl* and to determine what needed to be replaced or repaired. I consulted David Stookey, who ran an organization devoted to open-water rowing. David recommended a marine architect named Eric Sponberg. Eric came to Louisville to evaluate the boat.

The port gunwale had a gaping hole. I thought we could patch it, but Eric said we needed to cut away the gunwale and replace it. We cut away the port gunwale and dropped it on the floor. The starboard gunwale was cracked. Again, I thought we might patch it. Again, we removed the gunwale. There were two holes in the cabin roof. Gone was the roof. There were cracks in the cabin walls. Gone were the walls. There was a hole in the bow storage compartment. Gone was the bow storage compartment. When we were finished, there was nothing left of the *American Pearl* from the rowing deck up. Eric, Mac, and I finished the demolition in a single afternoon.

When it was over, Noreen Powers and Bob Hurley, the two people most responsible for the original work on the *American Pearl*, came by to see the boat. Their faces reflected everything I'd been feeling as I'd watched large sections of the boat drop to the garage floor. Bob and Noreen looked ill.

"Why didn't you just patch the holes?"

Eric explained that patching the holes would not have been safe. Neither Bob nor Noreen looked the least bit convinced. They left, disgust clearly painted on their faces. I felt like a fool. I'd surrendered all intelligence and authority to the "out-of-town expert." With *Pearl* parts lying all over the garage, the damage was done.

The next morning, Eric left town promising to send full-scale plans for the parts necessary to refit the boat. The plans he sent didn't fit together with one another. They didn't fit the boat. Eric meant well, but his measurements had not been adequate. In the end, we gave up on his plans and rebuilt the boat by shaping each new piece, part, panel, and plank with painstaking trial and error.

Mac worked with me every day. Scott Shoup, the teacher who'd helped with building the *American Pearl*, gave up a large portion of his summer vacation to the rebuilding. Bob Hurley and Noreen Powers helped when they could, and dozens of other folks gave up evenings and weekends to assist. Each time we ran into a seemingly insurmountable obstacle, the right person for the job seemed to appear. Each day seemed to have its own hero.

IT WOULD HAVE BEEN easier to follow the thread of the hero path if I'd been born with money. Several companies helped by donating hardware and equipment, but most things required cash. I ran my personal credit cards to their limits. I took a second mortgage on my house.

One day we were out of epoxy, and we needed to order another shipment of marine plywood. I opened my bank statement and skipped to the bottom line: I had $9.47 left. At the end of my proverbial rope, I decided that it was time to stop. I had to quit.

I resolved to break the news to my support team at our weekly breakfast. I went early to our usual breakfast spot, the Blue Dog Bakery. As I walked up to order my coffee, Kit Garrett, one of the owners, asked, "How is fund-raising going?"

The question caught me off guard, and the pain of what I intended to do that morning stung my eyes. "Not well," I said.

She handed me the coffee, and I went to our usual table. I sat staring at my notes. My friends were gathering. Just as I was about to begin the sad monologue I'd been practicing throughout the night, Kit walked up to the table. She said, "We really believe in what you are trying to do," and she handed me a piece of paper.

I opened the paper. In my hand was a check for a thousand dollars. I'm not sure I even managed to say "Thank you" before the sting in my eyes turned to tears. I ran to the restroom, locked the door, and stood there crying. It was enough money to pay for the epoxy and the shipment of plywood, but it didn't alter the fact that I was in serious financial trouble. *Quitting is still the only responsible thing to do, but how can I just give up? I could lose my house, my car, even my books. I can't live without my books.* I pulled out my wallet. I had three one-dollar bills, two credit cards (both at their limit), and my library card. As I gazed at the library card, I resolved to keep going.

A few weeks later, a friend secured a major sponsorship from the Brown-Forman Corporation. Not long after that, Fifth Third Bank became a corporate sponsor. Since Fifth Third Bank held the mortgages on my house, I hoped that they wouldn't foreclose while I was in the middle of the ocean. UPS agreed to ship the boat back to Europe at no cost to me. Along with these corporate sponsors came more than a hundred smaller donations from friends, friends of friends, and perfect strangers. Most were from the Louisville community. I felt the burden of these investments in me.

It would have been easier to follow the thread of the hero path if I'd been born male. Raising money for the row made me feel guilty. What difference would my rowing the Atlantic make in the world? The men in my life had no difficulty rationalizing the importance of raw athleticism. Top-level basketball, baseball, and football players made more money in fifteen minutes of playing ball than it would cost for me to row across the Atlantic Ocean. What is so useful about throwing a ball through an elevated hoop, hitting it over a fence, or plowing it into an end zone? It was not men who questioned the propriety of my intentions; it was other women.

I was not breaking new ground. A close reading of history will demonstrate that women have walked the hero path since the beginning of time, but we are supposed to walk it softly, and we are not supposed to walk it alone. When we do it, we do it for the benefit of others. If we climb mountains, we do it to raise awareness about breast cancer. If we hike the Appalachian Trail, it is to call attention to global warming. If we ride a bicycle across the country, we do it to feed hungry children in Africa. It would have been a simple thing to align my trip with some "cause of the week." I had done it before, but it would have been a fabrication. When I wanted to help the homeless, I helped the homeless. When I wanted to comfort people in need, I comforted people in need. Rowboats and oceans had nothing to do with such things.

Where men tend to be defined by their actions, women tend to be defined by their relationships. It is perfectly acceptable for a woman to follow her husband into the unknown. A woman may face down a lion in defense of her children. Pioneering women, ranching women, farming women have been as tough as nails when the situation demanded it. Nurses in war zones have exhibited unquestionable valor. When these women suffered, we saw them as victims of circumstance, innocent victims. I wouldn't be a victim of circumstance. I chose my circumstances, and because that choice was deliberate, I could never be innocent.

GÉRARD HAD TOLD ME that this trip was mine to do. Muhammad had counseled that I didn't want to go through life as the woman who almost rowed across an ocean. On the hero path, the protagonist typically gets advice from mentors and guides. Not heeding the advice often leads to trouble. I'd not always been good about listening to the wisdom of friends or mentors. *This time, things will be different.*

CHAPTER 23

Returning to Slay the Dragon

*In that day Yahweh will punish Leviathan the fleeing
serpent, with His fierce and great and mighty sword,
even Leviathan the twisted serpent; and He will kill
the dragon who lives in the sea.*

—Isaiah 27:1

BY THAT SUMMER, MAC AND I HAD BECOME NEARLY
inseparable . . . except for Thursdays. For some karmic reason, he and
I always fought on Thursday. Our first fight was over what to call a
particular type of screwdriver. I'd been cutting away some very foul,
very moldy urethane foam from under the rowing deck. I turned to
Mac and asked, "Could you pass me a flathead screwdriver?"

"A what?" said Mac.

I was wearing a full-face respirator. I thought perhaps my words
had not been distinct enough. Without removing my mask, I spoke
a bit louder and enunciated clearly: "Would you please pass me a
flathead screwdriver?"

"A what?" said Mac.

"A *flathead screwdriver*!"

"I don't know what you mean," he said. He was clearly not confused.

Pulling off my respirator and tossing it on the deck, I said, "I
need a flathead screwdriver."

"Could you possibly mean a slotted screwdriver?" asked Mac.

"It doesn't have a slotted head. It has a flat head," I said.

"The screwdriver you are asking for drives slotted screws. Flat-head screws can have slotted heads or Phillips heads," said Mac.

"Just give me the darned screwdriver!" I said, glaring.

Mac handed me the appropriate screwdriver. I pulled my respirator back on and shoved my head back under the rowing deck.

A FEW WEEKS LATER, again on a Thursday, Mac and I broke up over the construction of the dagger board. Bob Hurley and I wanted to build it one way, and Mac wanted to build it another way. Bob Hurley left the scene. Mac wouldn't budge. I wouldn't budge. Scott Shoup did his best to keep his head down to avoid hurled insults and flying power tools. Mac left, vowing never to return. I took him at his word.

The next morning, when I was supposed to be out on the Ohio River training in my rowing shell, I was sitting on the dock crying. Noreen Powers approached. She asked, "Tori, what's wrong?"

Between sobs I managed to get out the words, "I—I broke up with Mac. I broke up with Mac over the dagger board."

Noreen chuckled. "Yeah, well, Tori, that happens to all the women I know." I smiled. Noreen had a gift for well-placed sarcasm.

Then Noreen asked, "Is this a forever breakup or just a twenty-four-hour breakup?"

I didn't know there was such a thing as a twenty-four-hour break-up. Happily, it turned out to be a twenty-two-hour breakup.

THE LAST OF OUR memorable fights occurred just a few weeks before we were to ship the boat to the Canary Islands. Mac and I had been working on the boat all day. The temperature had been 104°F in the shade. He and I were in his kitchen. Mac was droning on and on about a one-eighth-inch gap between two sections of plywood that made up the new gunwale on the starboard side.

"I'm just going to fill it with epoxy and cover it with a layer of Kevlar on both sides," I insisted.

"It'll flex and it'll fail," Mac argued. He wanted the boat to be perfect, and nothing less would satisfy him.

As far as I was concerned, the time for seeking perfection was long past. "We've got to get the boat painted. We still have to mount all the hardware."

On and on he went about that darn eighth-of-an-inch gap in the plywood.

I started thinking about how hard it was going to be for me to leave Mac. How much I loved him, how difficult it would be to find myself alone again.

When I turned my attention back to Mac, he was still yakking about the gap in the plywood. That stupid eighth-inch gap was standing between us as if it were the Grand Canyon.

The next thing I knew, I was swearing. I didn't want to talk any more about plywood. I didn't want to hear any more about plywood. I didn't want to think any more about plywood.

"In a few weeks I'm going to leave. I'll be alone for months. I don't want to be alone. I'm tired of being alone. I don't want to spend the last of the time we have together fighting about *plywood*!"

In the next instant, I found myself indulging in a full-fledged, screaming hissy fit. I stomped out of the kitchen, headed for the front door. *Wait—I don't want to leave.* I turned, still stomping, but I wasn't sure of what to do next. The stomping was hurting my feet, so I fell on the floor and kicked my feet in the air.

Mac walked over and took me in his arms. "It's okay. It'll be okay. It's going to be all right. I love you."

A HALF HOUR LATER, I was mortified. Mac and I were back in his kitchen. I tried to apologize. "I am so sorry. I don't know what got into me. I've never behaved that way in my entire life. Not ever."

True to form, Mac replied simply, "That's okay, but if it happens again, I'm going to step over you and walk out of the room."

THE NEXT MORNING I went rowing with a group of women. After the row we went out for coffee together. Sitting at the table surrounded by women, I felt a sudden urge to brag. "I did something last night. I got in touch with my feminine side," I said, the pride swelling in me.

"How?" asked a friend.

"I had my very first screaming hissy fit."

It was Beth Brown who asked the next question. "Did you throw anything?"

"Well, no, I didn't throw anything," I admitted, somewhat deflated.

"It doesn't count if you didn't throw anything," said Beth.

OVER THE COURSE OF the summer, Kathy Steward and I took up a correspondence with the Norwegian rower Diana Hoff. Diana wanted to leave from the Canary Islands in early September. I argued that if we left in mid-October, hurricane season would pass before we reached the hurricane prone seas of the Caribbean. Diana dismissed the danger. She wanted to be in Barbados before Christmas.

On September 4, 1999, I left with Mac and several other friends for the Canary Islands. Thanks to UPS and Gérard d'Aboville, the *American Pearl* was waiting for us on the island of Tenerife. By September 8 we had the boat shipshape and ocean ready. Diana Hoff had some difficulty clearing her boat through customs. She worried that I would start without her, but I promised to wait. She and her supporters had the *Atlantic Star II* ready to go on September 12.

Diana selected September 13, 1999, as the day for our departure. This seemed oddly fitting. September 13, 1998, was the day that I'd arrived in Philadelphia aboard the *Independent Spirit*. I chose the time for our departure: dawn.

THE DIE WAS CAST, there was no turning back, but I dreaded saying goodbye. I hugged Kathy Steward, Joe Jacobi, and Noreen Powers. Then I turned to Mac. "I guess now wouldn't be a good time for a screaming hissy fit."

"You can if you want," said Mac. There was a hug, a last kiss, and a few tears. Then I let go of Mac and stepped into the *American Pearl*.

Diana and I rowed our boats out of the harbor. We were side by side until Kenneth Crutchlow of the Ocean Rowing Society called the start of what the media insisted on calling our "race." Press boats followed Diana and me for about a half an hour. Then, one by one, they turned around. After forty minutes, the last boat was headed back toward the harbor. In another hour, I lost sight of Diana. From that point on, I was alone.

I no longer enjoyed my solitary freedom. I missed Mac intensely. Once I cleared the islands, I found the mid-Atlantic to be a kinder and gentler ocean than the North Atlantic had been. My experiences on the second solo row were similar to the first row; only a few things had been different. On this trip I had four redundant communications systems, so I never lost communications. When we rebuilt the boat, we raised the ceiling in the cabin by four inches so I could sit upright. Because we had used a foam-core plywood the boat was a few hundred pounds lighter. Many small changes made the boat more comfortable. Kathy Steward had found reflective foil cloth, which we used to cover the roof to help keep the cabin cool.

Gérard had been right to worry about my sea anchors on the first trip. They hadn't been strong enough. This time I had three beefy parachute sea anchors. I named them Papa Bear, Mama Bear, and Baby Bear. Papa Bear was for good weather but adverse winds. Baby

Bear was my storm anchor, and Mama Bear was for the weather in between.

I packed along a wider variety of books and music. Dead white men were no longer enough for me. I brought along Langston Hughes, Toni Morrison, Maya Angelou, and Cornel West, and a healthy mix of others. For music I had Tina Turner, Barbra Streisand, Dolly Parton, and Cher. Each of these writers and musicians had followed the thread of the hero path, and I wanted each of them with me.

Although it had been a full year since Hurricane Danielle, not all of my injuries were completely healed. The lateral side of my right hamstring was still grumpy and discontented where it had been torn. My fingers had no trouble finding the hole in my left quadriceps muscle where my thigh had collided with the rib that supported the walls and roof of the cabin. My right shoulder ached from having been dislocated in the storm. I told myself these pains were psychosomatic, but when the wind came up and the seas turned ugly the fear in the pit of my stomach was dreadfully real.

I kept the same disciplined rowing schedule on the second trip as I had on the first. Unless wind and waves interfered, I rowed a minimum of twelve hours a day. Many people interpreted this self-imposed austerity as an exhibition of my competitive spirit. With every update on wind or weather came a report on the location of Diana Hoff.

I reached the halfway point on October 18. Diana Hoff reached the midpoint on November 5. While the media made a great deal out of the "race" between us, after the first week the idea had lost all its appeal for me. I can't imagine the idea of a race appealed to Diana either. In many ways, I think she and I were rowing for the same team.

I respected Diana, but I did not so much respect Peggy Bouchet. Peggy had not been ready to leave from the Canary Islands in September. She hoped to catch up with us by leaving from the Cape Verde islands, which are a thousand miles closer to the Caribbean. I didn't like the idea of racing Diana, but I was not about to let Peggy win by cutting a corner.

ON HALLOWEEN, THE OCEAN played a nasty trick on me. As I cooked dinner, dolphins arrived for a visit. I pulled out my video camera and put in a fresh battery. I wanted to see if I could put the face of the camera underwater to capture these creatures in their habitat. I sat at the edge of the deck and reached the camera over the side. As I did this, a dolphin came up from underneath the boat passing within inches of the camera. The swiftness of the dolphin startled me and for a brief second I let go of the camera. *Not to worry*, I told myself, *it is on its tether*. I glanced down at the deck; the camera's tether lay between my feet. I'd untied it when I changed the battery.

The camera had not moved six inches from where I'd let go of it, but in my haste to get a grip on it, I pounced. The camera bobbed beneath the surface and came up a few feet toward the stern of the boat. I pounced again. If only I'd reached out calmly, I could have easily retrieved it. The third pounce rammed my shoulder into the oarlock as I worked my way toward the stern of the boat. The fourth lunge sent me head first out of the boat. I panicked for half a second until, grasping at the waist belt of my harness, I assured myself that *my* tether was secure. It was. I would love to say that I swam with the dolphins, but the instant I fell flailing into the water, the dolphins disappeared.

I swam for the camera, but my tether pulled me up a few inches short. Recognizing the futility, I vaulted back into the boat as a circus performer vaults onto the back of a running horse. I did not bother to use my nylon climbing ladder. I shoved out the oars and attempted to turn the boat. Over the course of the afternoon the wind had come up and was now around twenty miles per hour. It seemed to take forever to turn the boat into the wind. In a racing single I could have easily retrieved the camera.

I spent the next hour rowing lazy circles around the camera. Twice I managed to get upwind of it, but each time I let the boat drift by the camera it was several yards away. Knowing I would need another swing, I took the time to put down my dagger board, but in the minute and a half it took me to lower the dagger board, I lost sight of the camera. I thought of all those heartrending man-overboard stories where competent captains with engines do circles around valued crew members only to lose sight of them in the swells.

It was only a camera. I had a spare, so in the grand scheme it was not such a huge deal. However, the camera belonged to my sponsor, Sector Sport Watches, and it was in a waterproof case. While I had a spare camera, I had no spare case. The fact that the camera did not belong to me compounded my sense of stupidity.

How could I have been so careless? How could I have been so clumsy? I don't do *things like that!* I resolved to be more careful. I was entering a phase in the trip in which it would be tempting to focus on the end instead of the moment at hand. My safety would depend on paying strict attention to the little things. Closing hatches, tying knots, securing tethers, and keeping things in good repair were as important as ever. It is my opinion that big mistakes don't kill people in the wilderness, little mistakes do. Little mistakes domino. I drop my camera; I dive overboard to get it; I'm not tethered. This would have been a fatal error. I would be more careful.

I ROWED HARD. By early November, it began to look as if I would set a new record for the fastest solo crossing. Not the fastest solo crossing for a woman, the fastest solo crossing for anyone. I was on track to break the record by more than a week. I let my ego run rampant until, on November 8, a low-pressure system formed over the Caribbean. After that, the trade winds began to blow backward. Just as it had when I lost the Gulf Stream, the boat stopped.

On November 13, I was 418 miles from Guadeloupe, but try as

I might, I just wasn't getting any closer to land. Typically, sunrise was my favorite time of day. Mariners have an adage: "Red sky in morning, sailors take warning." The dawn sky glowed like the coals of an old fire. It roiled with crimson, burgundy, and greenish purple. *Aurora may be the goddess of dawn, but I hate it when her hair is on fire.* Heavy black storm clouds swirled above me. I pulled out my video camera and commented, "Looks like the fire of Hades is coming for me." I didn't need a weather report; the burning sky told me far more than I'd wanted to know. Shakespeare's *Macbeth* came to mind: "By the pricking of my thumbs, something wicked this way comes."

Late in the afternoon, I phoned my support team. Diane Stege answered the telephone. Diane is always precise, but there was a strain in her voice. "Hold on while I get the weather report that Dane Clark sent." Then Diane read the report that she had clearly rehearsed. The low-pressure system over the Caribbean had become a hurricane. Hurricane Lenny was in the western Caribbean, and it was traveling from the west toward the east. Diane assured me that all the predictions were that the storm would move off to the north. Other than adverse winds keeping me offshore, I should be okay. Diane did her best to sound convincing.

It was with reluctance that I hung up the telephone. I'd studied hurricanes. I told myself, *At this latitude, hurricanes travel from east to west because the trade winds blow from east to west. The trade winds have blown from east to west for all of recorded history.* I opened the hatch and went out on deck. The wind was blowing from west to east, and that wind was bringing me a hurricane.

Hurricane Lenny hit the island of St. Croix as a category four. On November 18, I received word that Lenny had stalled near St. Martin, which was west-northwest of my position. At 7:30 P.M. on November 20, as I was about to eat dinner, I telephoned Mac just to say hello.

Mac didn't waste any time with pleasantries. "Lenny's turned again—it's headed straight for you. Dane Clark says you need to batten down the hatches and be prepared for anything." I went on deck to fill one of my two ballast tanks and to put out my big sea anchor, Papa Bear. I should have put out my storm anchor, Baby Bear, but I was more willing to test the strength of the Papa Bear and the roof cleats to which the anchor was tethered than I was to give up any more miles. After deploying the anchor, I climbed back inside to telephone Kathy Steward for a second opinion.

Kathy confirmed that Lenny was moving southwest on a collision course with me. The storm had lost much of its strength over Antigua and had been downgraded to a strong tropical storm. The sustained winds were just under seventy miles an hour. After my conversation with Kathy, I closed all the vents in my cabin, went out on deck, and filled my second ballast tank.

Just as I was about to return to eating my dinner, I heard an unusual wave. I looked out the cabin hatch to watch a fifteen-foot wave break over the port side of the bow. Several thousand gallons of water slapped into my starboard gunwale. The gunwale acted like a catcher's mitt. It caught the wave, went under water, and kept right on going. Because I was sitting on the starboard side, my body weight only added to the momentum. My feet went up over my head, and my knees hit the ceiling. I crawled toward the port side hoping to abort a complete rollover, but it didn't work. The boat did a full 360-degree roll with me skipping across the ceiling along with my pasta dinner.

The boat came upright quickly, but it took a minute or two for the water to drain out of the port scuppers. I had been lucky. Compared to other capsizes, this one seemed gentle. *Heels-over-head rolls are good. Head-over-heels rolls are bad.* With a heels-over-head roll, your knees hit the ceiling first. In a head-over-heels roll, your face hits the ceiling first. For this trip we'd padded it. On my first trip, I hadn't expected to spend so much time on the ceiling.

The waves were shaped like shark's teeth, and they had a nasty bite. I'd taken down my American flag, and I taped my wind gauge to the flagpole with duct tape. It registered gusts to eighty-eight miles per hour and average wind speeds of sixty-two miles per hour. The pyramidal waves looked to be eighteen to twenty feet high, with occasional waves that were much larger.

I'd lived in fear of this storm for more than five days. I was beginning to think that fear on the ocean is qualitatively different than most other fears. It lasts longer. If one is confronted by a grizzly bear (as I was once in Denali National Park) or a lion (Masai Mara National Game Reserve), one knows within minutes whether one is going to survive the encounter. If one falls into a crevasse (Mount Rainer) or stands in the track of an avalanche (in the Bolivian Andes), one's fate is decided in seconds. On the ocean, fear is more robust; it lives longer. It's like the cold of Antarctica, where after -40°F it all felt the same to me. I never became accustomed to it; I just grew tired of it. In Hurricane Danielle, I'd been scared to death. Lenny was no longer a full-fledged hurricane, but scared to death felt just like scared to death.

It's not supposed to hit me. It's supposed to go north. Every prediction was that the storm would turn and miss me by hundreds of miles. I rolled myself into a tight ball and cinched up the lee cloth to hold me next to the port wall. Since the floor of the cabin was my bed, the lee cloth was not intended to keep me from falling out of bed; it was to keep me from bouncing up the walls and visiting the ceiling. If I cinched the lee cloth tight enough, it cradled me firmly against the wall. When the boat fell to the starboard I swung in the protective hammock of the lee cloth, and when it fell to port I was snug against the plywood of the hull.

Every few minutes a wave would break over the roof, and it would tip the boat far over on its side, dipping the roof into the water. Lightning was all around. Even with my eyes shut, I could make out flashes. The storm was loud. The thunder bellowed and the waves smacked the sides of the boat.

Hours passed. In the cabin, I began to feel like some wild creature trapped in a corner. Over time, a suffocating sense of helplessness filled the air. It whispered to me, *You aren't going to make it. You'll fail. You'll fail again. You will lose, and the helplessness will win.* I'd come back out on the ocean intending to kill forever my sense of helplessness. Suddenly I was furious. The time had come for me to slay the dragon. "To hell with this storm," I said, and to the helplessness in my cabin I said, "To hell with you!"

I strapped on my life vest and scrambled out into the storm. A wave came over the boat as I clipped my tether into the safety cable. Blind to the insanity of my actions, I stood tall and defiant on the deck. The dark sky swirled like water running down a drain. Lightning crackled blue and purple. In my rage, I thought of Lamar and the blue and purple of our bruises. I remembered, with searing vividness, the times I'd failed to safeguard my brother and the times I'd failed to protect the many others who'd come after him. I had learned the speech from Shakespeare's *King Lear.* I'd shouted it for fun during snowstorms in the Antarctic and used it to entertain friends in the midst of rain-soaked rowing races. This time I did not play at the madness of Lear; I was the madness.

> *Blow, winds, and crack your cheeks! rage! blow!*
> *You cataracts and hurricanoes, spout*
> *Till you have drenched our steeples, drowned the cocks!*
> *You sulphurous and thought-executing fires,*
> *Vaunt-couriers to oak-cleaving thunderbolts,*
> *Singe my white head! And thou, all-shaking thunder,*
> *Strike flat the thick rotundity o' the world!*
> *Crack nature's molds, all germens spill at once*
> *That make ingrateful man!*

I'd been gearing up for this fight since I was a teenager. I outroared the wind. I dared the ocean to swat me down. I conjured the wrath of nature. But this was not enough for me. I turned my anger toward God. "It isn't fair for you to keep putting helplessness in my path," I bellowed. A wave slapped the boat hard, but I stood firm. "I've never taken the easy way, not once. What do you want from me?" I called God by the proper names the Harvard Divinity School had taught me: "Adonai, Allah, Brahman, Elohim, what am I supposed to do? Krishna, Marduk, Odin, Shang Ti, what do you want from me? Shiva, Vishnu, Yahweh, here I am." My voice turned raspy, and I switched to shouting at the lesser gods of wind, sea, and storm: "Adad, Donar, Dylan, Indra, come on! Neptune, Ramman, Rudra, Thor, and Yam."

Suddenly, I felt silly and self-conscious. Yam was a Phoenician god of the sea, but I couldn't help but think of the vegetable. *Here I am, standing out in a storm, picking a fight with a potato.* Part of me wanted to laugh, *No, I am angry.* "Yam rhymes with . . ." In the next instant I found myself swearing at the sky. My exercise in blasphemy didn't last long. It wasn't that I lacked the audacity to swear at God; I just couldn't come up with that many swear words.

A bolt of lightning struck the cabin behind me, and I fell to my knees. "I've helped the disabled. I've pulled homeless people out of Dumpsters. I've comforted individuals in distress. I've put myself out there time and again. How much more do you want from me? How much more can I give?"

I had been so sure that rowing across the ocean was part of my path that I'd almost taken it as a calling. Had I been wrong? Had it been nothing more than an exercise in haughtiness and self-delusion? Was this not mine to do?

My fury was spent.

I stayed on my knees and begged God's forgiveness. A tall wave washed over the deck, submerging me for a few seconds. I didn't move. As the water cleared, I began a long series of apologies. "I am sorry that I've been too small, too weak, too self-absorbed to make a difference." My arms and legs shook with my shame. "I'm sorry that I have not always been able to protect the people who needed my protection." Tears streamed down my face as I began to name all the people I'd let down. My brother Lamar was the first name on the list, but many others followed. The sorrow and disappointment poured out of me. After dozens of memories, I ran out of names. "The woman with gangrene, the man in the Dumpster who was lying in his vomit, the girl with Down syndrome who was pregnant by her father." Over and over, I apologized for my helplessness.

When I looked up from my prayer, the storm seemed to shine blue with electrical energy. It was then that I realized a sublime truth of what I had been missing. I'd intended to slay the sea monster of my helplessness. But I am, after all, a woman. We don't slay our dragons; we embrace them.

HELPLESSNESS WAS NOT SOMETHING outside me, some malevolent force that I had to defeat. Helplessness was a part of me. *I am a human being. It is our brokenness, our helplessness, which makes us human.* I thought I'd been trying to earn God's forgiveness, but the forgiveness I needed was my own. I had only to forgive myself.

I thought that rowing across the ocean would make me stronger, wiser, and less susceptible to the vicissitudes of human existence. What I did not realize is that rowing across an ocean wouldn't make me any less human. I needed to accept my dragons. I needed to make peace with my helplessness.

STILL ON MY KNEES, I prayed a prayer of thanksgiving. It was a prayer of atonement. Atonement: at-one-ment. I no longer felt alone. I felt at one with nature, with the storm, with myself, and with the rest of humanity. In that sense of oneness I felt a stronger love than anything I'd ever experienced. It was as if I could feel the good wishes of friends back home. I could feel the prayers of all the people who were hoping that I would weather the storm. *Our helplessness makes us human. Love is what makes our humanity bearable.* If there was to be any salvation for me, it would come through the redeeming gift of love.

I remembered my uncle's words: "A romance . . . the greatest stories in life are about romance."

CHAPTER 24

The Romance of Being
Merely Human

November 21, 1999
latitude north 17:10, longitude west 56:18
days at sea: 69
progress: 2,700 miles

ON NOVEMBER 21, AT 1:00 P.M., THE EYE OF WHAT HAD
been Hurricane Lenny passed directly over my boat. By evening, the
seas were beginning to calm, but there was still a strong headwind.
The headwind prevailed for the next several days. November 24,
the day before Thanksgiving, I sent out the following message via
e-mail:

> Before the wind stalled and then stopped me a few weeks
> ago, I planned to be on land before Thanksgiving. Had
> I arrived in the Caribbean when I was expected, Lenny
> would have still been a hurricane when it crossed me. So,
> I'm not sorry the wind stranded me out here. In fact, I am
> *thankful* I couldn't make any progress west. I do not think
> Lenny was meant for me any more than the sunrise is
> intended for me. However, I learned much from the storm
> and I dearly loved the sunrise that followed it.
>
> I am thankful for all the friends and others who
> prayed for my safety and sent me their thoughts and their
> energy. I am grateful for the sponsors who gave me the
> opportunity to return to the ocean. I still hope for and plan
> for a successful landing. It will just be a little later than

I charted a few weeks ago. Tomorrow, I will watch the sunrise. I will wash my shirt. I will eat a good freeze-dried meal and drink many cups of desalinated water. It will be a good day. Perhaps the wind will change and I will spend the day rowing toward home. This would make it an even better day.

On Thanksgiving Day, I had my usual breakfast of granola. The seas were calm enough for me to make some progress even against a fifteen-knot headwind. I felt a bit tender spending the day alone. I wanted to ask Mac a question, so I picked up the telephone. "Hello," said the familiar voice, sounding very chipper.

"Hey, Mac, it's Tori." I knew if I didn't get my question out quickly, Mac might run away with the conversation, and I'd lose my nerve.

"Mac, you know all this 'love pure and chaste from afar' stuff? Well, it's for the birds. I'm tired of being alone. When I get out of this rowboat, will you marry me?"

Mac was quiet for a moment. This Silence from Mac was daunting. When his answer came, it was entirely unpretentious: "Sure, why not?"

I can't say precisely what soaring prose I'd expected from my silver-tongued gentleman, but "Sure, why not?" wasn't it. Still, it meant yes, and that was the answer I had wanted.

Mac asked, "When do you want to do it?"

"Well, I don't know. I haven't thought that far," I admitted.

"Okay, I guess we'll figure it out," said Mac.

Mac went on to tell me about his plans for the day, but I was only half listening. *He said yes. He'll marry me after I get out of the boat, when I get home. I actually asked him, and he actually said yes. Well, not exactly—he said, "Sure, why not?"* I'm not sure I heard another word the man said for the rest of the telephone call. *Who'd have thought it, me proposing over the telephone? Wow.*

Headwind or no headwind, I am going home. I picked up the oars.

For the next several days I pretty much rowed around the clock. I took off a few minutes to eat, and an hour here and there to sleep, but I was highly motivated to get home.

At 3:00 P.M. on Wednesday, December 1, I noticed what looked like the sliver of a cloud on the horizon. The *American Pearl* would crest a wave and the cloud would appear, and as we settled into a trough the cloud would vanish. I cannot say why I thought the cloud was Guadeloupe, but I knew it was land. *Am I dreaming? Is it a mirage? Is that land I smell, or do I just need a bath?* It wasn't until nightfall that my certainty was confirmed. The island twinkled with lights.

The next morning, Gérard d'Aboville came out in a power boat to pay me a visit. My friends from Kentucky would not arrive until late in the evening. I had no intention of landing before my friends were there to meet me. "Civilization without my friends isn't worth coming home to," I told Gérard. He understood. The *American Pearl* was no longer just a boat; it represented a dream that was forged in the fires of friendship and devotion. And I was about to bring the pearl of that dream home.

Gérard and I agreed that I would row into the main port of Guadeloupe, Pointe-à-Pitre. As Gérard was about to motor back into port he said, "Enjoy your last day of solitude, Tori. Once you step ashore, your life will never be the same."

I knew Gérard was correct. *My life up to now has been a tragedy, a history, and a comedy, but going forward I will do my best to make it a romance.*

I rowed the *American Pearl* to within four miles of the harbor, and turned in for the evening. About 3:00 A.M. I noticed that the wind was up and the *American Pearl* was drifting uncomfortably close to land. I went on deck and was horrified to realize that I was no longer near the harbor on Grande-Terre (which is one of the main islands of Guadeloupe), but that a wind from the north had driven me south almost to another island, Marie-Galante. I was fifteen miles from the harbor and drifting farther away. I took up the oars immediately and once again found myself rowing into a headwind.

The morning of December 3, Gérard telephoned to say they were leaving the harbor in two boats to meet me. I explained that I was much farther away than we had planned. "Well, Tori, I guess you will just have to row a while longer." The sun rose, but I didn't see any boats. An hour passed. I kept rowing. Gérard called to say they were on the way and he asked for my position. Another hour passed. I kept rowing. Gérard called again to ask for a report on my position. I'd seen a large catamaran pass well to the north. The next time Gérard telephoned, he was clearly frustrated. The GPS on the chase vessel wasn't working. They didn't have a clue where I was. Instead of giving him the latitude and longitude, I tried describing the landmarks nearby.

About a half an hour later, Gérard was alongside. Standing beside Gérard was a tall, handsome man with very long white hair. It was Mac. He hadn't cut his hair since I'd left, and I thought, *Well, we both look like Tarzan.*

Soon a big motor-powered catamaran crowded with news people and friends joined us. Kathy Steward and Diane Stege were on deck with Beth Brown and Luckett Davidson. Joe Jacobi had been in Tenerife to see me off, and he'd come to see me in. Kathy Burr, who had been a trustworthy supporter, was aboard. Martha Barnett, a longtime friend and one of the best writers I know, had come to write a story. Louisville Collegiate School had sent two student representatives: Anne Greene and Alex Stege. Barry Bingham was standing toward the back, smiling broadly. Next to Barry, I saw someone I'd never expected. *No, it can't be. Am I seeing things?* Her bearing was regal. Standing erect, with her white hair blowing gently in the breeze, was my old history teacher, Helen Longley. *What a grand surprise!*

It was not the splendid entrance that Gérard and I had planned, but rather a slow slog with friends watching me drag the boat stroke after stroke toward the harbor. They'd been waiting for months. I guess having them watch for a few more hours was not too much to ask. When I paused for a moment to get out my raincoat, Mac asked, "What are you doing?"

I said, "It's going to rain."

Mac reported, "It's not supposed to rain until late this afternoon."

I started to point out the cloud just above Mac's head. I started to tell him that I'd been watching the weather for eighty-one days, and after rowing 3,333 miles of open ocean I darned well knew a rain cloud when I saw one. *No, keep silent. There's no need to pick a fight.* Five minutes passed. It started to rain. The rain didn't last long, just long enough to prove me correct.

When I reached the mooring, I tossed the bow rope to Mac and Joe Jacobi. The crowd was thick, and various people with cameras were vying for position. It seemed that there was barely any room for me to step ashore. Mac cleared a space for me to stand. I stepped into the crowd and Mac took me into his arms.

I had finished the journey. In the beginning, I thought I could not be worthy of love until I had beaten helplessness. In the end, I learned that my humanity is grounded in helplessness, and it is that very humanity that makes me lovable. I had expected to find enlightenment with my head, and in the end, I found all the enlightenment I need in my heart.

Afterword

DIANA HOFF LANDED IN Barbados on Wednesday, January 5, 2000. Later that same day, Peggy Bouchet landed in Martinique. While Diana wasn't racing, I was happy that she finished ahead of Peggy, even if it was just by a matter of hours.

I WOULD LOVE TO tell you that at the end of my journey the monomyth played out for me: that I returned home, ascended to the throne, married, and lived happily ever after. Much of this is true. I returned to Louisville, Kentucky. On January 7, 2000, less than one month after I reached home, I married Mac McClure in a ceremony described by one witness as a "microwedding." Including the priest, the photographer, Mac, and me, twelve people attended. I wore the long white gown I'd worn for my graduation from the Louisville Collegiate School. I regret that we didn't arrange to have any music, but then I'm not sure "The Star-Spangled Banner" is appropriate wedding music.

I have not ascended any thrones, but this is for the best. Thrones are like pedestals: cold, hard, unforgiving, and best avoided. I endeavor to be both willfully optimistic and willfully happy. There is one great benefit to having rowed a boat alone across an ocean: when helplessness wins more than I think it should, I can cry and no one dares to think of me as weak or feeble.

One afternoon, not long after my return, I was listening to the evening news. The news anchor reported that six hundred people had been killed by flooding in southeastern Africa. Then, without taking a breath, the anchor went on to report the score of a basketball game, describing the game as "a disaster."

I began to cry. I telephoned Mac, who had gone to the hardware store.

"Are you okay?" he asked.

"No," I sobbed.

"Do you want me to come home?" The concern was clear in his voice.

"Yes."

Mac left a full shopping cart at the hardware store and came home. What greater love can a man have than to leave a cart full of hardware for his wife?

LAMAR LIVES ABOUT TEN minutes from Mac and me. I remain my brother's guardian. I wish I could tell you that he adores me, but that simply isn't true. In fact, to hear him talk, you would think that I am the bane of Lamar's existence. "My sister not let me do nuthin. She not let me drive a car. She not let me get married. She not let me have children. She not take me to the *Star Trek* convention in Las Vegas."

We fight about the food he eats. Not so long ago I took him to the doctor, who asked, "Do you have any allergies?"

Lamar replied, "I allergic to cigarette smoke and vegetables."

Lamar works in a sheltered workshop with other developmentally disabled adults. He goes to church. Some days he's happy. Some days he's sad. Just like the rest of us.

ABOUT A YEAR AFTER my successful row, Mac and I had the good fortune to spend a few days with Thor Heyerdahl and his wife at a series of public events in Dijon, France. By that time I'd grown tired of talking about the trip. I thought, *If one more person asks me about a rowboat, I'm going to blow a gasket and fly around the room backward.* With this as my frame of mind, it was an invaluable gift to watch Thor Heyerdahl answer question after question about his voyage across the Pacific, which he wrote about in *Kon-Tiki*. He was in his mid-eighties and had been answering these same questions for more than fifty years. He was unerringly gracious. I watched him answer the same questions over and over as if it were entirely new each time. At the end of a long day, I asked, "What is it like having your life defined by a balsa raft?"

He was quiet for a long moment. He seemed to study my face. Then he answered softly, "If you didn't want to be known as the woman who rowed the boat, you shouldn't have rowed the boat." His tone was not at all condescending. The words were spoken with a tenderness and understanding that took me completely by surprise.

The following day, I was standing with Mac when Thor Heyerdahl came with a question for me. "Do you plan to write a book about your trip?" I admitted that I had considered it. He looked at Mac and then leaned in my direction. "Be sure to leave room enough to grow."

Many have asked why I waited so many years to write this book. The simplest answer is that I had to get comfortable with a life defined by something as small as a rowboat before I could write about it and still leave room enough to grow.

Acknowledgments

IN ROWING ACROSS AN OCEAN I LEARNED THAT SOME dreams are heavy and many friends may be required to carry them to fruition. Only a tiny selection of friends found their way into this telling of our story. A faculty member from my master's program in writing at Spalding University shared a troubling secret: "John Singer Sargent used to say, 'I paint a portrait and I lose a friend.' The same thing happens when you write a book. If your story is about a woman rowing a boat across an ocean, we need to learn about the woman, the rowboat, and the ocean. You must leave your friends behind." I hope this book will not lose me too many friends, but if someone tells you, "I helped her," it's probably true.

Many friends and colleagues read drafts of the manuscript along the way. In particular, I wish to thank my agent, Jillian Manus; my editor, Caroline Sutton; and the faculty, staff, and students of the brief-residency Master of Fine Arts in Writing at Spalding University: Sena Naslund, Karen Mann, Kathleen Driskell, Katy Yocom, Molly Peacock, Elaine Orr, Robert Finch, Charles Gaines, Roy Hoffman, and my classmates.

My rowing sisters patiently supported me throughout the writing journey: Margaret Handmaker, Judith Peoples, Jo Ann Rooney, Kay Vetter, and Joan Vandertoll. Friends and colleagues in the Louisville community provided constant encouragement: Lucy Freibert, Lisa Bash, Rick Barney, Steve Woodring, Dan Garvey, Michael Schmertzler, and many others.

The board of trustees, President Christ, and the senior staff of Smith College gave me advisors who unerringly call out the best in a woman. The board of trustees, John Gans, and the senior staff of the National Outdoor Leadership School gave me counselors who appreciate the call of wild places. Between these two institutions, I have been equipped to explore the wilderness of civilization and the civility of the wilderness.

Finally, I wish to remember the "pearls": Barry Bingham Jr.; Beth Brown; Diane Stege; Kathy Steward Jacobi; Luckett Davidson; Ann Hassett; Gérard d'Aboville; Helen Longley; Mac McClure; and the many other archfriends who have improved the course of my life.

51